Rubin "Hurricane" Carter and the American Justice System

Rubin "Hurricane" Carter and the American Justice System

Paul B. Wice

Rutgers University Press
New Brunswick, New Jersey, and London

Library of Congress Cataloging-in-Publication Data
Wice, Paul B.
    Rubin "Hurricane" Carter and the American justice system / Paul B. Wice.
        p. cm.
    Includes bibliographical references and index.
    ISBN 0-8135-2864-X (cloth : acid-free paper)
        1. Carter, Rubin, 1937—Trials, litigation, etc.   2. Trials (Murder)—New Jersey.
I. Title.
    KF224.C375 W53 2000
    345.73'02523—dc21

                                                                00-028086

British Cataloging-in-Publication data for this book is available from the British Library

Manufactured in the United States of America

To Richard Max Bockol, whose friendship, encouragement, and knowledge of the law have sustained me during the past thirty-five years and have provided invaluable guidance in the completion of this volume

Contents

Acknowledgments

 I have received much assistance and encouragement in the writing of this book. First, I am grateful to the late Professor Julius Mastro, my colleague and friend, who suggested the topic for this book and introduced me to some of the critical actors in the case. I also owe a deep debt of gratitude to the many individuals who were willing to be interviewed. Special thanks go to Judge Bruno Leopizzi, Lewis Steel, and Myron Beldock, who took time out from their busy schedules to assist me. Librarians at the Newark and Paterson public libraries were especially helpful in my research, particularly with the local newspapers. Marlie Wasserman, the director of the Rutgers University Press, provided a sharp critical eye that was very helpful in cleaning up the volume. The preparation of this manuscript could never have been completed without the selfless and intelligent assistance of my research assistant, Scott Ikeda. Thanks also go to Lydia Feldman, Ruvani Freeman, and my colleagues in the political science department at Drew University, who were all so supportive during the past two years as I tried to finish this project. Finally, I would like to thank my children, Andy, Matt, and Sara, whose love and faith in me is a constant source of inspiration.

Rubin "Hurricane" Carter and the American Justice System

Prologue

In June of 1966 America was tensed for a summer of racial unrest. The Watts riots in Los Angeles, California, in August 1965 served notice that other urban centers would likely undergo similar disturbances. The poverty and racism underlying these outbursts had not abated, and the long, hot summer about to commence was expected to ignite many additional urban conflagrations. Paterson, New Jersey (population 150,000), a grimy, economically declining smokestack city with a history of strained race relations and rust-belt malaise, was a prime candidate for a Watts-like disturbance. Early in 1966 the reform mayoral candidate, Laurence "Pat" Kramer, declared, "Paterson doesn't need a mayor, it needs a referee."

Early in the morning of June 17, 1966, the sound of gunfire echoed through Paterson's quiet streets as four people were shot, three fatally, inside the Lafayette Bar and Grill. Within an hour, Rubin "Hurricane" Carter, a prominent professional boxer ranked as the number-four contender for the middleweight crown, and a young companion, twenty-year-old John Artis, were arrested and charged with committing this brutal crime. This book is an examination of their case on its two-decade-long march through the legal labyrinth, first in New Jersey and then in the federal courts. The journey reaching its terminus in early 1988, when the acting prosecutor for Passaic County, John Goceljak, decided not to pursue a third trial following a federal reversal of the 1976 retrial.

It is an epic drama populated with a grand assortment of villains and a sprinkling of heroes (and more than a few characters who straddle that

divide), a case that illustrates many of the strengths and weaknesses of
our nation's criminal justice system and attests to the resilience of the human spirit. It shows what can happen when police and prosecutors do not
act professionally, critical witnesses lie, and the justice system is unwilling
to correct its errors or admit its mistakes. It offers a frightening look at
the inherent deficiencies of the adversarial basis of the American justice
system. The costs to the defendants were extraordinary. Both men lost the
major portion of their adult lives, robbed of the opportunity to experience the warmth of a happy family and social life and the chance to become productive members of society. Both suffered serious physical
debilities because of their lengthy confinement.

Although there were two defendants in this case, the story will focus
primarily upon Rubin Carter, who the police and prosecutors believed
was the driving force behind the heinous crime. John Artis appears simply
to have been along for the ride, both literally and figuratively. He suffered
the nearly fatal misfortune of being in the wrong place at the wrong time.
But Carter, because of his notoriety in the community, his national reputation as a professional boxer, and his outspoken criticism of the local
law-enforcement and judicial establishment, has been the lightning rod
for all the clashing passions and perceptions aroused by a murder case
that still fires in the popular imagination, as evidenced in Hollywood's
just-released—and highly fictionalized—account of the saga, *The Hurricane* (starring Denzel Washington). In furnishing a thorough, balanced
factual record, this book cannot correct the mistakes or redeem the suffering of the protagonists of this anguished odyssey. But it can, perhaps,
foster the insight that will help to forge a straighter, swifter path to justice
in the future.

1: The Fateful Night

The Slaughter at the Lafayette Bar and Grill, June 17, 1966

At approximately 8:15 P.M. on June 16, 1966, Frank Conforti walked angrily into the Waltz Inn, on Montgomery Street in a black neighborhood in Paterson, New Jersey. Conforti, a forty-eight-year-old white man and former owner of the Waltz Inn, had recently completed the sale of the bar to Roy Holloway. Conforti was upset, believing that he had not been fully paid. Holloway, who was black (like nearly all of the bar's clientele that night), stood motionless behind the bar as Conforti approached, armed with a shotgun. The two men argued for several minutes, and then Conforti pulled back the shotgun and fired. The first blast caught Holloway in the upper arm. Stunned, he attempted to stagger to safety, but Conforti fired a second round, this time delivering a fatal shot to Holloway's face and head. He was rushed to Barnert Memorial Hospital, where he was pronounced dead in the emergency room at 9:45 P.M.

Detective Edward Callahan had been driving in the vicinity when he heard the news of the shooting over his police radio and sped quickly to the scene. As he entered the bar with gun drawn, he nearly tripped over Holloway's body. He immediately spotted a man holding a shotgun and dove behind a pool table. He soon recognized the man as Frank Conforti, whom he had met several times before. Callahan called out to Conforti by name, asking him to put the shotgun down. Seemingly in a trance, Conforti complied, whereupon Callahan came forward and handcuffed him. Conforti offered no resistance. As Callahan escorted the suspect out of the bar, he was assisted by several police officers who had now arrived on the scene. A crowd had gathered outside the bar, and as Conforti passed, several men in the crowd shouted "Give him to us, we'll take care of him!" Conforti was driven to the police station and then arraigned before a magistrate early the same morning, pleading not guilty to the homicide. He was then taken to the county jail.

News of the murder spread quickly through the black community. An angry crowd gathered in front of the bar, where the victim's son-in-law, Eddie Rawls, demanded that the police and courts take swift action against Conforti. Rawls and two other angry onlookers drove to police headquarters to learn what the police planned to do with the suspect. Rawls sought out Callahan, and after locating him in the Detective Bureau, demanded to know what measures were going to be taken against Conforti. Callahan tried to calm Rawls down by telling him that the assailant would be handled by the proper authorities, but Rawls, unmollified, threatened, "You better do it, or we will goddam do something about it."[1] Lieutenant Al Lynch now spoke up, telling Rawls to calm down or he would be arrested. The three men began to leave quietly although Rawls shouted a final warning as they exited: "I will be back if something isn't done about this. We want to know what is going on, and we better goddam soon get some answers."

Although there was some degree of tension and anger in the black community, especially in the group of people gathering at the Nite Spot and Club La Petite, two popular black bars, there were no further incidents resulting from the Holloway murder. As the evening progressed, the neighborhood emotional state evolved toward sadness rather than bitterness. Rumors of a "shaking," local slang for a violent disturbance, circulated, but no action was taken.

THE LATE-NIGHT ACTIVITIES OF RUBIN CARTER AND JOHN ARTIS ON JUNE 16, 1966

The whereabouts of Rubin Carter immediately following the Holloway murder remain cloudy, even after two trials and extensive police investigation. The prosecution argued that after learning of Holloway's death and speaking with his enraged son-in-law, Eddie Rawls (an occasional member of Carter's training crew), Carter went out the same night trying to locate several weapons, including a shotgun that had been stolen from him a year earlier. Carter had recently heard a rumor from Annabelle Chandler that Neil Morrison, a longtime Carter friend, had stolen three

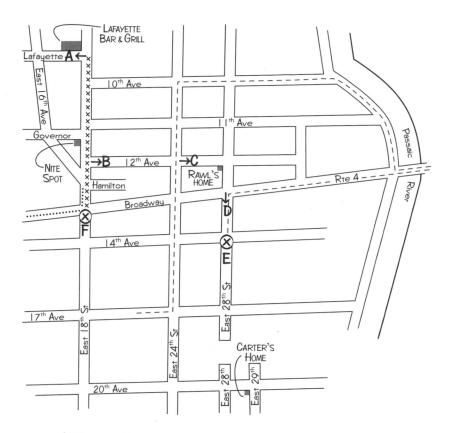

→   White car sighted.

⊗   White car containing Carter & Artis stopped.

······· Route taken by police officers Nativo & Tanis when they see a white car at **B**.

– – –   Route taken by police officers Capter & DeChellis when they see a white car at **C**, attempt to find it on Route 4, see a white car cross Broadway at **D** and stop Carter & Artis at **E**.

× × ×   Route taken by Capter & DeChellis when they stop Carter & Artis at **F** and escort them to the bar.

A   Mrs. Valentine sees white car drive away from the bar.

B   Nativo & Tanis see white car turn onto 12ᵗʰ Avenue from East 18ᵗʰ Street.

C   Capter & DeChellis see white car speed by on 12ᵗʰ Avenue at East 24ᵗʰ Street.

D   Capter & DeChellis see white car crossing Broadway on East 28ᵗʰ Street.

E   Capter & DeChellis pursue the white car and stop Carter & Artis on East 28ᵗʰ Street at 14ᵗʰ Avenue. The police let the car go and proceed to the bar.

F   Capter & DeChellis leave the bar, stop the Carter-Artis car at East 18ᵗʰ Street and Broadway and escort them to the bar.

This map is not drawn to scale. Streets not relevant to this case, e.g., 15ᵗʰ Avenue, and 16ᵗʰ Avenue, are omitted.

MARGARET WESTERGAARD

of his weapons from Carter's Chatham, New Jersey, training site: a .22 Winchester rifle, a bolt-action .22 rifle, and a 12-gauge pump shotgun. Around 11:00 P.M. on June 16, Carter ran into Morrison outside the Nite Spot bar and accused him of stealing the guns. Morrison denied the accusation. Carter, Morrison, and two other men then decided to drive over to Ms. Chandler's apartment to straighten out the matter.

That same evening George Andrews, a former Carter boxing trainer, also went to visit Ms. Chandler, who was gravely ill with cancer. As Andrews was about to enter her apartment in Paterson's Christopher Columbus projects, Carter, Morrison, and a third companion, Merrit Wimberly, were leaving. Everyone seemed calm and cordial even though, a few minutes earlier, Carter again had confronted Morrison about the weapon, upsetting the old woman. To avoid further disturbing Ms. Chandler, Carter accepted Morrison's denial and left the apartment, apparently satisfied that Morrison knew nothing about the missing weapons.

A short time earlier Carter had been relaxing in his home when he received a phone call from Nathan Sermond, who had just replaced Elwood Tuck as his personal advisor. He had received an offer for Carter to fight Rocky Rivero in South America, and Sermond wanted to meet Carter at the Club La Petite to discuss money matters. Carter was excited at the proposition because he was getting antsy, not having fought since March 8. Carter called his sparring partner, Wild Bill Hardney, and told him to meet him later that night at the Nite Spot, a bar owned by his old advisor, Elwood Tuck. Sermond was expecting Carter at ten o'clock, but the boxer was almost an hour late, having stopped first at the Nite Spot. As Carter drove toward Club La Petite, he spotted John "Bucks" Royster, a longtime friend and occasional drinking partner, and picked him up.

As Carter turned off Bridge Street and headed toward Club La Petite, he heard someone call his name, and he pulled over to the curb to find John Artis, a twenty-year-old of considerable athletic prowess whom Carter had met twice before. Artis leaned in the passenger-side window past Royster and asked Carter if he could have a ride to the Nite Spot. Carter said that he could but that he had to stop first at the Club La Petite for a while and take care of some business. John quickly climbed into the back seat. After arriving at the club around 10:45 P.M., Carter spoke with Sermond for approximately an hour. Sermond was ironing out arrangements for the upcoming fight in South America (Buenos Aires), and the local promoter would guarantee only two airfares, which meant that

Carter would be unable to bring along a sparring partner. This troubled Carter because he was rusty from the lengthy layoff and badly needed sparring to sharpen up. Sermond agreed to call the promoter and straighten out the problem. He told Carter to drop by later.

Carter, Royster, and Artis now left Club La Petite at around 11:30 P.M. for the Nite Spot, where Carter anticipated meeting up with his former sparring partner (Wild Bill Hardney) and his former manager, Elwood Tuck, who was working as a bartender. Carter dropped Artis off at the Nite Spot but did not immediately go in, deciding to make a brief detour to another nearby club, Richie's Hideaway, which was popular for its live music. He returned to the Nite Spot around two in the morning, where he met with Hardney, who had been waiting for him.

There are conflicting recollections about the course of the next critical forty-five minutes. Carter remembers remaining in the Nite Spot for only about fifteen or twenty minutes, at which point he volunteered to give a lift home to Cathy McGuire and her mother, Ms. Anna Mapes, a drive of only a few minutes. After taking the two women home, Carter returned directly to the Nite Spot. Carter and friends at the Nite Spot estimate the time of his return between 2:15 and 2:30 A.M.

Realizing he was running dangerously low on funds and wishing to continue partying with Bill Hardney, Carter decided he would drive home to pick up some cash and quietly slip back out without waking up his wife. He tried to convince Hardney to go with him, but Hardney was busy talking to his girlfriend and declined the invitation. Heading out of the Nite Spot toward his car, Carter saw John Artis and Buck Royster. He asked them if they wanted to accompany him on his drive home. Both said yes. Artis was interested in driving the late-model Dodge, so Carter tossed him the keys and climbed into the back seat. (The Dodge was a rental; his own car, a Cadillac Eldorado, was parked at home.)

The group now headed toward Carter's home, three miles to the north, but were stopped by a Paterson police car at Twenty-eighth Street and Fourteenth Avenue, four blocks from that destination. Sergeant Theodore Capter, a black officer who was one of the few local cops on friendly terms with Carter, came up to the driver, John Artis, and asked for his license and registration. Rubin told the sergeant from the back seat that the registration was on the steering column. Capter then shined his flashlight into the backseat and asked, "How you doing, Hurricane?" Carter inquired what the problem was. Capter responded, "Oh, nothing really.

We're just looking for a white car with two Negroes." He gave Artis back his driver's license and concluded the conversation by stating, "But you're okay, take care of yourself," and walked back to the police car. He was assisted in the stop by Officer Angelo De Chillis.

Sergeant Capter failed to disclose to Carter and his friends the real reason why they were stopped. At roughly 2:30 A.M., two Paterson police officers—Alexander Greenough and John Unger—received a frantic call over their car radio stating that four people had been shot at the Lafayette Bar and Grill on East Eighteenth Street at Franklin. Upon arriving at the scene, they were flagged down by an excited young man in his early twenties, later identified as Alfred Bello. Bello told the police officers that he had seen a white car with blue-and-yellow license plates speed away from the bar with two black males inside. Two other Paterson police officers, Sergeant Robert Tanis and Officer John Nativo, were also on patrol in the vicinity when they received a radio alert at 2:34 A.M. They had been driving west on Broadway heading east to East Eighteenth Avenue, but quickly turned their car around and began driving toward the scene of the crime. As they approached Hamilton Street, only four blocks from the Lafayette, they saw a white car turn onto Twelfth Avenue.

Sergeant Capter and his partner also heard the same radio alert with a description of the car. They were driving on Seventeenth Avenue near East Twenty-fourth Street and immediately headed toward the tavern. As they continued on Twenty-fourth Street, they saw a white car with out-of-state plates speeding eastward across East Twenty-fourth Street at Twelfth Avenue. Immediately after the car drove past, they received the radio alert describing the getaway as white and containing two black males. Believing that the car would likely be heading toward New York, the officers drove down Tenth Avenue, hoping this maneuver would allow them to reach the bridge over the Passaic River more rapidly than a car going down Thirteenth Avenue, which ended a few blocks west of the river. When the officers reached the bridge and Route 4, they lost sight of the white car. They then turned around and returned to Broadway, a continuation of Route 4. As they approached East Twenty-eighth, they saw a white car cross in front of them and quickly pulled it over. It was now 2:40 A.M., six minutes after the first radio alert. Cautiously approaching the car, Capter was relieved to learn it was Carter's car, driven by John Artis, with "Bucks" Royster sitting next to him in the front and with Carter leaning forward from the backseat.

After allowing Carter and his friends to go on their way, Capter proceeded on to the Lafayette Bar and Grill. He listened as Al Bello repeated his more detailed description of the car he had seen fleeing from the Lafayette Bar minutes earlier. Capter later testified that after hearing the description, "I looked at my partner, and he looked at me, and we took off looking for the car again." They now drove down East Eighteenth Street and spotted the Carter automobile at the intersection of Eighteenth and Broadway. They pulled the car over, seeing that now only Carter and Artis were in the car. Officers Tanis and Nativo soon arrived, and together they escorted Carter's vehicle back to the Lafayette Bar to see if this was the car Bello had seen leaving the bar earlier.

Carter later testified that after the initial stop by Capter, he had continued on to his home to pick up the needed cash. He next returned to the Nite Spot only to learn that Hardney and his friends were leaving to return to Newark. It was too late to do much else since most of the bars were closing, so Carter decided to call it quits for the evening and drive his companions home. After he dropped Buck Royster off and headed toward Artis's home, Sergeant Capter pulled in behind him, soon joined by another police car with its lights flashing.

It appeared obvious to Carter that Sergeant Capter didn't realize he had stopped Carter's car a second time. Carter described the scene in the following terms, showing the flashes of frustration and anger that erupted throughout his legal struggle:

> "Awwww shit! Hurricane," he said, shaking his head. "I didn't realize it was you." But before he could say anything else, patrol cars had come from everywhere but out of the sky. I never saw so many shotguns and pistols in my life. For a long moment I just stared at Sergeant Capter. I was disgusted. I didn't think he would do this to me. Although he did seem to be embarrassed about it, all it would have taken was for him to admit that he had made a mistake, that he had stopped us earlier with three people in the car, and miles away from where we were then. But for some reason, he didn't. Instead he told us to fall in behind his car, and to follow it, while the other cops fell in behind us.[2]

THE MASSACRE AT THE LAFAYETTE

The Lafayette Bar and Grill was a working-class establishment located in a racially mixed neighborhood at the intersection of Lafayette and Eighteenth Streets. At 2:25 A.M. on June 17, 1966, its bartender, James

Oliver, was serving the three remaining patrons and about to close. He walked over to the cash register and opened its drawer to begin counting the evening's receipts. Oliver, a fifty-one-year-old bachelor, lived in a third-floor apartment above the bar. He had been dating Betty Panagia, the widowed owner of the bar. Oliver had a reputation for decency and fairness, and although he had on occasion had run-ins with black customers whom he had refused to serve, he also had done favors for other blacks in the neighborhood. Although the bar was usually populated by whites, the blacks who went for an occasional drink were rarely made to feel uncomfortable.

As he began to tally the day's receipts, he looked forward to closing up quickly and going to a nearby diner for breakfast with one of his friendly customers, Fred Nauyoks, who was sitting on a barstool, patiently waiting for him to finish. "Cedar Grove Bob," as Nauyoks was affectionately called, was a middle-aged machinist. He had spent the evening listening to a local singing group and had stopped by the Lafayette on his way home. His wife was out of town, so he was in no hurry. He had been at the bar for several hours.

Two stools down from "Cedar Grove Bob" was Bill Marins. The two had been playing pool for most of the evening. Marins was a pleasant, sickly forty-two-year-old who had worked as a drill pressman at a local machine shop until a bout of tuberculosis followed by rheumatic fever forced him to retire. He was receiving a disability check and living with his father in a nearby apartment. Although not retarded, Marins was described by friends as being a little "slow." He was a regular at the bar, and on this fateful evening he had been there since around ten. That night, as was his custom, he lingered until closing time.

Sitting diagonally across from Marins and Nauyoks in the L-shaped bar (at the far end of the short stem) was Hazel Tanis, a fifty-one-year-old head waitress who had just come to the bar from her job at the exclusive Westmount Country Club in West Paterson. This night, Hazel had stopped by the bar to leave money for her friend Betty Panagia to pay for an upcoming convention of the local Bartenders, Waitresses, and Culinary Workers Union in Atlantic City. Despite Ms. Panagia's absence, Hazel decided to relax with a drink before continuing home to nearby Hawthorne.

Into this quiet, peaceful neighborhood bar burst two armed gunmen. The bartender, Jim Oliver, was the first to be aware of their presence as they threw open the front door. He reflexively threw a beer bottle at the ominous figures in the doorway and began to run toward the far end of the bar. Without any warning, the first gunman raised his shotgun and shot Oliver in the back, killing him instantly. Bill Marins turned toward the shooters as the second gunman fired his .32-caliber revolver, striking him in the left temple. Staggered by the impact, with blood pouring from the wound, Marins toppled off the barstool. Without pausing, the second gunman turned to Fred Nauyoks, firing into his skull at point blank range, killing him instantly. Nauyoks's lifeless form slumped over the bar. The assailants thought they had completed their job, but as they turned to leave, they spotted Hazel Tanis at the far end of the bar. Disregarding her pleas for life, they walked up to her and fired four bullets and a shotgun blast into her stomach, arm, and breast from less than a foot away. Amazingly, Hazel Tanis was not killed. She lay on the floor, still conscious but bleeding profusely from her five wounds.

As soon as the killers had finished firing into Hazel Tanis's body, they quickly turned around and fled from the bar. They had not spoken a single word. They had not taken a single cent. The only sounds now emanating from the ghastly scene were the moans and faint cries from William Marins and Hazel Tanis, who had both miraculously survived the brutal assault.

CRITICAL WITNESSES: BELLO AND VALENTINE

The barrage of gunfire startled two individuals whose testimony in the ensuing murder trial proved critical in convicting both defendants. One of these was Alfred Bello, a petty criminal who was serving as a lookout in a burglary a few blocks away. Bello was walking toward the bar in order to buy a pack of cigarettes when he heard the gunfire. Patricia Graham Valentine, the other witness, lived in an apartment over the bar and was awakened from her sleep by the shots. She jumped from the couch where she had fallen asleep and staggered over to a side window.

Both witnesses supplied the police with descriptions of the car driven by the murderers. Bello and Valentine provided the prosecution with the only evidence linking the defendants to the murder scene. The police had been unable to uncover any physical evidence, and the two victims who temporarily survived were unable to identify their assailants. Even the testimony of Bello and Valentine would barely survive the cross-examination of defense attorneys, evolving into a complex web of half-truths, distortions, and lies.

Alfred Bello's myriad versions of what happened that evening perplexed and frustrated prosecution and defense lawyers alike. This stocky, round-faced young man of twenty-three was down the street from the Lafayette Bar at 2:00 A.M. with his partners, Arthur Bradley and Kenny Kellogg, about to burglarize the Ace Sheet Metal Company. Bello, then on parole from New Jersey's Bordentown Youth Correctional Institute, had met Arthur Bradley through Sylvia Smith, a mutual friend. Bradley, a lanky, somewhat high-strung twenty-two-year-old, also had a criminal record. Earlier in the afternoon of June 16, both men met in Paterson at Smith's home, where Bradley explained his planned burglary of the Ace Sheet Metal Factory for later that evening. Along with a third partner, Kenny Kellog, who was a friend of Bradley's, the men departed for the factory shortly before 2:00 A.M.

Bello served as lookout while Bradley tried to force the door to the building open with a crowbar. Bello took a position on the corner of Sixteenth Street and Lafayette, two short blocks from the bar. While at his lookout post, he spotted a late-model white car with two black men inside, driving west on Lafayette Street. It slowed down as it went past him, and Bello jumped back nervously into the darkness as the car turned north on Sixteenth Street. Nervous about the car, Bello hustled back to Bradley, who was having trouble with the door and urged him to work faster. Bello then returned to his original position on the corner, where he saw the same car driving up Lafayette and again turning on Sixteenth Street.

Bello returned a second time to Bradley, who was still having trouble with the door, urging him to work faster. Bello decided he needed a pack of cigarettes. He thought he would be able to purchase them at the nearby Lafayette Bar but he first decided to get a soda from a vending machine at the gas station across the street. He recrossed the street and began walking east on Lafayette toward the bar. After a few steps he heard noises that could have been shots but dismissed the possibility, believing it was probably music coming from the bar. He lit up his cigarette and continued walking, and as he drew to within thirty feet of the bar, he viewed two black men coming around the corner walking toward him, one holding a shotgun and the other a pistol. At this point Bello became fearful and quickly did an about face, running as fast as he could back down

Lafayette. Bello soon spotted a darkened alleyway and ducked inside, nervously waiting for the two men to pass. In a moment he heard the screeching of tires. He then reappeared at the entrance to the alley, where he saw a white car speed by and hit its brakes before disappearing quickly around the corner. Bello would remember the unusual design of the brake lights. As soon as the car was out of sight, Bello ran to the bar and opened a side door.

Bello's testimony, shaky from the beginning, becomes increasingly suspect from this point on. This particular version of what he observed was his initial recollection of the facts, but as time progressed and he appeared before numerous investigative bodies and judicial proceedings, he offered additional, varying accounts. Bello testified at the first trial that once he entered the bar, he saw the horrible mayhem that had just occurred. He walked across the tile floor to get a clearer view of the total destruction. At this point Bello heard a woman enter the tavern from a side door and begin screaming. Bello told her to "stay there," but she ran forward to try and help the victims. Despite the horrors confronting him, Bello calmly went behind the bar, stepping over James Oliver's mangled body. Glancing around the bar he noticed the woman had disappeared. Reverting to his lifelong habit of petty thievery, Bello spotted the open cash register drawer and gathered up as much money as he could—approximately twenty-five dollars. He then ran out of the bar and back down the street to where Bradley was still laboring over the stubborn door. He gave Bradley the money and then felt compelled to return to the bar—a necessity since the woman in the bar could identify him. He told Bradley to flee the scene and quickly returned to the tavern, where he called the police and waited for them out on the sidewalk.

The young woman Bello saw briefly in the Lafayette Bar that night was Patty Graham (soon after she married her fiancé, Ray Valentine, and was thus identified in both trials as Patty Valentine). Although her testimony was later challenged and discredited on several points, overall she remained a fairly effective witness for the prosecution despite her lifetime family friendship with Lt. Vincent DeSimone, which raised the possibility of her having been coached from the earliest point in the investigation.

Earlier in the evening of June 16, Patty had gone shopping but returned to her apartment, which was directly above the Lafayette Bar and Grill just as her fiancé, Ray Valentine, was leaving to work the late shift. Patty put her young child to bed and stretched out on the living room couch at around 10:00 P.M., planning to relax in front of the TV. Within the hour she had drifted off to sleep. She was awakened around 2:30 A.M. by a loud noise that sounded like a door being slammed shut. Startled, she stood up and soon heard two more loud noises. Moving quickly to her front window to see what was happening, Patty saw that the Lafayette Bar sign was still on. The next sound she heard was a woman's voice crying "Oh no!" She then moved over to a bay window, which afforded her a view of Lafayette Street. She saw two black men dashing out to a late-model white car that pulled quickly away from the curb, slowed down as its brake lights came on, and then picked up speed again, vanishing into the darkness.

Patty hurriedly moved away from the window, threw a raincoat over her pajamas, and ran down the stairs, entering the eerily quiet bar from a side door. Once inside the bar, she screamed as she viewed the bloody scene. She also observed Al Bello standing by the front door. Despite his warning her to remain outside the tavern, she came into the bar and saw Bill Marins leaning against a pole in the middle of the room. He had one hand in his pocket, a bloody face, and was staring straight ahead as if in a trance, seemingly unaware of her presence. She tried to speak to Marins, whom she knew fairly well, but he remained zombielike, unable to communicate with her. She then continued to survey the bar room and spotted a body stretched under the air-conditioning unit. As she approached the body, Patty recognized it was Hazel Tanis. Covered in blood, she was able to talk, telling Patty, "I've been shot, call the police." Patty now ran back up to her apartment to call the police and quickly returned to offer assistance to Hazel, who asked her to call her boyfriend, Bob. Patty made another speedy trip upstairs, where she made the call, changed out of her pajamas, dressed, and went down the stairs, where she was greeted at the tavern door by a Paterson police officer, John Unger.

Officer Unger and his partner, Alexander Goodnough, had heard the call reporting the shootings at the Lafayette at 2:34 A.M. With Unger at the wheel, the car sped from Summer Street to Montgomery and turned left on Lafayette, racing toward the murder scene. Approaching the bar, they first saw Bello on the sidewalk waving his arms at their police car. Because they had parked on the wrong side of the street, Unger jumped out of the car first, sprinted into the bar, and returned immediately, telling officer Greenough to radio for at least two ambulances. He then returned to the bar, where he went first to Bob Nauyoks, still slumped over the bar.

Unger quickly determined Nauyoks was dead and then turned his attention to Hazel Tanis, crumpled on the floor and bleeding heavily from her wounds. He tried to comfort her, telling her help was on the way. Unger next moved on to Marins, who was walking around in a daze, blood still coming from the wound in his forehead. He tried to talk with Marins, hoping to learn what had happened, but soon realized it was futile. He helped Marins to a barstool. Believing he had tended to all the victims, Unger ran out to the car to locate a blanket for Hazel Tanis, who appeared to be in shock.

Officer Goodnough was speaking with Al Bello while Unger was surveying the damage inside the bar. Bello explained to the officer he had seen two black men leaving the area shortly after the gunfire in a new white car with blue license plates. Both men were black, of medium height (estimated at around five feet, eleven inches) and with thin builds. One was wearing a hat and sports jacket. Goodnough next observed Ms. Valentine running down the stairs from her apartment. He stopped her at the entrance to the bar, allowing her to go in and tell Hazel she had made the phone call to her boyfriend. He then escorted her back up to her apartment where he tried to calm her down and learn what she had observed. She described what she had viewed from the window, going into detail about the car and its unique taillights, which she sketched for him.

By now a large crowd gathered around the tavern, anxious to learn what had drawn all the police cars to the normally peaceful neighborhood. Metzler's Ambulance Service arrived at approximately 2:45 A.M. and rushed the two surviving victims to the hospital. Tanis was taken to Paterson General Hospital and Marins to Saint Joseph's Hospital, also located in Paterson. William Metzler, working with his older brother for his father's ambulance service, was amazed to see William Marins walking around, fairly coherent. Metzler remembers him stating that two people came in and said, "This is a holdup"; when the bartender went to get money, they started shooting. Also appearing at this time was the three-car caravan transporting Carter and Artis to the crime scene. Both men were removed from their car and placed up against the wall of the tavern and searched for weapons. They were handcuffed and placed in a police van that drove them back to police headquarters.

Paterson was stunned by the massacre at the Lafayette Bar and Grill. This was a generally peaceful establishment in a quiet neighborhood. Mayor Frank Graves called it "one of the most heinous crimes in the city's history." He vowed to have the case solved quickly, offering a reward of ten thousand dollars for information leading to the arrest of the guilty parties.

Carter and Artis reached the police station at about 3:00 A.M. and remained there briefly before being driven to Paterson's St. Joseph Hospital to see if William Marins could identify them. Detective Edward Callahan took both men up into Marins's room. It was now 5:00 A.M. Callahan first contacted the doctor in charge and asked if he could talk with Marins. The doctor answered that he could speak but only for a moment. Assisted by one of the nurses, Marins raised his head. Carter described the ensuing scene, which raised his hopes of exoneration:

> The man (Marins) was weak, pale, and seemed nearly dead; he had a ragged hole in his face where his left eye had been.
> "Can you see clearly, sir?" asked Callahan. "Can you make out these two men's faces?"
> The wounded man nodded weakly.
> "Are these the two men who shot you?"
> For what seemed an eternity, the injured man stared at me intently with his one remaining eye, glanced at John, then stared back at me some more. I almost cried with relief when he began to shake his head from side to side.

Carter and Artis were now led out of the hospital room and driven back to the Paterson Police Station. They were then placed in two separate small, windowless rooms within the Detective Bureau's interrogation room. At 9:30 A.M., over seven and a half hours after the shootings, Lt. Vincent DeSimone entered Artis's room. He introduced himself, saying he was from the prosecutor's office and that he wanted to ask him about his whereabouts that evening. He next mentioned that Artis did not have to say anything if he did not want to but that it would be better if they could clear this thing up. He warned him that he would be taking notes on everything he told him and that his remarks could be used against them in court.

DeSimone began the interrogation by having Artis give a brief personal history. Artis then began a detailed review of all the events of the preceding evening, beginning with his dinner at Grady's (a restaurant), at 6:00 P.M. After finishing with Artis, DeSimone began a similar interview with

Carter in the adjoining room. Carter, like Artis, was willing to talk to DeSimone and describe where he had been the previous evening. He was given the same warnings, but, as Carter wrote in his memoirs, "I sat there and told him everything he wanted to know (not out of any rising fear of him, but because I had done nothing to make me fear)." When asked if he wanted a lawyer, Carter answered, "I don't need a lawyer. I use my fists. I don't use guns."

Carter then related everything that had happened from his supper at home at 5:00 P.M. to the moment when he was stopped by the police at 2:40 A.M. After the interview, which lasted an hour and a half, DeSimone asked Carter if he would be willing to submit to a lie-detector test. Carter agreed but only on the condition that it be administered by someone other than the local police. DeSimone found that acceptable. He would arrange for an expert from the state police to give him the test. Interestingly, Carter also volunteered to take a paraffin test, which could theoretically detect the gunfire residue left by a recently fired weapon. The detective declined the offer because of the amount of time that had elapsed since the shooting as well as the test's lack of credibility among forensic experts.

At 3:00 P.M. the state trooper—Sergeant McGuire—arrived at the Paterson police station. The test took two hours, and when it was over, Carter was returned to the small interrogation room while the sergeant analyzed the results of the polygraph charts along with a similar exam he had given to Artis. After a short while Sergeant McGuire called Carter into his office and announced to him and Captain Gourly of the Paterson Police, "All the answers for the questions on the lines are the same. So you can turn him loose, Captain. And Artis too. Both of them are clean. They had nothing to do with the crime."

Years later, especially during the second trial, the prosecution argued that the test results were not so clearly exculpatory. The preceding quotation was from a recollection by Carter, and there is nothing that the police or prosecution has produced that appears to directly refute his statement. The absence of such concrete evidence is symptomatic of many missing police reports that either disappeared or were destroyed. Detective DeSimone, whose prominent role in the investigation cannot be underestimated, testified that some of his critical notes had either been lost or destroyed in a mysterious flood in the basement of police headquarters where much of the information had been stored. Similarly, written reports by Detective Callahan and Patrol Officer Goodnough had also disappeared.

Once the results of the polygraph tests were secured, the police were willing to release both Carter and Artis. Thus at 8:00 P.M. on June 17, both men walked out of the police station, seventeen hours after they had been dragged out of Carter's car and brought in for questioning. Assistant County Prosecutor Vincent Hull announced to the press that neither Carter nor Artis was even a suspect. Hull would not explain why the men were detained at the station and went on to state that there were no suspects in the case at that time although an extensive search for the murder weapon was being conducted.

On Monday, June 20, the *Paterson Evening News* ran the optimistic headline "Follow Hot Lead in Probe of Bar Murders." One police official was quoted as saying, "The pieces are now beginning to fall into place . . . and it now appears that the original motive of the gunmen was a holdup." The robbery, the police official surmised, turned violent after James Oliver, the bartender, had thrown a beer bottle and struck one of the men, causing him to begin shooting. Despite the headline, there were no subsequent arrests, and the memory of the traumatic scene at the Lafayette Bar began to fade from most people's memory. Carter resumed his boxing career, while Artis continued his preparations for entering the service. On August 6 Carter fought in Buenos Aires, Argentina, and lost a difficult ten-round decision to Rocky Rivero. It was to be the last fight of his boxing career.

A relieved Rubin Carter and John Artis went on with their lives after leaving police headquarters in the early evening of June 17, 1966. Carter worried about getting into decent shape for his upcoming fight while Artis pondered his upcoming enlistment in the army, only a week away. But for both men this was the calm before the storm. The Lafayette Bar massacre was a nightmare that was about to recur and bring them dangerously close to losing their lives.

2: Setting the Scene

The Paterson police investigated the Lafayette Bar and Grill murders for four months before finally arresting Rubin Carter and John Artis on October 15, 1966, and formally charging them with the heinous crime. Thus were these two men thrust into a twenty-two-year-long nightmare spent almost entirely behind bars.

The racially charged atmosphere of the times—rebellions in black urban ghettoes coupled with a surge in militant activist groups like the Student Nonviolent Coordinating Committee (SNCC)—combined with Carter's celebrity (he had fought for the world middleweight crown only eighteen months before the murder) to create the most notorious murder case since Bruno Hauptmann was convicted and sentenced to death in the Lindbergh kidnapping in 1935.

Paterson, New Jersey, is a study in rust-belt decay, a once-thriving working-class community moldering in the wake of industrial flight to the cheaper labor markets of the American South and the Third World. Located in northern New Jersey in Passaic County, between the more typically middle-class suburban communities of Totowa (to the west) and Clifton (to the southeast), Paterson is home to 140,000 people, about one quarter of whom live at or below the federal government's definition of poverty.

Although the size of the city has remained fairly steady for the past four decades, the ethnic and racial composition of the city has changed significantly. In 1967, 70 percent of Paterson was white, with the remainder of the population nearly evenly split between blacks and Hispanics. By 1994, the proportions had reversed: blacks (30 percent) and Hispanics (43 percent) now make up three-fourths of Paterson's population, whereas the white population has diminished to 27 percent.

Paterson is a city haunted by ruins of its past industrial might, its landscape dotted with large, long-abandoned red-brick textile factories. Its largely vacant, desolate downtown shopping area echoes emptily with the ghosts of an earlier generation's bustle. The city is still distinguished by the Paterson Falls, but the once mighty source of water power, capable of producing almost 90 million gallons of water a day, now trickles feebly, with 90 percent of its water supply diverted elsewhere.

Large, multistoried buildings, which once housed department stores, theaters, and banks are occupied, if at all, at the street level, with every third building being completely vacant. The few stores that remain open cater to the modest working-class salaries and ethnic tastes of the current population. Luncheonettes, beauty parlors, discount-clothing establishments, wig shops, and fast-food chains dominate the major downtown thoroughfares.

Modest efforts at urban redevelopment include a new community college, an impregnable, fortresslike justice-system complex (police station, municipal court, and so on), and a diminutive mall. But these token gestures are overwhelmed by the overall grayness, a sense of irrevocable superannuation.

As one moves westward toward Totowa and Wayne, the economic and housing conditions visibly improve. Similarly, driving southeast toward Fairlawn and Clifton, one soon sees a sharp rise in white middle-class homes and stores. Within Paterson itself, the two major ethnic and racial groups—blacks and Latinos—are clustered to the north and south of the downtown shopping district.

Despite the growth of the black and Hispanic communities during the 1960s, the city government remained under the control of the long-time Irish-American–dominated Democratic political machine. By the midsixties tensions between the black and Latino neighborhoods and city hall had reached the breaking point. Critics described Paterson as a police state. There were enough incidents of police brutality against minorities during the 1960s to force the state of New Jersey to convene a Passaic County Grand Jury to investigate the charges. Bill Norwood, author of *About Paterson*, wrote that the roots of these tensions were present "from the day the city was founded. . . . Paterson's failure was not one of simple democracy . . . it was a total failure in that the city's structure—its economy, government and natural resources—had no relation to its citizens." Norwood concludes his book with the pessimistic summation statement that the "city is ridden with confusing and contradictory passions, which are an essential part of its nature, but also make it nearly impossible for Paterson to function."

Rumors of an unholy alliance of police, politicians, and organized-crime figures haunted the police department through the sixties and seventies, a period of growing hostility between the police and the city's black and Hispanic communities. In 1964 Paterson was the scene of one of the first of that decade's many urban race riots as the black community staged a small uprising that was confined to the inner city.

Ironically, when other cities across the country later suffered far more serious rebellions—many of them with less serious racial problems than Paterson—Mayor Graves and his police were able to keep the city peaceful. This relative calm, however, masked the growing bitterness and frustration in both the white and the black neighborhoods, as the city nervously awaited the civil disturbance that never materialized. Nevertheless, this atmosphere did create a setting that, according to prosecutors in the Carter and Artis murder trials, was the catalyst for the Lafayette Bar and Grill murders.

Both defendants grew up and spent most of their lives in Paterson. Although this book will focus primarily on Rubin Carter, his codefendant, John Artis was equally devastated by the legal ordeal. Carter was the prominent figure that the police and prosecutors believed was the driving force behind the Lafayette Bar murders. John Artis just happened to have suffered the nearly fatal misfortune of being in the wrong place at the wrong time. It is because of Carter's stature as a successful professional boxer and an outspoken critic of the Paterson justice system that he became the key police target in the case.

Rubin Carter was born on May 6, 1937, in Delawanna, New Jersey, a small community just outside of Clifton in the north-central region of the state. Rubin was the fourth child born to Lloyd and Bertha Carter. Lloyd Jr. was his oldest sibling, followed by James and their sister Lilian. Four years after Rubin's birth, the family was completed with the addition of a baby sister, Beverly, whose birth necessitated a move to a larger apartment in Passaic.

Carter's father, Lloyd Sr., was a rather stern, religious man who served as a senior deacon in the local Baptist church. He often worked more than one job while contributing long hours to his church. Rubin's mother was equally devoted to the church but spent her days raising her growing family and maintaining their crowded home. Although the family had to watch their money carefully, Carter's childhood was not mired in poverty. Rubin, in his memoir *The Sixteenth Round*, describes a comfortable working-class childhood.[1]

Both parents came to New Jersey from rural Georgia. One of Rubin's earliest memories (around the age of five), was of the family sitting around a monstrous stove eating roasted peanuts that relatives had sent, while his father entertained them with strange stories about his childhood on the farm in rural Georgia. Even though some of the stories recounted frightening episodes about redneck white youngsters terrorizing and even brutalizing blacks, Rubin looked forward to these pleasant evenings.

Carter began his elementary school education in Paterson's P.S. 7. Despite his seemingly stable family background, he soon became a rebellious child and compiled a school record that repeatedly described him as "disobedient, disrespectful, truant, and a user of obscene language." It is possible, however, that his father's reliance upon physical beatings contributed to the youngster's heavy reliance on physical force to resolve difficult and frustrating situations.

Rubin, who was always undersized and somewhat introverted, developed a troublesome stutter that only aggravated his shyness and made school a difficult ordeal. He was often transferred into Paterson's adjustment school number 22, the city's special school for difficult children, especially those who had trouble with discipline.

One of Rubin's most traumatic early experiences occurred when he was five years old and was an early sign of his fighting abilities, especially his capacity to remain on the offensive while absorbing a tremendous beating. The fight was initiated by an older boy who lived in their building and would often sneak down into the basement and steal coal from his neighbors' bins. When Rubin's brother Jimmy surprised the older boy, nicknamed "Bully," in the act of stealing from their family's coal bin, he was badly beaten by the much larger thief. Jimmy returned to the apartment battered and told Rubin what had happened. Rubin, although younger and much smaller than Bully, went downstairs seeking revenge. He surprised the older boy and slugged it out with him, eventually landing several powerful blows to Bully's head, sending him home to tell his mother. Rubin felt exhilarated after the fight, describing his feelings many years later as "a shiver of fierce pleasure . . . a physical sensation in the pit of my stomach that kept shooting upward." That night, after Rubin's parents learned of the fight from Bully's angry mother, Carter's father beat his son viciously. Because of his speech impediment, Rubin could not clearly explain his side of the story. What angered him even more was his father's willingness to believe the worst about him. He could not understand how his father, who was such a religious man and prayed so devoutly to God, would also abuse his son so badly.

In 1943, Rubin's father bought a home in Paterson on Twelfth Street. It was in the "Up the Hill" section of town, a six-block area between Auburn and Carrol Streets. It was a racially mixed neighborhood at this time but extremely tough. The move was necessary because the family was expanding with the addition of another brother. In order to help pay for the new quarters, Rubin's father had to take a second job. He was also able to buy an ice business. Lloyd Carter now worked six days a week, delivering ice in the morning and then working an eight-hour shift at the Manhattan Rubber Company beginning at three in the afternoon.

In order to help their father, near collapse from his punishing schedule, the three oldest boys (Lloyd, Jimmy, and Rubin, aged fourteen, ten, and eight, respectively), took over the ice business at the suggestion of their mother. Using their father's truck to make deliveries, the two older brothers would carry the heavy blocks of ice up the numerous flights of stairs, while eight-year-old Rubin would shave the ice and serve the first-floor customers.

The three boys worked hard, and after returning home and cleaning up, they would venture out into the neighborhood to see their friends. Their immediate area was controlled by a tough gang of youths known as the Apaches. Rubin was an active member of the Apaches and developed a reputation as a good fighter. He was soon elected to the position of War Counselor, which meant he was responsible for choosing when and where a brawl would be fought as well as the weapons to be used. When a war was declared between rival gangs, the respective war counselors would meet and set the rules for the upcoming skirmish. On occasion the war counselors could settle a dispute by fighting among themselves.

Despite his relatively short stature and his stutter, Rubin was a successful brawler, able to withstand a great amount of pain yet persevere until he could overcome his opponent. Rubin was very proud of his position with the Apaches and enjoyed having his friends respect his fighting and leadership abilities.

The Apaches enjoyed raiding their rival gang's territory as well as battling any gang that was foolish enough to come into their neighborhood, violating the sacred territorial boundaries. Another preoccupation of the gang was to go on pillaging expeditions of the downtown Paterson stores, rowdy escapades that occasionally crossed the line into criminal vandalism or shoplifting. It was on one such caper that Rubin, then eleven years old, had his first brush with the law.

In March 1949 Rubin was returning from the movies with fifteen to twenty members of his gang when they decided to loot a sidewalk clothing rack outside of a local haberdashery. Rubin felt exhilarated as the gang ran past the racks, grabbing as much clothing as they could. Rubin collected several polo shirts and sweaters, none of which he was interested in wearing. He gave them to his excited siblings.

When his father came home that evening, he was surprised to see his children wearing new clothes. When he asked them for the source of their new garments, the children wilted under his harsh glare and quickly told him the truth. Rubin received the worst beating from his father he ever remembered. His father then called the police, who came to the house and brought Rubin downtown to the station house, where they tried to force him to give them the names of his fellow Apaches who had been involved in the thefts. Rubin first tried to lie his way out of the mess, but he was identified by the store owner. The police tried roughing him up but Rubin would not be intimidated, and continued to refuse to give up his friends.

After he was released by the police and returned home, his parents were told to bring Rubin back to the juvenile court (Paterson's Child Guidance Bureau) the following morning. Rubin was sentenced to two years' probation. The lenient sentence was due in large part to the role played by Rubin's father in notifying the police of his son's role in the robbery. Two years later, as Rubin turned fourteen, he was arrested again, this time for breaking into parking meters. He was referred back to the juvenile court, which placed him on probation and ordered him to make restitution for all of the stolen change.

Although Rubin's first two arrests grew out of youthful exuberance and peer pressure and did not involve any physical violence, his next entanglement with the law—just six weeks after the parking-meter incident—

was much more serious and landed him in a state reformatory. On an unusually warm day in late June, Rubin and several members of the Apache gang had been swimming in their special spot near the Paterson Falls, nicknamed the Tubbs. As the group was returning from their swim, they spotted an apparently drunk young white man sleeping in the grass near the path they were using. The man awoke as the boys approached, and staggered to his feet, walking toward the group. He first offered the boys his watch and then blocked their way on the narrow walkway. The boys tried to squeeze past the man, but he grabbed one of the smaller ones and tried to take off his pants. The boy resisted, and the man threw him to the ground. Rubin found a glass soda bottle nearby and threw it at the man's head. It struck him squarely, causing a deep laceration and sending him to the ground. The younger boys were all able to run away, but Rubin was trapped. The man grabbed him and threatened to throw him into the waterfalls. Rubin remembered that he had a scout knife in his pocket. He stabbed the man in his head but was thrown to the ground. They wrestled on the ground as the man attempted to grope him. Rubin broke free and began stabbing the man in the chest until he was able to roll out from under him. Rubin then fled home, where he lay in bed trembling with fear.

He was arrested five days later and charged with aggravated assault and robbery. He was brought before Judge Alexander MackLeod of the Passaic County Juvenile Court and in August 1951 was sentenced to three years at the Jamesburg Reform School. He was fourteen years old. He remained there until he escaped on July 1, 1954, just nine months short of completing his sentence. Three other boys were also charged in the incident.

Throughout his difficult three years at Jamesburg, Carter "just kept getting into trouble and they kept adding time," as he later told a reporter. Jamesburg was a large, rambling institution covering 725 acres in central New Jersey, a self-contained facility with its own farm, shops, and stores. The boys were housed in segregated cottages. There were children as young as eight who were status offenders—truants, runaways, and incorrigibles. The older boys were often serving sentences for serious violent crimes such as rape, murder, and aggravated assault.

Rubin's toughness was soon apparent, and he quickly rose to the leadership position as a "line sergeant" in the Reception Cottage where all newcomers were initially housed. Jamesburg operated as a quasi-military school. The boys marched everywhere, even conducting short-order drills with fake wooden rifles. Rubin was soon transferred to his permanent residence hall, Cottage Eight. Mr. Willis was the adult in charge (known as the Cottage Father). He was assisted by his two line sergeants, Chink and Line A. Carter hated Chink, whom he described as a sadist; he was, however, drawn to Line A, whom he found to be tough but decent.

Carter thought Jamesburg was like a punitive child-slavery pit, with the boys working long, hard days. The authorities apparently assumed that the youths were already incorrigibly hardened criminals. The only perceptible effect the institution had on him was to make him harder and even more embittered. He began to believe fatalistically that his life was following some preordained plan. He stoically accepted his fate although he continued to act out against the sadistic guards who challenged him and thus spent long intervals in the isolation unit. The worst such encounter was when Carter beat up a guard who had grabbed him and tried to force him to perform a task from which he had already been excused. The guard wound up in the hospital with broken arms and ribs.

Superintendent Moore, shifting from the stick to the carrot, advised Carter that if he could stay out of trouble for ninety days, he would be released. With five days to go, someone falsified an incident report about Carter. The superintendent was on vacation, and a guard who hated Carter was temporarily in charge and ratified the report, guaranteeing that Carter would forfeit his deal with the superintendent. Frustrated and angry, Carter and another inmate planned an escape. The next night— July 1, 1954—at eleven o'clock the boys left, hoping to have a three-hour head start before their absence would be noticed. Carter thought that he would simply cut across the woods until he hit a major highway and then run all the way home.

By three o'clock the next afternoon, Rubin had arrived in Newark. At this point the boys split up, with Rubin continuing on to Paterson, thirteen additional miles to the north. He finally arrived at his home around nightfall. When he walked into his house, he found his mother waiting for him. She had been notified of his escape by the Jamesburg officials. Rubin took a bath and put on new clothes. He notified his mother that he had decided to join the paratroopers. She served him a nice meal that she had already prepared. After eating, he went outside where his eldest sister Lillian was waiting for him. She handed him a packed suitcase, and they both entered a cab that would take him to Penn Station in New

York City. He quickly boarded a train for Philadelphia. There his cousin Hazel met him at the Thirtieth Street Station and took him to her home in West Philadelphia.

Ruminating over the bitter lessons learned in Jamesburg, Carter recounted in his memoirs that he fought "simply because I loved to fight, and in jail, that jungle of violence that bred either punks or young savages, I had found a fighting heaven." Carter explained that "it was bad enough that we inmates were beating, starving, and fucking each other in the ass, without the sadistic officers doing likewise. There's no justification for an inmate to pick on someone weaker than himself, but at least we were all in the same boat and things were a bit more balanced between us. But for a correction officer . . . to use his position and his badge to force young kids into degraded sexual acts—well, as far as I was concerned, there wasn't a tree high enough to hang the dirty sonafabitch."

HURRICANE IN THE ARMY

All went according to plan as Hazel met him at the station and drove him to her home. He met her husband, David, whom he had not met before, but was instantly drawn to, because David was also a stutterer. David and Hazel tried to talk Rubin out of joining the army because the Korean War, although winding down, was still claiming casualties.

But Rubin stuck with his plan, and two days later David took him downtown to the induction center. To conceal his criminal record, he told the induction officer that even though his birth certificate said he was born in New Jersey, he had lived in Philadelphia for nearly his whole life. He had his physical later that day and also passed a written exam. Two weeks later Carter boarded the special army train for Fort Jackson, South Carolina, where he began training to become a paratrooper with the famed 101st Airborne Division, better known as the Screaming Eagles. Rubin was amazed to find his train made up entirely of black recruits from New York and Pennsylvania. He did yet not grasp the fact that the army planned to abide by the segregationist policies of South Carolina.

Carter was assigned to basic training in Company C under the control of Master Sergeant Claude Hawkins. He was surprised to learn his experiences at the Jamesburg Reformatory had prepared him well for the rigors of army life. For one thing, he already knew how to march, count cadence, spit-shine his boots, and handle his weapon properly. He was also in great physical shape, impressing everyone with his strength and conditioning as the other recruits grunted and staggered through the push-ups, pull-ups, five-mile runs, and sixty-yard crawls. He didn't even complain about the food, as so many of the other recruits did. It was gourmet fare compared to what he had been eating at Jamesburg.

His first problem developed from a racial incident a few weeks after his arrival. After an early-morning footlocker inspection, at the subsequent line-up outside the barracks, Rubin forgot his hat. He was rebuked and then told to drop for fifty push-ups. Sergeant Hawkins did not think that Carter was moving fast enough and called him a "nigger." Carter was confused at first, not believing his ears, but he cleared his head and threw a punch that hit Hawkins on the chin, knocking him to the ground. The sergeant, a big and tough two-hundred-pounder, quickly jumped to his feet, and the two men fought for nearly an hour, as the other recruits looked on in amazement. Rubin finally knocked Hawkins out, and both men were totally exhausted.

A few hours later, Carter was ordered to report to the company commander, Captain Mendoza, where he was joined by Sergeant Hawkins. The sergeant lied on Rubin's behalf, stating that he had thrown Carter to the ground when he failed to obey an order fast enough. The captain decided not to take any further action, and both men were allowed to return to their barracks. The fight unexpectedly created a mutual respect between the two men. Hawkins appreciated Carter's ability to lead the platoon through their marching drills, barking a precise cadence. The remainder of his sixteen-week basic training was uneventful. He would now be ready to begin jump school at Fort Campbell in Kentucky, the home of the "Screaming Eagles." The training was difficult and intense. By the third week, they were already making jumps. Following his training, Rubin was assigned to the 11th Airborne, which was about to be transferred to Ausburg, Germany.

Carter had a rocky beginning with his new unit until he was befriended by Ali Hasson Muhammed, an Aswad Muslim originally from Sudan. Hasson had a calming effect on Carter as he began instructing him in the Muslim faith. One night, after drinking, the two friends were heading back to their barracks when they cut through a field house and saw the regimental boxing team working out. Carter bragged that he could beat any of the fighters he watched. Hasson went over and asked if he could give Carter a chance to come out for the team. Lt. Robert Mullick looked him over and told him to come back the next day for practice.

The lieutenant thought Carter would be humbled when faced with this team. Mullick did not like paratroopers, and he wanted to teach Carter a lesson. Carter showed up the next day, nervous because of his lack of experience at formal boxing. To guarantee Carter's humiliation, Mullick put him up against Nelson Glenn, a heavyweight who had been the all-army champion for the past two years.

Hasson was in Carter's corner as the fight began. Rubin quickly popped the muscular heavyweight with a left on the chin, and Glenn dropped to the canvas. He stood up, rather wobbly, and Carter moved quickly to finish him off, knocking him out for the full count.

The next day Lieutenant Mullick arranged to have Carter transferred to his Special Services detachment under his command. He was relieved of his paratrooper duties and was designated as a member of the army boxing team. It was an enviable position. The team had its own building for the twenty-five boxers. He was immediately accepted into the group as a "brother warrior." Carter now focused intently on boxing, stating, "I lived for boxing alone. It was the beginning, middle, and end of everything in my life." He was immediately successful, winning twenty of his first twenty-one fights, sixteen by knockouts.

Hasson was able to talk Rubin into going back to school. Together they enrolled in a Dale Carnegie correspondence course. Feeling good about himself, both mentally and physically, Carter soon noticed that his stutter had disappeared. He could speak with clarity and, as Hasson commented, "He never shut up." Rubin felt that his whole life was changing for the better, that even his boxing ability was on the rise. He began to develop a deep thirst for knowledge as Hasson continued to instruct him in Islam and the ways of the Koran.

His boxing accomplishments were especially noteworthy. He twice won the European amateur light-welterweight championships. He had won fifty-one of his fifty-six fights, with thirty-five knockouts. He was asked to try out for the Olympic team but that would have required him to reenlist. He was eager to return home. In June 1956 he was shipped to the United States, where he was discharged. On the ship home, his good fortune continued as he won $5,700 in various card games. Upon arrival back in the States, he was taken to Fort Dix, New Jersey, where he was mustered out of the army the next day.

A Return to Prison

He returned to Paterson and was appalled by the fallen condition of the city, a half ruin of filthy streets, abandoned buildings, and stripped-down cars. On his own street all of the trees had been chopped down. On the positive side, his entire family was back together. His brother Lloyd Jr., out of the service and married, lived a few doors down from his parents. Lillian's husband, Bob, had made it home from Korea. His brother Jimmy was going to Harvard University, and his sister Beverly was married and living in Passaic. His two younger sisters, Rosalie and Doris, were home attending high school.

Rubin had a wonderful couple of days acclimating himself to civilian life. Using his poker profits, he went on a shopping spree, buying a new Lincoln Continental and a new wardrobe. He was able to get a job driving a tractor-trailer for a local paper company. He even met and began dating an attractive woman named Regina.

Rubin's happy life took an unexpected downward turn a few days later as his troubled past returned to haunt him. On July 4, as Rubin and some friends were planning to drive down to Atlantic City to continue celebrating his return home, he was rearrested for his escape from Jamesburg Reformatory three years earlier. He was taken to Annandale, another youth correctional facility where he would serve the remaining nine months of his original sentence. Carter refused to wear his prison uniform or go to the mess hall with the other inmates. A violent confrontation with the guards ensued. He was able to meet with the superintendent of the facility, who was also puzzled over the legality of his forced return to confinement. Superintendent Goodman promised to look into the matter, but, before it could be resolved, he was promoted to become the new warden of Trenton State Prison. Carter was then plagued by a string of bad news. His car had been repossessed, his girlfriend Regina was now dating someone else, and the government had withdrawn his GI-bill benefits because he had entered the army illegally.

After serving ten frustrating months in Annandale, Rubin was so angry at being dragged back into prison that he felt like a walking time bomb, on the verge of exploding. He returned to Paterson, lapsing into a deep depression. He was humiliated by his poverty and ashamed of having had to spend more time in jail. He was able to find a job in a plastics factory, but except for going to work, he spent most of his time sleeping.

In the depths of his depression, walking home from work, he was awakened from his trance by a familiar voice. It was Little A (Alfred Harris), his closest friend for three years at Jamesburg Reformatory. Little A was driving a black Cadillac and was wearing a sharp suit. They immediately resumed their close friendship and began hanging out together.

A short time later, on July 1, 1957, one month after his release from Annandale, Rubin and Little A had a major lapse in judgment and committed a series of robberies that would put them back in prison for four years. The crimes made no sense since Carter had a decent job and did not need the money. Nevertheless, they spotted an elderly woman walking down the street and, on a lark, grabbed her purse and took off running. They next came upon a man named Roy Harrison, and they beat him up and took his wallet. (Police reported later that it took ten stitches to close his wounds.) They began running again until they reached their third victim, sixty-one-year-old Edward Simon, whom they knocked to the ground. They decided to end their crime spree at this point and went off in opposite directions.

Harris and Carter were arrested a week later. Two weeks after their arrest, both men pleaded guilty to the charges, hopeful of receiving more lenient sentences than if they would have gone to trial. Carter was sentenced to a three- to nine-year term at Trenton State Prison.

Carter remained in Trenton State for four years. Released in September 1961, he vowed that he would "never come back alive." The length of his prison time was due in large measure to his behavior while in prison. (Some defendants receiving similar sentences can expect to leave the prison after two years if they make no trouble.) Carter, however, was continually clashing with the prison authorities and was cited at least ten times between 1958 and 1961 for infractions ranging from refusing to obey an order to inciting a riot.

Even before Carter entered prison, law-enforcement officials had described him as a bitter, remorseless young man who appeared to be a future menace to society. John Feenan, Passaic County's probation officer, wrote in his presentencing report in late September 1957 that Carter showed no contrition or understanding of the seriousness of the charges. . . . In view of (his) juvenile delinquency record, his school record, and the present offense, the obvious conclusion that must be drawn is that Rubin Carter appears to be an aggressive, assaultive, bullying type of youth with sadistic tendencies.

Once in Trenton State, Carter was again evaluated, this time by the prison psychologist, C. J. Farrell, who concluded the following after a brief examination:

Because he is still young, the ability to ventilate his hostility through the socially acceptable ring endeavors might forestall future assaultive behaviors, although this is looked upon dubiously and only as a temporary thing. When the time arrives that Rubin's ring aspirations do not exist, he will become more aggressive and it is predicted that a repetition of the present involvement will occur.

A year later, on October 1, 1959, M. Borlin, another prison psychologist, described Carter as an

unstable, extremely aggressive, assaultive, hostile, antagonistic, immature, narcissistic, negativistic, impulsive, sadistic individual of average intelligence. This individual is almost completely lacking in controls, tending to act out impulsively the tremendous amount of hostility and aggression that is continuously boiling within him.

Despite the rather critical psychological reports, Carter's prison term turned out to be a time of physical, emotional, and intellectual growth. Although he began working in the prison's tailor shop, he soon refused to work anywhere in the prison. Instead, he began a regimen of training and physical conditioning in preparation for his return to the ring and the start of a professional boxing career. Carter also began tuning up his mind as well as his body. He commenced a reading program that included works by Freud, Jung, and Machiavelli. Out in the yard he would jog; in his cell he would do push-ups. After jogging he would go to the prison gym, where he worked on the heavy bag and the speed bag and tossed medicine balls. It felt like he was back in the army again with the boxing team, only the atmosphere was "a thousand times more intense." At the end of the day, after his evening meal, Rubin would return to reading and studying his books.

The time passed slowly, but Rubin felt himself growing stronger both physically and mentally. Prison officials refused to recognize the significant changes that were taking place in Carter's mental and emotional outlook. They persisted in categorizing him as a somewhat unstable inmate, always on the verge of exploding violently. Carter remained unaffected by the damaging psychological reports by prison officials. He could now see that freedom was only a few months away. He devoted himself even more ardently to preparing for his boxing career by practicing against all of the prison's best fighters.

Word soon spread through the grapevine, reaching outside, into the world of professional boxing, that Carter was ready to fight and would shortly be released from prison. Offers came to him from potential managers and trainers from Philadelphia, New York, Los Angeles, and Chicago. Promises of rich contracts, up-front money, and attractive jobs raised his spirits even more as his release date grew closer. He settled on Billy Legget as his manager because he knew him fairly well—Legget's full-time job was as a guard at Trenton State Prison. On September 21, 1961, Carter walked out of prison, realizing that he had spent nine of his twenty-four years locked behind bars.

SALVATION THROUGH BOXING

As Carter walked out of Trenton State Prison, he had rather mixed feelings:

> I didn't know where my next meal was coming from. With just ten dollars in my pocket and only the clothing on my back; with no prospects for a job and a new home in a city where I had no friends and with the burden of being an ex-convict to boot, I was a very likely candidate for jailing again before the night could fall.

Fortunately things were not quite so bad. True to his word, Billy Legget was waiting to meet him on the outside. Legget insisted it wasn't too late to begin a boxing career despite Carter's self-doubts. Legget made arrangements for him to live with Tommy Brown, a former prize fighter who had his own house.

The day after his release, Legget came by and asked Carter if he wanted to go down to Maryland with him and watch a fight between Virgil Atkins and Kenny Lane (Legget would be working in Atkins's corner). When they arrived, Carter went up into the stands to watch and began munching on hot dogs and drinking soda. A few minutes later Legget called to him to come down—he had a fight for him, right then and there. Things were complicated, however, because Carter did not have a boxing license yet. He met the Maryland commissioner, who was very dubious of the entire enterprise. Legget talked the commissioner into approving the fight. They hustled into the locker room, where he borrowed equipment from other fighters.

His opponent was Pike Reed, a decent middleweight from Washington, D.C., and a local favorite. They went toe to toe for three rounds and when the fight was over, Carter was declared the winner. He was so exhausted from his effort he couldn't get off the stool in his corner. He returned to the dressing room, where the commissioner asked him several questions. They couldn't believe he wasn't a professional and had never fought before.

Carter earned twenty dollars for the fight, but the money would not be paid to him until the Maryland Boxing Commission had verified his statements. He was frustrated as he left the stadium, but a reporter located him and began to interview him as he was walking across the parking lot. The reporter was very encouraging and moved by Carter's difficulties. He even gave Carter ten dollars.

Back in Trenton, Rubin followed a rigorous training routine to get back into fighting shape. Legget would come by at 4:00 A.M., and they would go running out on the highway. Carter would jog, sprint, and run at least ten miles per day. He never wanted to get tired again. In the evening he walked over to an old gym his manager owned.

Trenton was a boxing town. It was the hometown of Ike Williams, the lightweight champion. Bucky's gym had several good fighters training there. George Johnson and Winnie Winfred were his sparring partners. Winfred, a welterweight, was kind and patient with Carter. He was only seventeen and an amateur, but would soon turn pro.

Carter was frustrated because of his financial condition. His house was without heat. He was ready to go back to Paterson, where at least he had a warm home and good food waiting for him. Legget found him a job in Levittown, New Jersey, scrubbing floors, but one day on the job was all he could take. When he got home that night, Billy was waiting to take him to the gym for a workout, but Carter was too exhausted to train. Luckily his father and brother came down that evening on a surprise visit. They were appalled by the absence of food or heat in the house. They took him out to a grocery store, where they bought a stock of food. Next, they phoned the oil company, which promised to come by the next morning and fill the tank.

The following day Carter's boxing license arrived in the mail along with a contract to fight Holly Mims, a top-ranked middleweight, in a six-round fight. He was guaranteed a thousand dollars, and three hundred had already been advanced to his manager, Billy Legget. Carter was infuriated because Legget had been telling him they were broke, and Legget was sitting on three hundred dollars that Carter badly needed. Billy apologized, but Carter refused to fight on October 6 against Mims.

Legget waited for Carter's anger to cool, finally coming by his house on October 11 to ask him if he wanted to go to Reading, Pennsylvania, for a fight with a boxer not yet named. Carter agreed. He soon learned his opponent would be Philadelphia's tall, long-armed Joe Cooper, a local favorite. They would be the opening fight on that evening's card. Carter wasted no time, knocking Cooper out in the first round with a powerful barrage of punches that sent his opponent tumbling through the ropes and falling out of the ring. The crowd was stunned. Carter's father, who had driven down from Paterson, excitedly jumped into the ring and hugged his son, both men glowing with happiness.

His first loss was a six-round decision to Herschell Jacobs, a light heavyweight. This was his second fight with Jacobs, and it made no sense. All of this was being orchestrated, not by Billy Legget, but by Carmen Tedeschi, a contractor who walked into his dressing room that night. Legget stated that Carmen was Carter's new manager. Carter was fighting every couple of weeks in Jersey City, Union City, and at St. Nicholas Arena in New York. By the end of October 1962, Carter had won twelve of his first fourteen fights, ten by knockouts. His furious fighting style earned him his famous nickname, "Hurricane."

Around this time another stroke of good fortune graced Carter: he met and fell in love with his future wife, Mae Thelma Bosket. Carter described her as his soul mate. She was slim and very attractive and possessed a stubborn streak to match his. Their whirlwind romance and marriage withstood very difficult times throughout the decade they remained married, until the strain of his seemingly endless imprisonment finally ended the marriage in 1976, shortly after his second trial.

On October 27, 1962, a little more than a year after he left Trenton State Prison, Carter made the big time: a nationally televised fight in Madison Square Garden, which he won decisively with a brutal first-round knockout of Florentino Fernandez. Over the ensuing year Carter's next seven bouts were all televised and yielded increasingly lucrative winnings. As 1963 drew to a close, Carter had become the number-one contender in the middleweight division.

He signed to fight Emile Griffith, former welterweight champion, on December 20, 1963, in Pittsburgh's Civic Arena. Carter was good friends with Griffith, who had just been voted fighter of the year. Carter needed a strategy to stop Griffith from dancing away from his punishing body punches, so before the fight he began taunting Griffith to come after him. Carter's ploy was successful—Griffith abandoned his normally cautious style and waded into the "Hurricane" with reckless abandon. Carter seized the opportunity, unleashing a punishing series of jabs and hooks, and knocking out the former champion in the first round.

Carter received even better news six weeks later, when his wife gave birth to their first child, a daughter named Theodora. Rubin had now set up his training in Chatham, New Jersey, a quiet suburban town. He began spending more and more time at the peaceful training facility during the next two years. By the spring of 1964, Carter had risen to become the number-one middleweight contender for the championship crown. He was so angered by the way the press had treated him during his difficulties with Paterson police that he refused all interviews.

Across the Hudson from Carter's Paterson home, a seemingly unrelated minor riot in Harlem caused even more problems for him. On April 17, 1964, for no apparent reason, random violence spread through Harlem. Some thought it might be related to several children turning over a fruit stand, although the police believed it was sparked by the murder of a shopkeeper by six teenagers. Carter, during an interview with Hyman Gross of the *Saturday Evening Post*, contended that the rioting was caused by the police flooding into Harlem after the murder, beating and kicking black kids in the neighborhood. Carter stated that the black community should have fought back against this police violence, even to the death if necessary. Carter added a final comment that he believed was off the record: "During last summer's riots, I told Elwood Tuck, let's get our own guns and go up there and get us some of those cops. I know I can get four or five before they get me. How many can you get?"[2]

Despite Carter's insistence that his comments were stated strictly in jest, many police officers, particularly those in Paterson and throughout Passaic County, did not see any humor in his statement. It was clear that they would retaliate against Carter at the first opportunity. Carter was surprised his quip created such an uproar. He failed to appreciate that he was now a famous boxer, on the edge of winning a championship, and was therefore good copy. The boxing legend Sugar Ray Robinson called him in after the article was published and told him he should have never said those things. Even though his words may have been taken out of context, the damage was done. Carter had several friends on the Paterson Police Force, both black and white officers, and they all warned him to be careful.

After a difficult summer, Carter finally was able to arrange for a title bout with the champion, Joey Giardello, in Philadelphia in late December. Carter decided to totally revamp his support team. Elwood Tuck, a long-time friend from Paterson, was his adviser. The new manager was Patty Amato, and the new trainer was Jimmy Wilde who had worked with five former champions.

The Giardello fight would bring Carter the richest purse of his career— $12,500. Giardello also had a troubled background; a brawler from the tough South Philly neighborhood, he was trying to forge a new middle-class suburban life with his wife and three kids in Cherry Hill, New Jersey.

The fight took place on December 14, 1964, in Philadelphia's Convention Hall. As the fight began, Carter took his usual aggressive approach, stalking Giardello, who danced clockwise away from Carter's lethal left hook. In the fourth round Carter staggered the champ with several head shots and opened a cut over Giardello's left eye. Still Giardello was able to dodge his powerful punches for the next eleven rounds, and Carter began to tire. In the thirteenth, Giardello staggered Carter with a series of hooks and continued pounding Carter's head and body in the next two rounds. Despite his clear domination of the first ten rounds, Carter lost the fight. A comparison of the fighters' faces—Giardello's bleeding and battered, Carter's untouched—cast doubt on the official outcome. It was, many thought, a "Philadelphia decision."

It became increasingly obvious to Carter that all of the police and media attention was wearing him down. He even discovered that the FBI had been following him around. When he checked into his hotel in Los Angeles before the Rodriguez fight, the police chief, William Parker, called Rubin and asked him to come downtown to police headquarters to register as an ex-convict, as required by California law. Parker boasted to Carter that he had known Carter was coming to town because the FBI had notified him. They had been trailing him for quite a while, according to Parker. Carter's time in Los Angeles was marred by the outbreak of the Watts rebellion. Needing a rest after that nightmare, he traveled to South America the next month to fight Joe "The Killer" Ngidi.

Carter had an exhausting year in 1965, traveling around the globe for his nine fights. Although he won six of the fights, five by knockouts, Carter knew he was no longer as sharp as he once was. By January 1966 Rubin was still only twenty-eight years old but he had fought thirty bouts in the past four years, a pace that had taken a heavy toll on his body. Nevertheless, he resumed the hectic pace and fought five more times, traveling from Chicago to Honolulu and back to South Africa. Again, his record suffered as a result of the frantic pace—he won only two of the five fights. Rubin was tired of traveling and living out of suitcases. He missed his family and just wanted to go home and have a well-earned vacation with his wife and daughter. He was just beginning to enjoy relaxing with his friends and family when the fateful events of June 17, 1966, began to unfold.

THE SECOND DEFENDANT—JOHN ARTIS

The second defendant in the Lafayette Bar murder case was John Artis, then a recent high school graduate preparing to enter the U.S. Army. Although Carter's name dominates the public's memory of this case, it was John Artis who was charged by the prosecution with shooting three people inside the bar at nearly point-blank range, firing five rounds into one victim as she lay pleading for her life.

It has never been easy for the prosecution to reconcile these acts with the quiet, soft-spoken personality of John Artis. How could a young man without any trace of a criminal record, with a strong attachment to the local Baptist Church and the good possibility of a college scholarship, choose to go into a bar he had never been in before, in the company of a man he barely knew, and without the slightest provocation shoot three innocent people to death?

Nothing in John Artis's brief life could shed any light on this mystery. He was born in Portsmouth, Virginia, in 1946 and moved to Paterson four years later. He graduated from the city's Central High School in 1964 and was twenty years old when he was arrested for the Lafayette Bar and Grill homicides. While attending Central High, he distinguished himself in athletics (football and track) and was awarded a college scholarship for his prowess in track. Unfortunately, shortly after graduation his mother died, and his college plans had to be postponed. He was greatly affected by her death and, as he stated, "I didn't really feel like doing anything."

He held several jobs over the following year, the longest one being with the Maigar Car Corporation in Paterson, where he worked as a brakeman. In early 1966 he grew dissatisfied and took a leave of absence, looking for some other type of opportunity. Another factor affecting his future plans was the war in Vietnam. He believed he would soon be drafted. He reasoned that it might be best simply to enlist, complete his obligation, and then go to college. He planned to visit his high school track coach in a few days to discuss the feasibility of his new timetable. He hoped the coach would assist him in speaking to the college and requesting a postponement on his scholarship until after he completed his military service.[3]

According to Reverend Roger L. Douglas, pastor of the New Christian Missionary Baptist Church, Artis was remembered as a "law-abiding and very fine young man." John especially enjoyed singing and was an active member of Paterson's Young People's Choir. His other main interest was his participation in several town basketball leagues.

Into this seemingly unremarkable but promising young life marched the events of June 17, 1966. After that date he lost his scholarship, his career prospects, his freedom, and even several appendages. For the next fourteen years John Artis was confined in a New Jersey state prison, where he contracted Buerger's disease, a rare circulatory illness that led to the amputation of several of his toes and fingers.

3: The First Trial
May 1967

On June 29, 1966, a grand jury convened to hear testimony from a select group of potential witnesses in the case of the Lafayette Bar and Grill murders, but nothing significant was uncovered. Detective Vincent DeSimone, who was in charge of the investigation of the Lafayette Bar shootings, testified that, based on the limited descriptions the police had gathered from a few witnesses, no suspects could be determined. This exclusion applied to Carter and Artis, who "weren't even close," according to DeSimone. Even the ten-thousand-dollar reward failed to elicit any leads—just a scattering of crank informants. A woman from Florida was taken seriously when she said she knew the killers. She was flown up to Paterson, where she accused two brothers of the crime. After being detained for two months as a material witness, she admitted she had been lying, hoping that she could lay claim to the reward money.

As the hot summer days passed and fall began, rumors of an initial break in the case circulated. By the second week in October, the gossip had grown to the point that the *Paterson Evening News* printed an article hinting that a group of policemen had been seen escorting a short, heavy-set young man through the Alexander Hamilton Hotel. Subsequent stories reported that this mysterious person had been led out of the hotel and relocated in a more secluded locale, a rooming house in the Broadway Hill section of Paterson, where police were observed guarding the house. Who was the person demanding such police protection? What did he know about the Lafayette murders, and who would he implicate?

AL BELLO COMES FORWARD, AND ARRESTS ARE MADE

Unlike most rumors concerning the case, these had substance. The mysterious individual under protective custody was none other than Alfred Bello, the lookout on a small-time robbery who had been waiting for the first police car as it rushed to the scene of the crime. His initial statements to the police provided only a vague description of two black men and their white car leaving the bar following the shooting. Bello, it appeared, had more to say, and his testimony proved critical in prosecution efforts to convict Carter and Artis in both trials. The only new aspect to the case was the unexpected death of one of the victims, Hazel Tanis, on July 14. Although her wounds were very serious, she had begun to gain strength and doctors were cautiously optimistic. Unfortunately, she took a drastic turn for the worse and quickly expired on July 14.

Bello had been nervous since the early morning hours of June 17, when he inadvertently became involved in the case. He realized that Patty Valentine had spotted him inside the bar as she ran down the stairs and entered the tavern after hearing gunshots. An additional problem was the burglary that he and his buddies had been attempting just two blocks away. As police questioned Ms. Valentine, Bello tried to detect whether she was telling them about his presence. To his relief she did not mention him at that moment, but he could not be sure that upon further interrogation she would not reveal his whereabouts. As the crowd around the Lafayette Bar grew larger with the arrival of more police and rescue equipment, Bello slipped back into the group of spectators for a few minutes longer and then went back to find Bradley so they could join Kellogg in the getaway car and leave the area. At this point the police had only obtained a description of a white car speeding away from the Lafayette but no clear description of the shooters.

The first break in the case came in July, when Bello bumped into a Paterson patrolman, Donald LaConte, in a local bar, Frankie's Play Pen. According to Bello's testimony at Carter's retrial in 1976, the two men were conversing when he told LaConte, who he knew had been at the Lafayette Bar shootings, that he (Bello) had not been alone that evening when he gave the police the description of the getaway car. LaConte asked who had been with him, and Bello identified Arthur Dexter Bradley.

The following day Bello was asked to come down to the police station. When he arrived at the station, he noticed Bradley was also there. Bello was questioned by LaConte and several detectives. He admitted to them that he had been in the area that evening "to do a job at the Ace Metal Company," although he did not reveal the identity of his coconspirators. Bello later explained that the reason for his decision not to give up his partners was because he was on parole, had a brother in prison, and had stolen money from the open cash register at the Lafayette Bar.[1]

It is puzzling that with all of these concerns, Bello nevertheless was willing to offer the Paterson police this opening crack in solving the Lafayette slayings. Why say anything at all, especially if you were already in trouble and had all of these fears? Two possible explanations emerge, although neither one is easily provable. First, Bello may have been fishing around for help with his parole, since he did subsequently ask Detective DeSimone to have his parole transferred from Passaic to Bergen County. He was also interested in the possibility of cashing in on the reward money, now raised to twelve thousand dollars, and he was testing the waters to see if the police would guarantee at least a partial payment.

A second reason relates to his natural volubility. He enjoyed playing the role of a big shot or at least posturing as an inside dopester. By dropping these hints, he quickly gained the spotlight and the intense interest of the Paterson police. Bello's loose tongue and craving for attention continued to frustrate and confuse both defense and prosecution efforts for years to come.

Despite this initial break in the case, the Paterson police did not pursue the lead, possibly because they viewed Bello as an unreliable source or because they doubted his story's relevance to the murders. Their investigation stagnated for two more months until Bello ran into LaConte a second time. It was now October 3, and Bello was relaxing in Joe From's Bar in Totowa, a Paterson suburb, when Officer LaConte came over to him and they began talking. According to Bello, he told LaConte that "you had the two guys and let them go." LaConte tried to elicit their names and additional information, but Bello was reluctant to discuss it further. He was willing to talk to LaConte's superiors with the specified exception of Detective DeSimone. Bello later explained that he thought DeSimone believed him to the be the prime suspect in what was viewed as a robbery/murder. It is also likely that Bello thought that DeSimone, an aggressive detective with a citywide reputation for toughness, would force him to disclose more than he desired. From the very beginning of the investigation, DeSimone made it clear to Bello that he knew Bello had stolen money from the open cash drawer. A meeting was arranged for later that evening at Paterson's City Line Diner. LaConte would bring his boss, Detective Robert Mohl.

A short time later, meeting with LaConte and Mohl, Bello dropped a bombshell that reverberated throughout the New Jersey justice system for the next two decades. According to Bello, he told the police officers the details of everything he had witnessed in the early morning hours outside the Lafayette Bar, including the identity of the two men he had seen fleeing from inside the bar. He identified them as Rubin Carter and John Artis, the same two men Bello had seen being brought back to the bar in their white car after the shooting. Despite the critical nature of Bello's disclosures, it was never clear whether he reached any understanding with Detective Mohl as to what bearing this information would have on his parole problems or his eligibility for the reward money. The conversations were not recorded on tape or in the form of notes by either police officer. We are forced to rely on the fluid, constantly shifting testimony of Alfred Bello, a person whose credibility waned as the case progressed.

Eight days later, Bello had the opportunity to meet with the feared DeSimone (as well as LaConte and Mohl) and give a more complete oral statement at the Wayne police station. (The parties decided a neutral site would be prudent, not wishing to alert the press and public to the recent developments in the case.) Bello repeated his story, at least the same account he had given Mohl and LaConte the week before, in which he implicated Carter and Artis. Supposedly unbeknownst to Bello, the conversation was being taped—a recorder was fixed under the table, hidden from view.[2] They also discussed in a rather perfunctory fashion Bello's request for some assistance from DeSimone in having his parole transferred to a safer jurisdiction. The gruff detective said he would look into it but did not promise anything definite.

The defense attorneys I interviewed doubted the spontaneity of these taped conversations, insinuating that they most likely had been rehearsed earlier or simply prior to the tape recorder being turned on. Given the questionable credibility of all participants, such skepticism is probably warranted. In any event, the Paterson police now had the evidence necessary to arrest Carter and Artis and announce to a still grieving, angry Paterson that the Lafayette Bar murders had finally been solved. The police waited three more days before bringing Bello back in again, this time taking a formal statement from him and Arthur Dexter Bradley naming

Carter and Artis as the two men they saw exiting the Lafayette Bar and then driving away in a white car. As soon as his statement was given, Bello was placed in protective custody under heavy police guard.

On the day after Bello and Bradley formally identified Carter and Artis—October 15, 1966—both men were arrested in the early morning hours and placed in the maximum security section of the Passaic County jail. Carter was arrested at 2:30 A.M., Artis four hours earlier. The two men were taken from their separate isolation cells at 9:00 A.M. the next day to be arraigned in Paterson Municipal Court by Magistrate Charles Alfano. The magistrate notified both men of their constitutional rights and accepted not-guilty pleas from the defendants. Carter had already selected Raymond Brown, accomplished Newark defense attorney, to be his lawyer.

The men were held without bail pending a tentative preliminary hearing scheduled for October 25. Assistant Prosecutor Hull, who headed the investigation, would not comment on a possible motive for the slayings. Ten days later, a grand jury was convened in the basement of the local YMCA. Although there were a number of witnesses offering testimony, the critical witness was Al Bello, the mysterious person the police had been holding in seclusion for two weeks. Within three days the grand jury indicted the two defendants, and the interminable legal struggle began.

THE TRIAL BEGINS—JURY SELECTION AND OPENING STATEMENTS

Although Thelma Carter had been able to obtain the services of Raymond Brown within one day of her husband's arrest, Carter did not meet with him until February 1967, four months later. Carter was aware of Brown's reputation as an experienced, shrewd defense attorney, but he was not very reassured upon seeing him for the first time. Carter, in his autobiography, describes the scene in detail:

He didn't appear very spectacular as he ambled into the consultation room, wearing a dumpy brown suit. He was tall, and high yellow in complexion—what most black people refer to as a redbone. His hair was short and kinky, dust colored, and he walked with a slouch, like he was ready to sit down at every step. I learned later that his appearance was deceptive and that there was nothing slouchy about his mind. He was sharp, and I felt that I was in good hands. . . . One thing did bother me though: I had been writing him regularly . . . but this was the first time I had seen or heard from him—only one month before my trial was to begin. Somehow, this just didn't grab me right. It didn't feel good at all.

Artis had chosen Arnold Stein for his attorney. Stein, a short, bespectacled man in his midforties, had an excellent reputation as a theorist and tactician, whereas Brown was the showman who would do the bulk of the actual arguing. Stein looked more like a law professor than an aggressive courtroom litigator. In this trial, Stein played a secondary role, rarely taking the floor. (Stein later went on to a distinguished career on the bench, serving both as a superior court judge and as a member of the appeals court.)

Brown's adversary was the assistant prosecutor Vincent Hull, a young, promising, well-connected lawyer (his father had been a New Jersey state senator) who later used this case as a career steppingstone—he eventually wound up as a superior court judge. Seated beside him throughout the trial was his chief investigator, Detective Vincent DeSimone. The judge was Samuel Larner, who had recently been appointed to the superior court in Essex County but had been transferred over to Passaic County to temporarily replace a vacationing judge. As the trial was about to commence, Larner had been on the bench less than a month. He appeared to most observers to be rather short-tempered and anxious to move the proceedings along as quickly as possible. Larner and Brown were no strangers to each other, having served as cocounsels, defending two men in a major conspiracy case to commit espionage.

Jury selection was to begin on April 15, but the first order of business was notification by Hull to the court that the state would seek the death penalty for both defendants. Judge Larner instructed the ninety-six prospective jurors at the Passaic County Courthouse that under New Jersey law a first-degree murder conviction without a recommendation of mercy automatically calls for the death penalty, whereas a recommendation of mercy means a life sentence. Larner also explained that jurors must not be hampered by their personal feelings about the death penalty "but be willing to follow the state law and vote a murder conviction without recommending mercy if, in your opinion, the evidence warrants it." Nevertheless, two potential jurors were excused the first day by the judge because of their adamant opposition to the death penalty.

The jury selection dragged on for the next three weeks until the required fourteen jurors were selected. (At the conclusion of the trial, lots are drawn, and two of the jurors are removed while the remaining twelve deliberate the case.) By the time the final juror had been selected, 377 potential jurors had been questioned. Considering that in New Jersey the defense is allowed twenty peremptory challenges and the prosecution twelve, most of the potential jurors were dismissed for cause. (A peremptory challenge need not be based upon any specific reason, merely a hunch that a juror will not be sympathetic to one's case.) The defense utilized all twenty of its peremptory challenges, while the prosecution used only eight.

Although several jurors were able to convince the judge that because the trial would probably be rather lengthy, their service on the jury would cause them serious personal or financial difficulties, the overwhelming majority of jurors were eliminated because they had already reached a definite conclusion about the guilt or innocence of the defendants on the basis of pretrial media coverage. Both of the local newspapers, the *Paterson Morning Call* and the *Evening News*, had been covering the case rather thoroughly from its inception. Local radio stations had also been discussing the case since mid-June. Thus, any juror who wished to get off the jury had a ready-made excuse. The possibility of having to impose the death penalty raised an additional reason for disqualification, although only a handful of individuals employed this excuse.

The final fourteen persons chosen for the jury included ten men and four women. Only one black person was chosen, who ended up as one of the two individuals eliminated at the end of the trial by random lot and thereby excluded from the final deliberations. Nearly all of the jurors were either mid-level, white-collar employees or skilled laborers. Half of the jurors lived in either Paterson or neighboring Clifton. The remainder resided in small suburban communities outside of Paterson such as Wayne, Pompton Lakes, or Teterboro.

The final juror chosen, Natalie Congdon, a press operator from Wanaque, was named on Tuesday, May 9. The trial began later that same day, with opening statements from the prosecution and defense. Hull said that he would present both direct and circumstantial evidence to prove beyond a reasonable doubt that Carter and Artis had committed the murders. The direct evidence was in large measure the eyewitness testimony of Alfred Bello and Arthur Bradley, who said they had spotted the defendants leaving the bar and walking toward them.

Hull acknowledged that his witnesses were not very upstanding citizens and, in fact, were "up to no good" on the early morning hours of June 17. In fact, they were attempting to break into the Ace Sheet Metal Company around the corner on East Sixteenth Street. Even more damning was Hull's admission that Bello entered the tavern after the shootings and rifled the open cash register, stealing approximately twenty-five to thirty dollars. An important third witness announced by the state was Patty Graham Valentine, who lived above the tavern and observed the getaway car through her second-story window.

The only contentious portion of the prosecutor's opening statement was when Hull claimed that the state would be able to show that the police had recovered a 12-gauge shotgun shell and live Smith and Wesson .32-caliber bullets from Carter's automobile. Hull stated that the state would be able to link the shell and bullet to the weapons used by the murderers. The defense quickly objected, with Brown arguing that the admissibility of this evidence was pending in pretrial motions regarding the legality of the search. Judge Larner rejected the defense attorney's argument, stating that "this issue was determined on pretrial application as far as I know, and counsel can refer to that which he intends. If he doesn't prove it, it is up to the jury to disregard it. I will not limit (the prosecutor) in that connection."

The ruling by Larner was a bad omen for the defense, but it was now time for Brown and Stein to rise and offer their own version of the case through their opening statements. Brown went first and spoke for nearly a half hour. Dressed in a wrinkled gray suit with his Ben Franklin–style glasses about to slip off the end of his nose, he ambled over to the jury box and began to speak, arguing forcefully that the defense would present an absolute denial of the prosecution's allegations. He was especially critical of the state's star witnesses, whom he described as "two thieves," with Mr. Bello receiving the additional characterization of "ghoul," even hinting that Bello himself might have been responsible for the heinous crime. He also emphasized the fact that Carter had been cooperating with the police from the time of the crime until his indictment in November. He told the jury that as the case develops they will "find so many unanswered questions in your mind that I know that reasonable doubt on top of reasonable doubt will exist." Brown concluded his opening statement with a description of the defense's version of the events of June 16 and 17, hammering away at the credibility of Bello and Bradley.

After Brown sat down, Arnold Stein was given an opportunity to present his brief opening statement, which in large part reiterated the major points raised by his colleague. Stein closed by saying that "John Artis was not in the tavern. He does not belong in this courtroom today as a criminal defendant . . . so you (the jury) should explore this whole case when you listen to it in the context of what conceivable reason this young man . . . would have to be in that tavern shooting down four innocent people with whom he had no contact at all."

With the conclusion of the opening statements, the morning session of the trial's first day ended. In the afternoon the prosecution began to argue its case, presenting a wide array of witnesses.

THE PROSECUTION PRESENTS ITS CASE

The first witness for the prosecution was Charles Geiger, an engineer who explained, through the use of charts, blueprints, and photographs, the layout of the bar and immediate neighborhood surrounding the Lafayette Bar and Grill. A few additional witnesses, mainly police officers who were present at the crime scene immediately after the shootings, were also called. Several gruesome photographs of the victims were shown to the jury at this time.

During cross-examination, Brown was able to portray a rather sloppy, lackadaisical effort by police investigators working the crime scene. No fingerprints were taken, nor were paraffin tests given to anyone. The failure to check for fingerprints seemed especially egregious considering the police initially believed that robbery was the primary motive and the cash register was wide open.[3]

The first witness on the trial's second day was William Marins, the sole survivor of the Lafayette slaughter. A stolid, balding man in his midforties, he began to recount the deadly events that claimed the lives of his three friends. He was not sure of the exact time—somewhere between 2:30 and 3:00 A.M.—when two black men came into the bar and began firing their weapons. One had a shotgun, while the other one, who was standing behind him, held a pistol. Both men appeared to be about six feet tall. He was unable to provide a detailed description of the men other than stating that the one holding a shotgun had a thin moustache. Shortly after hearing the initial gunfire, Marins turned toward the doorway and immediately felt a sharp pain in the left side of his head. He remembers noticing smoke coming out of the barrel of the gun just before he passed out on the bar. He regained consciousness within a few minutes, just before the police arrived. He clearly remembers their assisting him out of the bar to the waiting ambulance and being driven to St. Joseph's Hospital.

Throughout the questioning by Prosecutor Hull, Marins tried to emphasize how groggy he was following the shooting, believing himself to be in a state of shock for several hours, including the period of his initial questioning by the police at the hospital. He emphasized his fuzziness throughout this entire interval, indicating that it was not possible for him to clearly know what he was saying to the police while he was receiving medical attention at the hospital. He also felt that he could not have been very certain about failing to identify Carter and Artis because of his impaired mental and physical condition. It was clear that the prosecutor had carefully prepped this important eyewitness to the shooting. Because his earlier statements to the police, especially to Detective Callahan in the hospital, tended to exculpate Carter and Artis, Marins now had to modify his initial description of two fairly tall, light-colored black men. It was all too obvious that Carter, five feet seven inches tall, dark-skinned, and with a short, powerful build, did not even come close to fitting the description of the shooters Marins saw in the Lafayette Bar.

The prosecution concluded its direct examination of Marins by again emphasizing his medical condition. Because of his shock and heavy medication, the prosecution urged the jury to minimize the importance of Marins's failure to identify Carter and Artis when they were presented to him in the hospital.

The defense, now about to begin its cross-examination of Marins, would have to resurrect his refusal to identify Carter and Artis in the hospital room. It was more than mere semantics, for if the jury did believe his initial exoneration of the defendants, it would significantly improve their chances of an acquittal.

Raymond Brown was armed with six different statements made by Marins that supported the defense position. Of prime importance was his statement to the police in the hospital but, but he also cited a corroborating deposition that Marins had given in a civil suit that he had initiated against the bar. As Brown began to confront Marins with the contradictions between his earlier statements and his just-concluded testimony as a prosecution witness, Marins became increasingly agitated. In his autobiography Carter described the tightrope upon which Brown was walking as his questions became more pointed:

> He (Marins) was really hostile now, sullen, short-tempered, and vicious. It was a frightening thing to watch. He knew the killers were supposed to be black, and he seemed willing to send us to the electric chair just because John and I happened to be black, not because he thought we were guilty of the crime. He knew the jury would be more sympathetic to him and his lost eye, and to those three dead people, than to anything that we had to say. And Brown knew it too. He didn't want to push this man around, but he had to. Otherwise the witness just might change-up completely, and claim that John and I were definitely the ones who shot those people.

After Marins's lengthy testimony, he stepped down from the witness stand, his face florid with anger. The court was adjourned for the day. How receptive had the jury been to Marin's evolving interpretation of what he saw that night? Which version would they find most believable?

The newspaper accounts of the first two days of the trial evince a clear anti-Carter slant, reflecting, perhaps, Paterson's long history of racial tensions. During the 1960s these tensions were evident in the simmering antagonism between the Italian and Irish ruling elite and the increasingly black and Hispanic populace. An example of this attitude is an article by Everitt Harvey on May 10 (one month before the trial was scheduled to begin) in the *Paterson Morning Call*. The article describes Carter as a man obsessed with guns and violence. It also reminded the city of Carter's juvenile record, which included a lengthy sentence to Jamesburg Reformatory for a brutal assault with a knife.

The first witness on the third day of the trial was Patricia Graham Valentine (known to most of her friends as Patty), the woman who lived above the tavern at the time of the shootings. Ms. Valentine, thirty-three years old and so soft-spoken that she could barely be heard, described how she had fallen asleep watching television and was awakened by a loud noise. She went to the front window, where she heard two more noises followed by a women's voice moaning, "Oh, no!" She then moved to her bedroom window, where she saw two black men running toward a white car parked on the side street. As the car pulled away from the curb, she noticed that the taillights were shaped like triangles or butterflies. As the car vanished into the night, she went downstairs, entering the bar through a side door.

Once inside she saw a young man (Al Bello) standing by the front door. As she surveyed the bloody scene, she recognized all four victims. She remembers screaming and dashing up the stairs to call the police. As she went out the side door, she noticed Bello had moved to the end of the bar near the cash register. When she came back down the stairs she moved across the barroom to try and offer some assistance to Hazel Tanis, a long-time friend. Hazel asked her to phone her boyfriend. As Ms. Valentine went outside to go upstairs and make the requested call, she saw Bello running on Lafayette toward the bar. After making the call, she went downstairs for a third time. By this time the police had arrived.

During an aggressive cross-examination, Ray Brown challenged the accuracy of Ms. Valentine's observation as well as her overall credibility. She had stated that she had awakened at 2:30 A.M., at which time she heard voices. But Brown showed that she had somehow divined the time because although the television set was still on, all of the shows had now gone off the air. It was also determined that she knew Bello fairly well and that he had in fact visited her on several occasions.

In retrospect, Valentine's testimony at the first trial appears to have been carefully rehearsed. As an important witness who was on friendly terms with Detective DeSimone, it is likely that her observations were crafted by the detective to be maximally useful to the prosecution. In later years Valentine's testimony seemed increasingly tainted.

Brown's strident style of cross-examination appeared to be wearing on Judge Larner, and by the time the defense attorney began to attack Ms. Valentine's wavering and at times questionable testimony, Larner rose to her defense, warning Brown to ease up. Raymond Brown was not intimidated by the sharpness of the judge's comment, coming back at the judge with his own acerbic retorts. There were several instances where it looked like Brown would be held in contempt, but he would invariably reduce his level of contentiousness.

The next witness presented by the state was Ronald Ruggiero, a twenty-four-year old professional boxer who had trained with Carter and knew him fairly well. Ruggiero's testimony was important because he could substantiate Bello's movements up and down Lafayette Street at the time of the shootings. He lived near the bar, at 251 Lafayette Street, and on the morning of the shootings, he observed a white car containing two black men gliding down Lafayette. Ruggiero then saw Bello walk quickly down the street and return a minute later, heading toward the bar. He added that he saw Bello later that evening, milling around in the crowd that had gathered outside of the tavern. He was certain it was Bello he had spotted out on Lafayette because he knew him from a local gym.

Before the prosecution's star witness, Alfred Bello, could take the stand, the defense attempted to prevent him from testifying. Brown and Stein argued that there had been such blatant contradictions between the different statements that Bello had given to the police and the grand jury as to destroy his credibility as a viable witness. Brown raised the obvious question of why Bello had waited four months before coming forward to identify Carter and Artis. Could it have been related to Bello's efforts to obtain special treatment from the Paterson police and prosecutors? Bello was concerned over his current parole status as well as the possibility of his being charged for the attempted burglary of the Ace Metal Shop or the theft of twenty-five dollars from the open Lafayette Bar cash register. Bello was even hopeful of collecting a large portion of the twelve-thousand-dollar reward offered by the city of Paterson. Raymond Brown wondered aloud how someone as reprehensible as Bello might easily be willing to alter his testimony in order to satisfy the prosecution in exchange for favorable treatment in any of his previously noted difficulties.

Judge Larner agreed with the prosecution that the reason for these discrepancies was Bello's fear of retaliation from Carter as well as a concern for how the police would view his role in the burglary of the Ace Metal Company on the night of the shootings.

As Bello made his grand entrance into the courtroom, the police officers standing behind Carter edged closer to him in anticipation of a violent confrontation, but Carter remained calm. Bello proceeded to the witness stand, where the prosecutor was waiting for him. Bello's jet-black hair shone atop a stocky body perched upon elevator shoes (with exaggerated heels) as he confidently moved past the jury and took his seat.

Hull decided it was best to inform the jurors of Bello's unsavory background before he began to testify as to what he had seen on June 17. The jury learned that Bello had done time in both Annandale and Bordentown state reformatories. In 1962 he was convicted of robbery, breaking and entering, and larceny. In 1963 and again in 1964, he was convicted of larceny. He was currently on parole from the 1964 larceny conviction. At one point in his testimony he described himself simply as "a thief."

With Bello's mea culpa completed, Hull now asked him to describe the events in the early morning hours of June 17. He candidly explained that he and his two associates, Kenny Kellogg and Arthur Dexter Bradley, were near the Lafayette Grill, attempting to burglarize the Ace Sheet Metal Company on Sixteenth Street. While Bradley was trying to break in, Bello served as lookout, and Kellogg waited down the street in the getaway car. While waiting for Bradley to force the door open, Bello spotted a white Dodge driving slowly past with two black men and what appeared to be the barrel of a rifle sticking up between them. Growing fidgety, Bello decided to go for a pack of cigarettes at the Lafayette Bar just around the corner, two blocks away. As he started down Eighteenth Street, he heard two shots. He continued walking, heard two more shots, and then saw two black men coming toward him, one carrying a pistol and the other a shotgun. He knew they recognized him since he was less than twenty feet away. so he quickly turned around and ran. They chased him briefly but then jumped in their white car and drove off. At this point Hull asked Bello if he could point out those two men in the courtroom, and he identified Carter and Artis. Carter, he claimed, had been holding the shotgun and Artis the pistol.

Following the dramatic identification of the defendants, Bello continued to describe how he again began to walk to the Lafayette after the white car drove away. Bello next described the bloody scene inside the bar. He also observed the open cash-register drawer. Since he needed change to call the police, he quickly scooped up some change as well as an extra twenty-five dollars in bills. Just as he was exiting the bar, he heard Ms. Valentine scream and then quickly leave. He ran down the street to give the money to Bradley and then returned to the bar, realizing that the woman had seen him inside and might confuse him with the actual murderers. Police were now arriving on the scene, and he gave them a description of the white car. A short time later the police brought Carter and Artis back to the bar, at which time Bello told the police he could not identify them as the men he had seen in the car.

It was now time for defense attorney Raymond Brown to cross-examine Bello. Still appearing self-confident, Bello had a difficult time answering Brown's questions, which were designed to underscore the many inconsistencies between Bello's courtroom testimony and earlier statements he had given to the police and grand jury. After being caught in a series of contradictions, Bello became both acerbic and evasive, continually blaming his faulty memory for the numerous conflicts. As Brown pressed Bello on his having pilfered the money from the Lafayette Bar, the agitated witness responded, "Basically I am a thief. I admit that. I'm not an assassin, remember that."[4]

Brown now turned the interrogation toward the identification of the defendants. He confronted Bello with the fact that on the morning of June 17, he had told Sergeant Capter that he had not seen the faces of the two black men who emerged from the bar and drove away in the white car. In fact, he admitted that the two had not actually chased him or even walked close enough to him to make a positive identification. Brown also elicited Bello's acknowledgment that when Detective DeSimone brought the two defendants up to him (after the police had escorted them back to the bar), Bello told DeSimone he had not seen their faces and therefore could not identify them.

Bello's only retort to the blistering cross-examination by Brown was that his reason for not identifying them at the scene and waiting four months to come forward was his fear of retaliation from Carter and his friends and a fear of implicating himself in the burglary that he and Bradley were undertaking at the time. Brown then reacted bitterly to Bello's explanation, declaring that the real reason he had changed his testimony was to collect the reward money and gain help in the disposition of his recent criminal activities.

Bello had weathered a grueling two-day grilling from Brown. It was now time for Bello's partner to take the stand and verify his account of that evening's activities. His partner was Arthur Dexter Bradley, a slender twenty-two-year-old petty criminal with a criminal history that surpassed Bello's, although it included the same type of crimes: robbery, larceny, and burglary. In contrast to Bello, who spoke out forcefully and appeared to be playing to an audience, Bradley was very ill at ease and spoke so softly that the judge and jury had to lean forward to hear him.

Bradley testified that he had spotted Carter twice that evening but could not identify Artis. The first time was when he was trying to break into the Ace Metal Company and saw a white car drive by with four blacks, one of which he recognized as Carter. (Carter had been pointed out to him in 1964 when Bradley and a friend were cruising around Paterson late one evening. He later saw Carter's picture in a boxing magazine.) The second time was a short while later, after hearing gunshots and walking toward the bar, where he thought he would find Bello, who soon appeared in front of him. Just as Bradley was about to catch up to Bello, more gunshots rang out from the bar, and he saw two black men heading in their direction. He recognized the one holding either a rifle or a shotgun as Carter. Bradley could not recognize the other man since he — Bradley — quickly turned around and began running back toward the Ace Sheet Metal Company.

A short time later, Bello returned to the Metal Company, giving Bradley the money he had pilfered from the cash register. Bradley now decided it was time to evacuate the area and started walking away, looking for Kellogg with the getaway car. Eventually he found himself across from the bar, where the police and a large crowd had gathered. He crossed to the street to be with Bello, whom he now spotted by the bar. Two detectives, Lawless and Ruggiero, were taking Bello downtown to the police station, so Bradley hitched a ride with them. Bradley was dropped off just before they reached the station. He took a cab to Sylvia Smith's apartment, where he caught up with their wheelman, Kenny Kellogg. They then decided to go back and finish the burglary. Bradley completed the break-in, but when he located the safe, he was unable to open it. The frustrated group decided to give up on the job and go back home. They were becoming increasingly nervous because of the growing police presence in the neighborhood in the wake of the Lafayette Bar shooting.

Brown's cross-examination of Bradley paralleled his earlier efforts with Bello. He tried to show the jury that both men's lengthy criminal records cast a shadow over their testimony. Like Bello, Bradley admitted that he had lied in earlier statements to the police and in statements before the grand jury. (Even though he had committed perjury, he had never been charged.) Brown drove home the point that Bradley had even more to gain from changing his story because in October, when he came forward to give a statement to the police, he was facing charges on four armed robberies, two breaking-and-entering larcenies, one auto theft, and one possession of stolen property.

Brown closed the interrogation with a series of questions related to Bradley's ability to identify Carter with such certainty given the fact that he had only seen him once before and had glanced briefly at his picture in a sports magazine. The defense attorney was able to show the jury that Detective DeSimone, who was in charge of the investigation, had not spoken with Bradley until October 14, the day Carter and Artis were arrested. Bradley was in the Bordentown reformatory at the time, and at the time of the trial Bradley was confined in the Morris County Jail. As Bradley stepped down, the first week of the trial concluded.

The trial continued on Monday, May 16, with the testimony of the final member of the burglary trio, Kent Kellogg, the twenty-two-year-old "wheelman." Kellogg, now working as a short-order cook, told the jury he had gone to the Lafayette Bar immediately after parking the car, allowing Bello and Bradley to walk over to the Ace Metal Company and begin the burglary. He observed four people inside the tavern, but he quickly left, realizing he had no money. He went back to his car parked on Franklin Street and laid down in the back seat. He then heard a series of shots coming from the tavern. Kellogg's testimony generally corroborated much of what Bello and Bradley had told the court the preceding week.

The prosecution now proceeded to bring forward a series of Paterson police officers to describe the scene at the Lafayette as well as detail the capture of Artis and Carter. The first policeman to testify was Alexander Greenough, the initial officer to arrive at the murder scene. Greenough spoke first with Patty Valentine, who gave him a description of the car. She supposedly also drew a sketch of the unusual taillights, but the police officer unfortunately misplaced it. Greenough also spoke with Bello, who told him he saw two black men, both about five-feet-eleven, who chased him down an alley.

Sergeant Ted Capter took the stand next and explained in detail the two stops of Carter's car that morning. During his cross-examination by Brown, Capter also told the courtroom of another car he and his partner had unsuccessfully chased, before stopping Carter. The car had eluded them by speeding onto a ramp for Route 4, heading toward New York City. After Capter, most of the policemen testifying described minor points in the early morning investigation of the shooting.

One officer, however, Detective Edward Callahan, did state that he had visited Hazel Tanis in the hospital, and she had given him a statement that Hull characterized as a "dying declaration." The declarations are carefully restricted because once given by a witness who subsequently dies, they cannot be refuted through cross-examination. As soon as Raymond Brown heard Callahan begin to describe his hospital conversation with the critically ill Hazel Tanis, he requested that the jury be excluded from the courtroom while the lawyers debated the admissibility of the

Callahan-Tanis conversation. The judge agreed to Brown's motion to remove the jury.

Callahan then told the judge that Tanis had told him it was not an attempted hold-up. Two black men came into the bar and "just shot her."
She then gave him a vague description of the two men, stating that one
was armed with a shotgun and the other had a pistol. Callahan spoke
with her again, five days later in the hospital, showing her a number of
police department mug shots.

Ray Brown was successful in blocking the introduction of this information into the trial record by showing that it did not qualify under the provisions of the "dying declaration" statutory requirements. Brown showed
Judge Larner hospital records that indicated that she was not close to dying at that time and, in fact, appeared to be on the road to recovery before
an unexpected reversal.

Judge Larner also supported Brown's motion to block the introduction
of a rough composite sketch supposedly made by Tanis. The drawing was
so vague it could have been any young, clean-shaven black man. It was
one of the judge's few rulings throughout the entire trial that favored the
defense.

The prosecution next brought forward several police officers to verify
the ballistic evidence. Patrolman Phillip LaPadura identified the shotgun
shell as well as the lead portions of three .32-caliber bullets found in the
bar after the shooting. Detective Joseph Rafferty supported LaPadura's
identification of the shell and bullet fragments. Although no weapons had
been recovered, the prosecution argued that Carter fired the shotgun
while Artis fired the pistol.

Detectives Rafferty and Lynch took the stand next, and, under cross-
examination by Brown admitted that they had not taken any fingerprints
in the tavern or performed paraffin tests on the defendants. Detective Rafferty explained that the state police in Trenton had advised the Paterson
police that such tests were inconclusive.

Patrolman Edward McSheffrey testified that he had driven the defendant's car from the bar to the police garage that morning. After parking
the car at the garage, he rolled up the windows and locked the door. He
also noted under cross-examination that he had failed to search the car at
that time.

According to the subsequent testimony of Detective Emil DiRobbio,

Carter's car was searched at the garage at 3:45 A.M. on June 17. When DiRobbio opened the front door, he found a .32-caliber lead bullet on the floor under the passenger seat. He next opened the trunk, where he found a Super X Smith and Wesson 12-gauge shotgun shell under some boxing equipment.

Further testimony in the afternoon by ballistic experts lessened the importance of Detective DiRobbio's discovery. The ammunition was similar but, as the state trooper ballistic experts testified, it was clearly different from the ammunition used in the shootings at the Lafayette Bar and Grill, which, the experts stated, consisted of .32 S&W copper-coated bullets and Remington Express plastic shells clearly distinguished from the lead-bullets and the riot-type Super X Wesson shell that DiRobbio had found in the car. After learning this testimony from the firearms experts, Judge Larner excluded the shotgun shell from evidence but inexplicably allowed the lead bullet into evidence despite protests by the defense.

The prosecution closed its case on Friday, May 19, as it brought forward Passaic County Detective Vincent DeSimone. He had interviewed Artis and Carter shortly after they were brought to the Paterson police station on June 17. Before his testimony could be presented, however, the judge had to rule on the defense contention that DeSimone had violated the requirements of the Miranda case that had been decided only four days earlier. This U.S. Supreme Court decision requires the police to inform defendants of their right to counsel (Sixth Amendment) as well as their right to remain silent (Fifth Amendment). Brown and Stein argued that their clients had made incriminating statements without the presence of an attorney and without receiving any warnings from Detective DeSimone. The detective told the court that he had given both men their warnings. He showed the court a sheet of paper on which he had written down the necessary warning the day after the Supreme Court decision was handed down. Judge Larner was not swayed by the defense arguments and stated that he believed the detective and that the constitutional requirements had been satisfied.

DeSimone continued to reconstruct his conversations with both defendants, which indicated several discrepancies between their recollections of their activities earlier in the evening. DeSimone was reconstructing conversations that had been held nearly a year earlier and at which he had taken no notes. DeSimone claimed he had misplaced the original notes on the same morning he had conducted the interrogations.[5] The defense again attempted to challenge the admission of the detective's recollections, but Judge Larner overruled their objections.

The defense began to present its case on Monday, May 22. In a surprise move, Brown had Rubin Carter appear as his first witness. Wearing a light tan jacket, black vest and trousers, the same outfit he was wearing on June 17, 1966, Carter took the witness stand and denied any involvement in the crime.

During questioning that lasted two and a half hours, Carter described his activities during the time when the shootings at the Lafayette were taking place. He had been to the Nite Spot Tavern several times early in the morning of June 17. He had met Cathy McGuire and her mother, Ms. Anna Mapes, and had driven them home from the bar, a distance of only about three blocks, between 2:15 and 2:20 A.M. Ms. McGuire was aware of the time because her mother had to go to work the next day and kept looking at her watch. After a brief conversation at their home, he returned to the Nite Spot at approximately 2:30 A.M. At this point he began chatting with Bill Hardney, his former sparring partner, who had driven from Newark to see him. Carter had an upcoming fight in Argentina and was trying to figure out how to take a sparring partner along with him. Carter then left the bar with John Artis and John "Bucks" Royster and began to drive home to get some additional money. Carter said he was stopped by Sergeant Capter at Broadway and East Twenty-eighth Street. They were allowed to continue after their registration was checked. He continued to his house, where he picked up some cash and then returned to the Nite Spot, arriving between 2:45 and 2:50 A.M. After a few drinks and some brief conversations, Carter left the bar to drive first Royster and then Artis to their respective homes. The car was stopped again by Sergeant Capter, this time at Broadway and East Eighteenth Street. They were now taken to the murder scene at the Lafayette Bar.

The next witness for the defense was Elwood Tuck, the manager of the Nite Spot and a former adviser to Carter. Tuck stated that Carter had been "in and out' of his tavern that night. He clearly remembered checking a clock in the bar around the last time he saw Carter and remembered it was 2:15 A.M. (2:30 bar time, since he always set it fifteen minutes fast).

Next Ms. McGuire and Ms. Mapes testified that Carter had brought them home that night in his white car, verifying his account. Prosecutor Hull conducted an effective cross-examination of both women. Hull was able to show several instances where the courtroom testimony of the women contradicted statements they had given earlier to Detective De-Simone. Ms. Mapes, an elderly black woman, was especially rattled by DeSimone's aggressive style of interrogation and became confused over the exact date on which Carter had driven her and her daughter home.

In his autobiography Carter states his belief that DeSimone's aggressive tactics intimidated many of his potential witnesses in the black community. Carter wrote that Wild Bill Hardney, who could have been very helpful to the defense, left town as soon as he was listed as a witness. Carter contends that the police knew that Hardney would probably leave town rather than face a grilling from DeSimone and his cohorts. Carter noted that John Royster was similarly intimidated and so nervous that "he hid out in his attic for most of the trial."

After Carter testified, Brown brought forward ten additional witnesses. Their purpose was either to verify Carter's presence at the Nite Spot or to serve as character witnesses. Joseph Peter Rush, a member of the U.S. Secret Service living in Chatham, New Jersey, and former National Boxing Association president Anthony Petronella of Providence, Rhode Island, both appeared as character witnesses. Rush said Carter was highly thought of in the Chatham area, where he had established a training camp.

On Tuesday afternoon, May 23, John Artis took the stand and was questioned by his attorney, Arnold Stein. Artis stated, "I never shot anybody" and then basically corroborated the testimony given by Carter earlier about their activities on the night of June 16 and the early morning of June 17. Under questioning by his lawyer, Artis stated he did not know the victims, never owned a shotgun or revolver, and was never in the Lafayette Bar and Grill.

The end of the trial was fast approaching as the defense concluded its presentation of witnesses and prepared to do battle with the prosecution on Wednesday, when a series of critical rebuttal witnesses was scheduled. All that remained was the presentation of summations by both sides on Thursday. At that pace the case would go to the jury on Friday.

The first order of business on Wednesday was the prosecution's presentation of two rebuttal witnesses whose testimony challenged the accuracy of statements made by Ms. McGuire and Ms. Mapes about the time and date they were supposedly driven home by Carter. Hull brought forward Henry Ludeman, a laundry supervisor at Bergen Pines Hospital in Paramus, where Ann Mapes was employed; he also called Detective De-

Simone. Ludeman testified that Mapes was not at work on Friday, June 17, because it was her day off, thus contradicting the testimony that the reason she was so acutely aware of the time Carter had driven her and her daughter home was that it was getting so late and she had to work the next day. DeSimone testified that when he spoke with Mapes, she had been confused about the date she had been to the Nite Spot with her daughter. Her recollection was that it was Friday night, June 17. She testified later at the trial that it was actually late Thursday evening. Although the testimony of the two women was crucial in establishing an alibi for Carter, the prosecution succeeded in showing that the elderly woman was confused over whether she should have referred to the date as very late in the evening of June 16 or early in the morning of June 17.

The prosecution also brought back John "Bucks" Royster, also a defense witness. (Royster had been in Carter's car when it was stopped the first time by Sergeant Capter.) Hull questioned Royster about the exact date he had been with Carter. Royster's testimony before the grand jury, ten days after the crime, indicated he thought he had received the ride in the early morning hours of Saturday, June 18, rather than on the night of the shootings, which is what he claimed at the trial. Because Royster had been drinking heavily that night and had periodically fallen asleep in Carter's car, his recollection of specific times during the early morning hours was not likely to impress the jury.

The defense also had the opportunity to bring in additional witnesses on the final day of testimony. They first brought back Arthur Bradley for additional examination. Bradley's identification of Carter was a critical element in the prosecution's case. Brown wanted to bring Bradley back on the stand in order to remind the jury of the multitude of pending criminal charges facing him that gave him ample incentive to curry favor with the county prosecutor. John Artis's attorney, Arnold Stein, used the final day to present four character witnesses for his client.

On Thursday, May 25, the thirtieth day of the trial, the defense and prosecution presented their summations to the jury. Raymond Brown, speaking for the defense, went first. He spoke for ninety minutes in a mostly measured manner, yet at several times he slipped into a highly emotional style, attacking the credibility of Bello and Bradley and pointing out the pervasive prejudice contaminating the proceedings. Brown went so far as to declare that "these men (the defendants) wouldn't be here if they weren't black." Brown contrasted his own witnesses who came forward voluntarily (including the defendants) with Bello and Bradley:

> I would not try to apply reason to a Bello. I would not try to apply reason to a Bradley because that alone will not answer it. How can one believe them? Who can determine why a Bradley at his tender age already has *six* convictions? Who can determine why a Bello, who is on parole and knows that his maximum is 1969, will deliberately go to break in when he says he is working—why he will go down and admittedly commit two acts of thieving—a very patronizing young man, quite confident, suave in dress and very self-assured. How does one account for that? I don't know—well tell me, can you believe him?

Brown grew more emotional when he began to address the perceived racial bias in the case. He declared,

> That's all you have here—Negro, Negro, Negro. I have heard it until I am—I have heard it from Bradley and from Bello and heard it from every living soul here. Apparently that means you are either suspect or more guilty. I don't know what it means, but in this case, ladies and gentlemen, if we are to reach the high plateau this court demands, it can't mean anything. It can't!

Brown's summation concluded with an exhortation to the jury to carefully reason and question how the prosecution could possibly prove its case beyond a reasonable doubt, the degree of proof necessary to convict.

> Can you believe that this man (Carter) who did not run, who did not hide, did these things? How can one believe this? These are terrible photographs. This is a stark tragedy. Could this man have done this? But that is not the question, is it? The question is, did the state prove it beyond a reasonable doubt, and of course, you have to answer "no." And what do you say about Patricia Graham Valentine? She couldn't identify them within ten feet. What do you say of William Marin's five feet eleven, light-skinned? What do you say of Bello's five feet eleven, light-skinned? Do you write all that off?

Arnold Stein also delivered a summation for the defense, speaking quietly and in what the *Paterson Evening News* described as a near monotone delivery that lasted fifty minutes. Like Brown, Stein devoted most of his address to attacking the credibility of the state's key witnesses, questioning why they waited four months before coming to the police to identify Carter and Artis. The answer to this question, stated Stein, was to receive help in their numerous pending cases with the authorities.

The court recessed briefly for lunch, returning in the afternoon to hear the prosecution's summation. Speaking for seventy minutes, Hull emphasized both the strength of the prosecution's case as well as the enormity of the tragedy. Hull began dramatically holding up the .32-caliber bullet that was found at the scene. He declared that

> after you (the jury) deliberate upon the facts in this case—that bullet, small in size will get larger and larger and larger and that bullet will call out to you and say to you Bello and Bradley told the truth. That bullet will call out to you and say to you Carter and Artis lied, and that bullet will get louder and larger and it will cry out to you like three voices from the dead, and it will say to you Rubin Carter and John Artis are guilty of murder in the first degree.

Hull continued to hold the jury's rapt attention as he emptied three bags of bloody clothing on the table. Alongside each bag he placed pictures of the deceased victims lying on gurneys in the morgue. He then identified each victim, describing how each was murdered. He concluded his summation by declaring forcefully that "the facts in this case clearly indicate the defendants have forfeited their right to live—I ask you to extend to them the same mercy extended to James Oliver, Fred Nauyoks, and Hazel Tanis by sending them to the electric chair."

With the completion of the summations, Judge Larner adjourned for the day, to resume the next morning (Friday, May 26) when the jury would begin deliberations. Before delivering his charges, the court would have to select the jury's foreman and choose which two jurors of the fourteen would not be included in the final deliberations. Cornelius Sullivan from Wanaque was selected as foreman, while George Griffith and Ronald Paturno were not selected and were excused from the proceedings.

Following state law, Judge Larner's law clerk, Regina Sportelly, selected twelve of the fourteen slips of paper from a lottery box. The loss of Griffith was a serious blow to defense hopes. Brown throughout the trial had directed his presentation at Griffith, the sole black on the jury. Thinking that Griffith might be most sympathetic to their case and skeptical of police testimony, he was the defense's strongest possibility for voting for acquittal. The defense knew that with Griffith's removal, their chance for at least achieving a deadlocked jury was significantly diminished. Several years later, in an interview, Griffith affirmed the defense's estimation of his sympathetic disposition. He stated that he did not believe Bello and would have therefore voted for acquittal. This would have resulted in a hung jury, and the judge would have been forced to declare a mistrial.

Judge Larner's charge to the jury outlined the four possible verdicts they might reach: not guilty, guilty in the second degree with punishment at the discretion of the court, guilty in the first degree with a recommendation for life imprisonment, and guilty in the first degree without a recommendation—the last option amounting to the death penalty. Judge Larner's instructions lasted slightly over an hour. He explained that the evidence presented by the state was primarily circumstantial but added that the law makes no distinction between direct and circumstantial, and that in some instances, circumstantial evidence may be even more satisfying and persuasive than direct. He told the jury not to be concerned that there was no demonstrable motive. The tone of the judge's instructions cast a dark shadow over the already depressed defense team.

The jury left the courtroom to begin deliberations at noon, settling into four and a half hours of discussion. At four o'clock the jury notified the court that they had a question about a portion of Bello's testimony and were given the relevant part of the transcript.

An hour later they informed the judge that they had reached a verdict and reentered the courtroom. At 5:35 P.M. the jury foreman, Sullivan, rose and stated that the jury had found the defendants guilty with the recommendation of life imprisonment. Two of the four women jurors had tears in their eyes as the jurors filed out of the courtroom. Judge Larner declared a ten-minute recess to allow them to leave the building.

As the verdict was announced, Mae Thelma Carter, Rubin's wife, began sobbing loudly and was helped from the courtroom. Both defendants appeared visibly shaken when the verdict was announced although neither made a sound. While the court was briefly recessed, Artis stood up and lit a cigarette, walking from the counsel table to the wall, staring into the gallery. Carter remained seated and leaned forward placing his head in his hands. After the ten-minute recess, Judge Larner returned to the bench to declare June 29 for sentencing.

On June 29 Carter and Artis were transported to a high-security Passaic County courthouse. The defendants were placed under heavy guard as eight court bailiffs brought them into a nearly empty courtroom, with only the defendants' immediate family members and courthouse personnel present.

Carter was the first to be sentenced, and his attorney stepped forward, contending that he should not receive more than one life sentence (since he had been convicted of three counts of first-degree murder, Carter faced the possibility of receiving three separate life terms, each one to be served either consecutively or concurrently). A life sentence in New Jersey meant that an inmate would only serve an average of eighteen years in prison and would be eligible for parole in fourteen years. Brown argued that if Carter received more than one life sentence it would usurp the power of the parole board. His attorney went on to state that Carter had been self-controlled and respectable during the trial and that a triple sentence would bury him for life.

Judge Larner, apparently unmoved by Brown's comments, sentenced Carter to two consecutive life terms. Before delivering his sentence, Larner offered his rationale for handing down the severe sentence:

> From my analysis of the evidence and the witnesses, I have no hesitancy in stating that the jury verdict was fully warranted by the proofs submitted during the trial. The killings for which you were indicted and tried resulted from a cold-blooded massacre of innocent victims wholly unknown to you. There is not a single factor in these killings that can mitigate the heinousness of the offense. There is totally absent any understandable reason or motive that can be said to have impelled you to commit this horrible crime.

It was now Artis's turn to receive his sentence. His attorney, Arnold Stein, stepped forward to describe Artis's exemplary record, leadership qualities, and youth work. Judge Larner admitted that he was having difficulty reconciling Artis's earlier background with the violent crime of which he had just been convicted. He concluded that he agreed with Stein that "because of his clean record and decent background, he would give him the opportunity to start life anew in the future." Larner then gave Artis one life sentence with the other two to run concurrently. He also gave him credit for the 259 days he had spent in jail awaiting disposition of his case.

Following his sentencing of John Artis, Judge Larner concluded the historic trial by completing a few administrative details and stepped off the bench. His tumultuous tour of duty in Paterson was over. Immediately transferred back to Essex County, he later happily left the criminal courts, rejoining the civil part to which he had originally been assigned.

Despite the apparent finality of the jury's decision, Carter and Artis's struggle to regain their freedom was far from over. Their attorneys would soon file a notice of appeal, commencing a frustrating and seemingly interminable process. Many important questions remained unanswered. The most puzzling aspect of the case was the failure of the prosecution to provide a motive. They never addressed the question directly. Their efforts were aimed at proving that Carter and Artis were seen coming out of the bar carrying weapons and were therefore responsible for the slaughter. Earlier statements by the police, as reported in the Paterson papers, said it was a robbery. The cash register was open, and it would be difficult to determine if money had actually been taken.

An alternative motive, which was hinted at after Carter and Artis were charged with the crime, was that the shootings were meant to avenge the death of Roy Holloway, who had been murdered earlier that same evening. Nevertheless, the prosecution presented no evidence directly linking Carter and Artis with this earlier shooting, nor did Hull ever specifically state publicly that this was the motive.

There were rumors circulating after the shooting that James Oliver, the bartender at the Lafayette, was the primary target of the killers. He had supposedly been taking bets and doing policy (numbers), and a local gang who believed they had a monopoly on these illegal activities shot him as a lesson to anyone else wishing to challenge their monopoly. Other variations on this theme hypothesized that Oliver had been skimming money off the top of his operation or had failed to pay the gang the protection money required of anyone running gambling operations within the area. The other three victims simply happened to be in the wrong place at the wrong time and had to be eliminated as possible witnesses. Although the issue of motive was not raised during the first trial, it would reemerge as an important issue during subsequent legal proceedings.

A second problem area was the questionable behavior of the police. Beyond their rather sloppy investigation of the crime scene (e.g., neglecting to dust for fingerprints), the detectives investigating the shootings seemed to lose their notes whenever it was convenient for the prosecution, and they were rarely able to substantiate their conclusions with direct evidence. The timely discovery of the bullets and shotgun shell in Carter's car also appeared to add to the skepticism of many observers. It seemed strange that the search was delayed until the car had been taken to the police garage. Also puzzling was the fact that the shell and bullets were similar to the ones recovered at the scene but certainly not an exact match. Equally suspect was the detectives' claim that Hazel Tanis had given a dying declaration and had completed a roughly drawn sketch of her murderer. Again, no written documentation was provided.

The most fundamental question was the credibility of Bello and Bradley. Why did they wait so long before coming in and identifying Carter and Artis? What was their motivation for cooperating with the investigation? Later events cast additional doubts on their veracity and that of Patricia Valentine.

There were also grounds for doubting the truthfulness of some defense witnesses, particularly the testimony involving Carter's whereabouts during the late night of June 16 and the early morning hours of June 17. Was Carter driving around in search of his missing shotgun or simply visiting an old friend who was in poor health? The testimony of Ms. McGuire, Ms. Mapes, Bill Hardney, and John Royster appears somewhat questionable at several critical points during the trial. In future legal proceedings these alibi witnesses were subjected to even harsher scrutiny. It remains very difficult to conclude exactly where Rubin Carter was between 2:00 A.M. and 2:45 A.M. on June 17, 1966.

Appellate review and future trials wrestled with these questions for the next two decades.

4: Between Trials
1967–1976

Two days after Carter and Artis were sentenced, Rubin entered the aged, massive Trenton State Prison. The oldest active prison in the nation, established in 1798, it housed the state's most dangerous criminals. Carter had been here before, five years earlier, but in the interim had seemingly put his life back together thanks to his successful boxing career, which had taken him to the brink of the world middleweight championship. When the slaughter began at the Lafayette Bar and Grill on June 17, 1966, Carter was still ranked as the number-four contender in the world. It was now July 1, 1967, and the state of New Jersey justice system had decreed that he would spend the rest of his life behind bars.

Carter observed that little had changed during his five-year absence from Trenton State Prison. He later wrote,

I found it to be the same obsolete hole of depravity and death that it was when I'd left it five years before. The little racist guards that I'd left behind were all big-shot guards now, working in the upper echelons of the administration. They controlled the jail with an iron fist of brutality, a minimum of compassion, and a maximum of security. The deliberate execution of each inmate's personality seemed to be their favorite pastime. A generation of young kids now made up the prison's population. All the old-timers were gone, free, dead or shipped out to the farms, while this new breed of whatchamacallits staggered around the jailhouse with nothing on their minds. There were no clear lines of demarcation anymore between the men and the homosexuals in the joint or between the stool pigeons and the jailhouse punks. Trenton State Prison now was just one great big happy family of fools.[1]

Carter would "not stoop to this prison's ungodly level of non-existence." He believed the police and prosecutors hoped that his burning rage and inclination for violent outbursts would send him on a deadly rampage which would likely cost him his life.[2] Vowing to frustrate the state officials who waited for his imminent self-destruction, he turned in on himself, meditating, studying the law, and eventually writing a book about his life, hoping to draw the public's attention to his case.

Carter explained his immediate game plan in the following terms:

For the entire month of July I stayed locked away in my cell in deep med-itation, gathering up all three of my souls—Rubin, Hurricane and Carter—and wondering what we should do. But as usual, we couldn't seem to come to terms—although we all agreed, for the moment, to con-tinue with our fight to be free. Rubin, being the quick learner of the three, decided to study the law and get us back to the court that way, if he could, while the Hurricane just said, "Fuck it!" and was ready to de-molish everything in the prison; but, Carter, usually the most quiet and reserved of all, thought he ought to write a book and bring our case be-fore the public. Because one thing was accepted by us all, and that was we would definitely not submit to this prison's nastiness. We would study the law and write this book and if that didn't work, then let the Hurricane take over and do what must be done.[3]

Despite Carter's efforts to retreat from the violence permeating Trenton State Prison, the prison psychologist noted on July 29, during his intake interview, that "Carter was belligerent, held himself aloof and refused to discuss himself." The psychologist, Stanley Milgram, concluded "that Carter will have difficulty adjusting to incarceration. It is assumed that he will be manipulative and violent and obtain his self-centered desires." Given Milgram's brief exposure to Carter and his seemingly preconceived notions, his diagnosis is of minimal value in unraveling Carter's complex personality. Milgram was probably frustrated by Carter's reluctance to cooperate during the interview and his threatening countenance. Carter, for his part, objected to the psychologist's intrusion into the privacy of his inner thoughts. Based on his past experiences with prison officials, even psychologists, Carter greeted their intervention with a large measure of skepticism.[4]

THE OPENING ROUND IN THE NEW JERSEY APPELLATE COURTS

Following the trial, the defense attorneys began working on an appeal, trying to flee from Judge Larner's jurisdiction as quickly as possible. According to New Jersey law, however, their initial motion for a new trial would have to go first through Larner. Given his strong belief in Carter's guilt—"There is not a single factor in these killings which can serve as mitigation of the heinousness of the offense"[5]—as expressed in his speech during the sentencing hearing, it came as no surprise when he rejected the defense motion. Following a few perfunctory and preliminary legal moves, the lawyers decided to appeal directly to the State Supreme Court for a new trial. The case was argued before the court on May 12, 1969, and on July 15, 1969, the court affirmed Carter's conviction in a 7–0 decision.

The court rejected all of the defense's arguments. The first issue discussed was the failure of the Paterson police to follow the recently decided standards set by the U.S. Supreme Court in the landmark case of *Miranda v. Arizona*. The defense argued that when the defendants were arrested and were being interrogated, the detective's recollection of their oral statements concerning their activities during the night of the homicides should have not been admissible in court. The statements were not a verbatim record but simply the detectives' rough efforts to record the essence of their statements. The State Supreme Court held that the importance of these statements was "virtually nil." Neither defendant admitted to committing any of the homicides nor did they implicate each other in their admission to the police—they simply accounted for their whereabouts that evening.

Second, the defense charged that the bullet and shotgun shell found by the police should have been excluded as evidence because the search of Carter's car was illegal. They argued that the police lacked the necessary probable cause for an arrest and that the search of the car was incidental to the arrest. Chief Justice Joseph Weintraub rejected this argument as well:

As to the arrest, the trial court correctly held that probable cause existed. Whether the arrest occurred when defendants were ordered to drive in the convoy to the tavern or when they were placed in the police van at the tavern is not critical. Probable cause existed at both times, and the search, which took place after the second event, was incidental to it.[6]

A related third issue raised by Raymond Brown was Judge Larner's decision to permit the prosecution to comment about the shotgun shell (in addition to the bullets) after he had granted a pretrial motion excluding its introduction into the trial. The supreme court dismissed the significance of its impact upon the jury's decision to convict the defendants, categorizing it as merely a "harmless error."

The defense contended that the severity of the sentences violated the Eighth Amendment's prohibition against cruel and unusual punishment. Carter, in particular, was ordered to serve two consecutive life terms. Both defendants were being punished separately for each of the three murders. Weintraub rejected the defense's argument that there was in actuality only one offense, all three victims being murdered in one simultaneous barrage of bullets. The chief justice thought it evident that there were three distinctive homicides, committed as separate criminal acts. It was analogous to a case of arson causing multiple deaths, each one to be considered as a separate homicide. With the final defense argument rejected, the State Supreme Court affirmed the trial court judgment. The first round of appeals had ended, and a disheartened pair of defendants faced the prospect of spending the rest of their lives behind bars.

Shortly after hearing the disappointing New Jersey Supreme Court decision, which rejected his request for a new trial, Carter began to consider changing attorneys. The more he thought about the quality of his defense, ruminating in the morbid solitude of his prison cell, the more determined he became to replace Brown. He realized that although Ray Brown had done a decent job, especially his oral presentations, Carter began to sour on some of his strategic decisions, which had either backfired or resulted in lost opportunities. Carter felt strongly that they should have fought more doggedly to have a change of venue. It was obvious, even before the trial actually began, that the Passaic County newspapers (the *Evening News* and the *Morning Call*) were convinced of Carter's guilt and slanted nearly all of their articles on the case with that bias. Carter wrote that the press presented "highly publicized accounts of a racially motivated triple murder of white citizens by two Negroes made it impossible for us to receive a fair trial in Paterson, and Brown should have asked for an immediate change of venue. At least, I'm convinced of that." Both papers seemed to accept police and prosecutorial interpretations of the case at face value. They acted as if their beloved city was on trial and needed the assistance of the Fourth Estate to protect the city against outside agitators. This posture persisted for the next twenty years, growing in rigidity and fervor the closer the case came to being overturned.

A second problem for Carter was the failure of Raymond Brown to capitalize on the testimony of Hector Martinez. Martinez had been involved in several robberies of motels with Arthur Bradley, and in the summer of 1967 they were serving time together at Bordentown. Martinez told Raymond Brown before the trial that Bradley had bragged to him how he was going to use the Carter case in order to force the Passaic authorities to help him with numerous pending criminal matters. Bradley admitted to Martinez that he had never seen Carter or Artis coming out of the Lafayette Bar after the shooting. Unfortunately for the defense, Brown never laid a sufficient foundation for bringing Martinez into the case to testify as he was cross-examining Bradley. With Judge Larner's ruling preventing Martinez's testimony, Bradley's credibility survived. A critical opportunity to impeach a potentially vulnerable state witness had been missed, and Carter held Brown responsible.

The third and possibly most egregious error, Carter believed, was Brown's mishandling of his alibi witnesses, especially the two women, Mapes and McGuire. Carter understood the intense pressure the police and Lieutenant DeSimone could put upon his witnesses. These women would be particularly vulnerable to their intimidating tactics. Carter and Brown knew that beginning in mid-October, following his arrest, both women had been very nervous about their forthcoming testimony because of the intense grilling they had already received from DeSimone. It would be extremely important for Brown to comfort and reassure them. Carter thought that Brown had been remiss in their preparation for the hostile cross-examination they were certain to face. The prosecution had been successful in rattling the women, especially Ms. Mapes, whose inconsistent testimony created serious doubts in the minds of the jurors about the accuracy of her recollections.

This combination of factors convinced Carter and Artis by 1970 that they needed better legal representation for their appeal. Although neither defendant had the financial resources to hire a private attorney, they were willing to take their chances with legal representation from the state's public-defender program. The program was under the capable direction of Stanley Van Ness and had an excellent reputation. Their appeal was soon turned over to Paul Feldman and John Noonan.

One unfortunate consequence of Ray Brown's involvement in the Carter case was the prosecution's assertion that he had attempted to convince defense witnesses to perjure themselves in order to gain an acquittal for Carter. There was supposedly one such meeting at the Thunderbird Motel in Newark and other meetings in his law offices where the strategy of deception was allegedly planned. In attendance at these meetings were Ms. Mapes, Ms. McGuire, and others whose testimony could provide an alibi for Carter during the time of the shooting. Despite charges raised by Hull following the trial and threats to bring the entire sordid affair before a grand jury or a state bar panel, no such action was taken.

PRISON LIFE

Within a week of the rejection of his appeal by the New Jersey Supreme Court, Carter was transferred to Rahway State Prison, a maximum security institution a few miles south of Elizabeth. It was a better place to serve time than Trenton. It was larger, less crowded, operated numerous programs to keep the prisoners busy, and allowed contact visits (which were not permitted at Trenton). In his autobiography Carter offers an interesting description of life at his new home:

> There was no brutality or racism when I got to Rahway in 1969—only apathy in the form of overindulgence. Everything that the other institutions lacked, Rahway had: contact visits every Sunday, which was equal to mouth-to-mouth resuscitation for us inmates. Rahway, then, was a beehive of activity. There were so many places to go at once, and so many things to occupy one's mind, that few people really knew if they were coming or going. If ever a more subtle form of compliance has been employed to dehumanize a man than those techniques used at Rahway, I would surely like to see it. The inmates were allowed to run wild, and they thought they were hip and getting over. Meanwhile the only person really getting over was Warren Pinto, the superintendent, who let the fools run themselves ragged and never had a day of trouble.[7]

Despite the abundance of activities occupying most inmates, Rubin chose to work on his writing in isolation. He was uninterested in participating in the fractious inmate politics that the prison authorities tolerated insofar as it facilitated their control over the inmates—a tactic which Carter had accurately assessed as a successful divide-and-conquer strategy. Although Carter had a few minor scrapes with the guards and other inmates, he primarily studied the law and wrote his autobiography. He was cited a dozen times for disciplinary infractions, but most were early in his stay, before the staff and other men had acclimated themselves to Carter's rigid regimen.

Carter's quiet and narrowly focused existence was shattered on Thanksgiving Day 1971, when a violent prison riot erupted. Two hundred inmates gained control of two of the prison's five wings, holding hostage the warden along with seven guards. Peace was restored after twenty-seven hours, but only after the warden had been stabbed and beaten. Although the Rahway uprising paled by comparison with the infamous Attica, New York, riot a few months earlier, it was nevertheless regarded as the worst in New Jersey history.

The disturbance began innocuously at 9:30 P.M. on November 24, 1971, when an inmate, Clay Thomas, a thirty-six-year-old former heavyweight professional boxer from Paterson, walked into the auditorium, where prisoners were watching a movie. He was angry over what he perceived as the abuse of a close friend of his who had his "still" confiscated by the guards and dragged out of his cell. An irate Thomas threw a chair through the movie screen, climbed on the stage, and began addressing the crowd with an incendiary harangue about the treatment of black inmates by the guards.

Warden Vukcevich came onto the stage to try to reason with Thomas, but Thomas assaulted him, and both men fell off the stage. Once on the floor Vukcevich was hit with a chair, kicked repeatedly, and stabbed numerous times in the back. James Garret, an inmate, miraculously dragged the bleeding warden to the safety of his cell where he used his training as an army medic to close his wound with a safety pin and thread.

Rubin Carter helped to keep the two hundred rioters restricted to just two wings by blocking a door, thereby preventing them from spreading the disturbance into the remaining wings. Carter, interviewed on the twenty-fifth anniversary of the riot, said his actions were based on self-preservation. He was aware of the slaughter that had just occurred at Attica and was concerned that if the Rahway riot escalated, there would be a violent reprisal, and he imagined that he would likely be killed because of this status as a celebrity inmate. Carter remembered, "I had to block the door, there was a corrections officer locked in there with us. People from outside were trying to get at the officer. I could not permit that."[8]

Most of the remaining time Carter spent at Rahway was uneventful with the exception of a minor incident in April 1974 which resulted in his transfer to the Vroom Building at Trenton State, a psychiatric hospital for the criminally insane. Carter had become active in an inmate group known as the People's Council, organized by Tom Trantino. They were deeply interested in prisoners' concerns, especially the death penalty. As chairman of the group, Carter had been asked by Trantino to address the inmates in the cafeteria. Carter spoke critically of the prison authorities and urged prisoners to bring their grievances to the People's Council. Later that evening, Carter, Trantino, and two other leaders of their organization were transferred down to the Vroom Building. Carter brought a civil suit in the federal courts challenging the constitutionality of his transfer, and, although it was denied, he was transferred back to Rahway a few months later.

The most impressive aspect of Carter's years of confinement, beyond his ability to endure the physical and emotional hardship, was his intellectual growth. His formal education ended at age thirteen when he was sent to Jamesburg Juvenile Reformatory. Yet Carter's innate intelligence and force of will drove him to consume books voraciously, not merely criminal law volumes but philosophical and historical treatises as well. Additionally, he conquered the stuttering that had undermined his academic efforts in elementary school. Carter may have been confined in a maximum-security prison, but from 1969 to 1974, he experienced a remarkable intellectual, emotional, and spiritual renewal. The spark that ignited Carter's renewed commitment to his personal growth and his legal struggle came from a very surprising source—a young white Irish-American and former police officer who had just returned from military service in Germany.

FRED HOGAN AND RICHARD SOLOMON: THE FIRST GLIMMERS OF HOPE

Fred Hogan was a boxing fan who was especially attracted to Hurricane Carter, the flashy middleweight contender from Paterson. Hogan enjoyed driving out to Carter's training camp in Chatham and watching him spar as he prepared for an upcoming fight. He remembered Carter as being open and friendly. Hogan had left his police position in the midsixties to enter the military and was assigned to a military police unit in Germany until his discharge in 1969. He was shocked to learn of Carter's conviction, disbelieving that the "Hurricane" was capable of such a cold-blooded, murderous act. Shortly after Hogan returned to the United States, he became an investigator with the Monmouth County Public Defender's Office. He also began to study the Carter case and eventually visited him in Rahway. Carter barely remembered Hogan from his Chatham training days and was reluctant to open up to him, but after six months of regular visits from Hogan every Saturday morning, Carter began to talk about the case.

Hogan spent every spare moment investigating the case, hoping to uncover new evidence that would justify a new trial. He began to bring a tape recorder on his visits to Rahway as he and Carter went over the entire case in painstaking detail from arrest to sentencing. Hogan soon believed in Carter's innocence and started working to develop evidence that would lead to a new trial. Hogan had located Hector Martinez, who told him that Bradley had been bragging about how he lied in order to dupe the state into giving him a break on his multitude of pending robberies and burglaries awaiting disposition. Even though Martinez was unable to participate in the initial trial, Hogan thought that if he kept digging, it was likely that he could uncover other individuals who had had similar conversations with Bradley. He therefore began tracking down Bradley's prison whereabouts for the preceding years.

Hogan was able to locate a police captain in Bergen County and a correctional officer in Morris County who told him that Bradley had been telling inmates that he had lied in court. This hearsay evidence was of no probative value and could not be used in court, but it allowed Hogan to focus more precisely on those inmates who had spoken with Bradley. Carter, meanwhile, was writing a legal brief focusing on search and seizure and self-incrimination. Hogan had already notified Gerald Foley, who was in charge of the appellate section of the State Public Defender's Office, of their progress and the startling new facts he was uncovering. Hogan's relentless investigation located several inmates who had been with Bradley in the Bergen, Morris, and Union County jails. They had heard Bradley brag about his role in Carter's conviction. Bradley also told them how angry he was at both Al Bello and Passaic County officials, who had failed to deliver on their promises.

Although nearly all of this information was only hearsay and not admissible in a criminal court, it nevertheless drew the interest of Stanley Van Ness, the public defender for the state of New Jersey. After carefully reviewing the information provided him by Carter and Hogan, Van Ness decided to visit Carter. He and Hogan showed up at Rahway the day after the Thanksgiving Day riots and notified a startled Carter that the Public Defender's Office would accept his case.

Hogan was not the only person to discover "The Hurricane" and become enthralled with the case. At about the same time, Richard Solomon, a freelance filmmaker, became interested in Carter's predicament, envisioning a documentary film on the former middleweight contender and his plight. Solomon soon reached the same conclusion as Hogan about Carter's innocence. He began to develop a publicity campaign designed to make others aware of the injustice perpetrated upon Carter. Initial efforts were unsuccessful, leading to rebuffs from ABC Sports and the *New York Daily News*. Some publications, such as *Sports Illustrated* and the *Village Voice*, exhibited early interest but declined to join Solomon's crusade.

The sole success was in convincing Viking Press to take a closer look at the autobiography Carter had been writing. After reading portions of a rough draft, Viking sent an editor, Linda Yablonski, to help Carter put the book into publishable form. The book, entitled *The Sixteenth Round*, was eventually published by Viking in 1974. It was a candid recounting of Carter's life, and it received decent reviews. The *Library Journal* wrote that "Rubin Carter presents a compelling case for his freedom. *The Sixteenth Round* is a tough and brutal book that presents a different account of criminal justice in action." The book had modest sales but did not become a best-seller. The book did earn him a ten-thousand-dollar advance, which Carter turned over to Fred Hogan to manage, a decision that proved to be unwise.

The book failed to produce the desired public outcry despite its moving conclusion: "Now, the only chance I have is in appealing directly to you, the people, and showing you the wrongs that have yet to be righted; the injustice that has been done to me. For the first time in my entire existence, I'm saying that I need some help. Otherwise there will be no tomorrow for me."[9]

Solomon's persistence helped to convince David Anderson, the renowned sports columnist for the *New York Times,* to come out to Rahway to visit with Carter. On December 23, 1972, Anderson wrote an extremely moving column in the *Times* based on his visit with Carter, entitled "Christmas at Rahway." Anderson quoted Carter as declaring, "I didn't commit the crime. I was cleared by a man wounded by the killers, I passed a lie detector test that I took voluntarily, the description of the killers fit neither me nor John Artis. . . . I sit here and look at these bars holding me in here."[10]

Even Anderson's moving account of his visit with Carter failed to elicit the desired public response. Another *Times* reporter, Selwyn Raab, later became deeply involved in the case and became a catalyst for projecting Carter into the national limelight as well as helping to prod the New Jersey judicial system into granting Carter a retrial. In 1973 Raab was an investigative reporter working for a WNET television news show, *The 51st State.* Raab was a Brooklyn native who had done some amateur boxing in his youth. Solomon contacted Raab because of his role in the case of George Whitmore, a young black convicted in 1963 of killing two New York City "career girls," Janice Wylie and Emily Hoffert. Whitmore had confessed but later insisted that the police had beaten his admissions out of him. The charges were eventually dropped, but he was arrested again, charged with rape, and convicted after three trials. Raab was convinced that Whitmore was innocent of the rape charge and was able to bring in new evidence that led to the district attorney's dropping the charge. Raab wrote a book about the case, *Justice in the Backroom.*

After learning of Raab's role in the Whitmore case, Richard Solomon contacted him and asked him if he would investigate the Lafayette Bar and Grill murders. Raab became fascinated with the case and told Solomon he would begin looking into it. Raab read the trial transcript, visited the scene of the crime, and after further interviews and research became convinced that Bradley had been lying, which meant that it was equally plausible that Bello had also fabricated his testimony.

Raab's next step was to try and contact Bello, who was serving a nine-month sentence in the Passaic County Jail for breaking and entering. Bello wrote him a tantalizing brief note: "I'd like to talk to you but I can't. If I could tell you the whole story, it's quite a story."[11] The elusive Bello was released from jail before Raab could reach him and immediately disappeared. Raab's professional life now became more complicated because of his promotion to executive director of the *51st State* show.

Raab's new responsibilities necessitated his turning over the Carter file to Hal Levinson, one of his reporters.

Levinson worked with Fred Hogan and located Hector Martinez in Little Falls, New Jersey. Because of Ray Brown's strategic miscues, he had been unable to use Martinez's testimony to impeach Bradley's eyewitness identification. Martinez cooperated with Levinson and Hogan, giving them a sworn affidavit reiterating what Bradley had told him at Annandale Reformatory. The investigators checked out the details of Martinez's account and were convinced of its veracity.

The investigative team now had to locate Bradley and confront him with the Martinez affidavit. In May 1974 they located Bradley in Wayne, New Jersey, in a parking lot next to his home, and he talked with them for four hours before Bradley finally admitted that his 1967 testimony had been fabricated. They quickly drove Bradley to the law offices of Michael Blacker, an attorney who knew Hogan. He had Bradley sign a sworn statement recanting his 1967 testimony.

It was now critical for the investigators to find Bello and have him also recant his earlier testimony. During the summer Selwyn Raab left WNET, moving on to a position with the *New York Times,* and Levinson shifted over to another television station. Despite these career changes, the trio continued working together and located Bello in the Bergen County Jail, where they immediately attempted to convince him to recant his identification of the defendants. Bello consented to a meeting with Raab on September 10, 1974. Raab followed this up with a second meeting a week later in which Bello said he was ready to talk. Raab now called Hogan, who quickly drove up to the jail and had Bello sign an affidavit attesting that his 1967 testimony was a lie. Raab rushed back to the *Times* to write the story and on September 27, 1974, nearly five years after Hogan and Solomon began working on the case, the sensational story reached the public.

THE RECANTATIONS AND THEIR AFTERMATH

The page-one headline in the *New York Times* read "Murder Case Witnesses Recant Seven Years After Two Got Life Terms." Not only did Raab's lengthy article present the recantations and review the 1967 murder trial, but it also offered statements from Bradley and Bello explaining why they had been convinced to lie. Blame was placed primarily on the police. They both accused Lieutenant Vincent DeSimone of the Passaic County Prosecutor's Office of being primarily responsible for pressuring them. Bradley explained, "There's only one reason. That was all the time (the long sentence). They (the police) never would have got me to talk otherwise. I saw a way out of my own mess." Simply stated, Bradley admitted, "I lied to save myself."

The more voluble Bello declared that the police promised "they would take care of me if I got jammed up (rearrested) again." He had also hoped to collect the $10,500 reward but thus far had been unsuccessful. Bello admitted that he had seen the actual murderers but that his identification of Artis and Carter had been a "grave mistake."[12] He blamed persistent police pressure for his deceptive testimony. Bello was serving a nine-month sentence in the Bergen County Jail in Hackensack for burglary. Bello and Bradley stated they had been deeply bothered by their false testimony but had hesitated recanting because of fear of police retaliation in Passaic County. Now that the five-year statute of limitations for perjury had passed, they could at least evade that charge.

Bello described in detail his interrogation on the night of the murders. He insisted that "I tried to tell it right, but they (the police) wouldn't listen. They'd go over the story and kept saying 'These (Carter and Artis) are the guys.'" He was warned by detectives that he might become a suspect in the murders if he refused to cooperate by incriminating Carter and Artis. By October 1966, four months after the shootings, Bello capitulated to the police demands. Shortly before the trial, according to Bello, Lieutenant DeSimone advised him to "take the money (the $10,500 reward) and split (leave Paterson). They promised me they'd take care of me if I got 'jammed up.'" The pair tried to collect the reward after the trial was concluded but were told it was not available because Carter had filed an appeal. Neither Bello nor Bradley was ever prosecuted for the attempted burglary of the Ace Metal Company on June 17, 1966.

Bello continued to be very nervous about possible repercussions from his recantation given that he was currently imprisoned on a burglary charge. He said he had spoken with Lieutenant DeSimone the previous August (1974) in the Passaic County Jail and had told the detective that his original testimony in the Carter case had been a mistake. Bello recounted that DeSimone had warned him, "I'm going to tell you something. If you open your mouth you're going to do 100 years."[13] DeSimone angrily denied the charges that he had tried to browbeat them into falsely identifying the defendants.

Repercussions from the *Times* front-page article announcing the recantations were immediate and far-reaching. Attorneys for Carter and Artis from the state's public defender's office announced that they would immediately file a writ requesting a retrial.

The former county prosecutor, Vincent Hull, labeled the accusations "categorically untrue," but the case was now in the hands of his replacement, Joseph Gourley. Gourley informed the media that he would personally handle the case. In reference to charges leveled against Lieutenant DeSimone and others who had worked on the Carter case, Gourley told the press, "I don't believe that they would coerce any individual in order to secure a conviction. Lt. DeSimone feels he did everything correctly and only asked Bello and Bradley to tell the truth." He closed the interview with the announcement that he would "resist strenuously" any attempt to obtain a second trial.

The next day Stanley Van Ness, the New Jersey public defender, not only requested a new trial as a result of the newly discovered evidence, but also asked for an independent investigation of the accusations by the two eyewitnesses that they had been coerced into identifying Carter and Artis by Lieutenant DeSimone. In two related incidents, Arthur Bradley, apparently feeling the pressure from his recantations, was accused by his mother of attacking her and was arrested. Additionally, Governor Brendan Byrne of New Jersey announced that he would commence talks with the state's attorney general and public defender to reopen the Carter-Artis case.[14] Two days later the public defender assigned private counsel, Paul Feldman of Asbury Park and John Noonan of Newark, to represent Carter and Artis, respectively.

The hearing to determine if the new evidence justified a retrial was scheduled for October 29 before Judge Samuel Larner (the original trial judge) in his Hudson County courtroom in Jersey City. Two weeks before the hearing, in an unexpected break for the defense, Judge Larner ordered the Passaic County prosecutor to turn over to the defense a group of secret police records, including tape recordings related to their investigation of the Lafayette Bar homicides. These police and prosecution materials had been unavailable to the defense for use in the 1967 trial, but recent reforms in New Jersey discovery rules had expanded the rights of the defendants, granting them much broader access to these records. Judge Larner ordered that the new discovery requirements be complied with by the prosecution prior to the scheduled October 29 hearing. The defense attorneys waited expectantly for this new information, hopeful that it would prove beneficial to their demands for a new trial.

A Second Round of Appeals and the "Ring of Truth"

Before a packed courtroom, on the ninth floor of the Hudson County Courthouse on October 29, Judge Larner began the hearing to determine if the recent recantations by Bello and Bradley as well as fresh disclosures from police and prosecution records warranted a new trial for Carter and Artis. Bello testified first, stating that he had lied seven years before in the original trial. He said he had hesitated coming forward earlier because of feared reprisals by the Passaic County Prosecutor's Office and Lieutenant DeSimone, whom he blamed for coercing him into testifying falsely.

On October 30, the second day of the hearing, the defense attorneys played an intriguing tape recording from the material that Judge Larner had ordered the prosecution to turn over to Carter's attorneys. Recorded secretly on October 11, 1966, at the Wayne police headquarters, the tape reveals detectives Mohl and DeSimone promising to go to the "top people in the state" in order to assist Bello in his then-pending case. There was a clear inference that the detectives would also forget about Bello's attempted burglary the same night as the murders. It was also clear that Bello was at first uncertain about his ability to identify Artis and Carter after being shown a photograph of John Artis. Bradley was questioned after Bello left the witness stand and was cross-examined for nearly two hours. He repeated again that he had lied at the first trial in order to get a reduced sentence for four armed robbery charges, unrelated to the Carter case.

On the next day of the hearing, the former prosecutor, Vincent Hull, took the stand, testifying that he had made no promises to either Bello or Bradley. He admitted that he had not pressed burglary charges against the duo but that this was not part of any promise or guarantee. He did acknowledge that he was aware that Lieutenant DeSimone was trying to help them receive lighter sentences.

The hearing resumed on Monday, November 5, with the prosecution playing the secret tapes. The assistant prosecutor, John Goceljak, argued that Bello had voluntarily implicated Carter and Artis in the Lafayette Bar slayings. Goceljak next emphasized that the defense had only played selected portions of the tapes that were largely being taken out of context. The entire taped session at the Wayne police station on October 11, 1966, does not unambiguously demonstrate coercion. The following is an example of a key passage from the tapes selected by the prosecutors to validate this point:

> *Detective Capt. Robert C. Mohl:* Can you tell the lieutenant (DeSimone) whether this was Rubin Carter or wasn't Rubin Carter?
>
> *Mr. Bello:* Well, it was Rubin Carter as far as I know, or his brother.
>
> *Lieutenant DeSimone:* Now in regard to John Artis, the other one, you likewise saw him. In your mind, can you honestly say that this was the man that was with him, with Rubin Carter?
>
> *Mr. Bello:* Yes.
>
> *Lieutenant DeSimone:* In other words, in your mind it was definitely Rubin Carter and John Artis who came around the corner on that morning?
>
> *Mr. Bello:* Yes.[15]

On Tuesday, November 6, the defense was able to show that less than two days after the triple murder, Bello was unable to identify either of the defendants as the killers. Under intense cross-examination Lieutenant DeSimone admitted that he had withheld this information from both the prosecution *and* the defense. The prosecution continued to try to convince Judge Larner that Bello had been unwilling to initially identify Carter because he feared retaliation. On the final day of the hearing (November 7), both sides presented their summations.

Even before Judge Larner announced his decision, another twist in the case raised more doubts about the impartiality of the original police investigation. Selwyn Raab of the *New York Times* discovered a discrepancy in the official records that the prosecution had recently been ordered to reveal to the defense. The findings challenged Detective Emil DiRobbio's sworn testimony at the 1967 trial that he had found a bullet and shotgun shell in Carter's impounded car when he searched it approximately seventy-five minutes after the murders. Although Carter and his attorneys had suggested that the police had planted the ammunition, Raab's new evidence gave greater credence to their accusations. The *Times* investigative team discovered that the bullet was not recorded in the property clerk's voucher until five days later. Moreover, the bullet, although similar to the ammunition found at the scene of the crime, was clearly distinguishable. A copper-plated bullet had been used in the holdup, whereas the one placed in the property clerk's voucher was lead-plated.

Unfortunately, this new evidence was uncovered too late to be presented at the hearing. Detective DiRobbio insisted that he had found it on that first day, and somehow the property clerk, who had since died, must have simply delayed recording its placement in his office files.

Exactly one month after the bullet discrepancy was discovered (on December 12, 1974), Judge Larner delivered his opinion rejecting the defendant's motion for a new trial. In his judgment the new testimony from Bello and Bradley was "patently untrue," not believable, and lacked the necessary "ring of truth." Therefore the recantation did not provide a basis for a new trial. Larner concluded that the two eyewitnesses had not lied at the trial in 1967 when questioned about any promises having been made to them concerning the prosecution of unrelated criminal charges against them. The judge also ruled that the failure of the prosecutor to present the defendants with a tape recording that provided evidence of certain statements made to one witness (Alfred Bello) concerning offenses which he was believed to have committed did not amount to a denial of due process. Larner wrote that this failure to turn the tape recording over to the defense for use at the trial involved only a minor discovery problem. Larner wrote that the failure of the state to prosecute Bello for an unrelated crime—the attempted burglary—did not prove the existence of a promise made prior to his testimony against the defendants or prove that he had lied at the trial about not receiving special treatment in exchange for his testimony.

The judge expressed his belief that Bello had changed his testimony because he was upset at not having received the $10,500 reward money and was trying to embarrass and gain revenge against Lieutenant DeSimone, whom he held responsible. Larner concluded that the defendants were entitled only to a fair trial, not a perfect trial, and he found they had not been denied any fundamental right.

Carter, interviewed following the decision, reacted stoically, stating he had not expected the judge to reverse himself. Carter told George Vecsey of the *New York Times*, "I wasn't looking for anything—not from him— if he set a new trial, it would be like investigating himself."

Despite the setback, Carter indicated that his attorneys would be appealing to higher courts. This new legal action, however, would be directed by a new team of attorneys. Carter had been critical of Paul Feldman, the attorney selected by the State Public Defender's Office. Carter was especially upset with his lawyer's failure to call several witnesses who he thought would help his appeal.

NEW APPEALS, NEW LAWYERS

Carter was anxious to find a high-powered attorney, preferably one from outside New Jersey. He felt his previous attorney had been overwhelmed by local pressure. Carter mentioned his concerns to Raab, who recommended the New York attorney Myron Beldock. Raab was impressed by Beldock's work on the Whitmore case.

Artis was also able to obtain a New York attorney with excellent credentials: Lewis Steel, a young attorney who had already established a fine reputation as a civil rights attorney. He had recently worked with William Kunstler during the infamous Attica prison riot 1971. Like Beldock, he had helped reverse the conviction of a defendant (William Maynard) in a highly publicized murder case by unearthing exculpatory evidence. Both attorneys had volunteered their services on a pro bono basis.

One week after Judge Larner had denied their motion for a new trial, Beldock and Steel announced that they were filing a second motion for a retrial based on new evidence—the discrepancy in the date the bullet was recorded in the police department's property book. Beldock realized that his motion would initially have little chance of success since it had to be again argued before Judge Larner, but, according to New Jersey law, the only way for the defense to eventually extricate itself from Larner's jurisdiction and reach the State Supreme Court was to first obtain a ruling from Larner. The new appeal by Beldock and Steel stated that Larner had "misapprehended the issues." The defense was asking the judge to reverse himself because at least four important legal points had been inadequately covered at the previous hearing in October. The response of the Passaic County prosecutor was to oppose the motion, arguing that nothing significant was offered in the newly discovered material and that all of the critical points in the case had been sufficiently argued and decided.

On the eve of the second round of requests for a retrial, Joseph Gourley asked Judge Larner to prevent Beldock and Steel from representing Carter and Artis. Gourley questioned the "good faith" motives of the defense attorneys and asked them to explain to the court how they became involved

in the case. Carter explained to Judge Larner that he and Artis had dismissed the attorneys who had been selected by the State's Public Defend-
ers Office because of a serious disagreement over legal strategy. Carter
also thought it was very difficult for someone to receive justice in a New
Jersey court when he was being represented by attorneys who had to de-
pend upon that very system for their livelihood—i.e., working for the
State Public Defender's Office. No action was taken on the prosecution's
request by Judge Larner, who focused only on the defense motion requesting him to reconsider his previous decision denying a retrial, made a
month earlier.

The hearing began on a contentious note when the new defense team of
Beldock and Steel requested that Larner disqualify himself from the hearing because he had adopted "a partisan attitude" and was unable to remain impartial. Steel went so far as to accuse the judge of "prejudging the
issues" and exhibiting a predisposition to disbelieve the defendants.
Larner reacted to the accusations angrily, responding, "This is a hot air
discussion of abstract principles that have nothing to do with the case."
He then informed the attorneys that he would not disqualify himself and
he also rejected their request to permit Carter and Artis to attend the
hearing, explaining that it would be wholly unnecessary and a ridiculous
expense in time and money to transport them from prison to the courtroom.[16]

For the remainder of the three-hour hearing, the team of defense attorneys presented what they argued were new points of evidence that had allegedly been suppressed by the prosecution. The following are the six
critical pieces of evidence that the defense attorneys believed were excluded in the first trial:

- A bullet allegedly found in Carter's car the day after the murders
was not turned in to the police property clerk's office until five days
later.
- A contradiction in statements by witness Alfred Bello, who reportedly told investigators the previous year that he had been inside
the bar where the killings occurred just before the murders, although
he testified that he had been outside and seen Carter's car circling the
block.
- A statement by Passaic County Detective Vincent DiSimone,
who, at the hearing last fall, revealed for the first time that on August

4, 1966, there was another man in custody who was suspected of the crime.

•   A police tape recording of an interview with Bello in which he could not identify Carter and Artis.

•   A police report on another interview with Bello in which he could not identify Carter's car as the one he testified he saw.

•   The record of possible promises of leniency made by police to Bello.

John Goceljak, representing the prosecutor's office, argued that the jury had had all of the information necessary to reach a proper verdict at the initial trial.

Approximately two weeks later, on February 12, 1975, Judge Larner rejected for the second time the defense's motion for a retrial based on the newly uncovered evidence. Larner held that the prior defense counsel's failure to call six witnesses to the hearing for a new trial was not a sufficient reason for a reopening despite the wishes of the new counsel. He further ruled that the withholding of certain investigative materials which were not exculpatory in nature did not require a new trial and that the fact that the bullet and shell found in the defendant's auto were registered with the police property clerk five days later than originally claimed by Detective DiRobbio did not suffice to qualify as newly discovered evidence.

Not surprised by the outcome, Beldock and Steel immediately began plans for a direct appeal to the New Jersey Supreme Court, hopeful that once outside of Larner's bailiwick, they would have a much better chance for a new trial. The defense attorneys told the press that their appeal would focus on three critical issues: (1) the prejudicial behavior of the trial judge; (2) the suppressed evidence; and (3) the judge's error in restricting the original retrial hearing to just the recantation issue since he was thereby unable to hear other relevant evidence. Gourley, the Passaic County prosecutor, defended his office's position by referring to 1967 New Jersey Court rules that, he argued, legally authorized the withholding of the police files by his office. He further contended that, in his opinion, this information would have been worthless to the defense. The defense rejected Gourley's interpretation because it gave the prosecution unilateral control over the release of documents without allowing the defense to have an opportunity to make their independent evaluation.

In early September 1975 Beldock and Steel were ready to file their appeal requesting that the State Appellate Division of the Superior Court grant them a new trial. On September 2 the defense lawyers delivered their 125-page brief to the Appellate Division in Trenton. Ironically, Larner himself had, in the interim, just been appointed to the Appellate Division after having served eight years on the trial bench. The defense lawyers indicated that they would expect Judge Larner to disqualify himself if the appeal came before his section of the Appellate Division.[17]

After seven years of frustrating defeats, the defense was encouraged to hear in late August that the state's Attorney General's Office would not oppose the Carter-Artis appeal. Matthew Boylan, the director of the Criminal Justice Division of the Attorney General's Office stated that the state would not join Passaic County prosecutors in opposing defense motions for a new trial. Even though it was customary for Boylan's office to handle appeals for county prosecutors, he said they would sidestep the Carter case since it might eventually have to investigate possible prosecutorial improprieties.[18]

Three months later, Carter and the defense team received an even more important piece of good news. On November 6 the New Jersey Supreme Court announced that it would directly review the Carter-Artis appeal, permitting them to bypass the Appellate Division of the Superior Court. The decision would probably cut at least six months from the already tedious process, although it was unlikely to be heard by them before January 1, 1976, according to the clerk's office.

Legal experts thought the supreme court's decision to expedite the Carter appeal was at least partially in response to the groundswell of public support, which had been growing since Bello and Bradley recanted their initial testimony. In a related move, Carter and Artis decided to ask Governor Brendan Byrne for executive clemency. Lewis Steel, Artis's attorney, requested that the governor act quickly on their request because there was likely to be a long legal struggle before the case could be resolved.

GENERATING PUBLIC SUPPORT—A DEFENSE STRATEGY

Despite having Judge Larner twice reject their requests for a new trial, the defense was beginning to make advances in the court of public opinion. The most critical step in this process had been taken a year earlier, when Selwyn Raab began his series of reports in the *New York Times*.

The Carter forces now had a sympathetic voice on the country's most important newspaper.

The publicity campaign had stalled during the winter of 1974–75, when Judge Larner rejected a series of defense motions. However, by the fall of 1975, with an aggressive, experienced team of defense attorneys and a surprise decision from the State Supreme Court, public support began to grow again. On September 1, the *New York Times* reported that a Newark-based group had collected fifteen thousand signatures requesting a new trial for Carter and Artis. Carolyn Kelley was identified as the executive director of the organization calling itself the New Jersey Defense Committee for Rubin Carter and John Artis. At about the same time, across the Hudson, a group of New Yorkers headed by George Lois, a successful advertising executive, formed the Hurricane Defense Fund. Their stated goal was to raise $500,000 for his legal expenses.[19]

Lois had become interested in the Carter case after a visit from Richard Solomon, who had been active earlier, in the investigative phase of the campaign, but who now turned his considerable energies to organizing a viable publicity campaign. Lois's talents as a marketing and advertising executive were an important force in developing increased interest and support for the cause.

Solomon now sought a celebrity who would lend his or her name to the publicity campaign. He decided he would go after Bob Dylan, the folk-rock icon who had been involved in the civil rights movement since the early sixties. Solomon mailed Dylan a copy of Carter's autobiography and invited him to meet Carter and learn more about his case. Dylan took Solomon up on his invitation. After returning from a European concert tour, he stopped in Trenton and contacted Solomon, who arranged a visit to the prison.

Dylan spent nine hours talking with "The Hurricane." Dylan said he felt an instant rapport with Carter. After the meeting, Dylan wrote, "I realized that the man's philosophy and my philosophy were running on the same road and you don't meet too many people like that." He was also convinced of his innocence and soon after the meeting wrote a powerful song, "The Ballad of the Hurricane," characterized as "eleven one-two punch stanzas to the body of New Jersey injustice." Carter and Artis would now have their plight communicated to millions through the medium of Dylan's powerful ballad.

Solomon and Lois continued to mount their campaign to raise the nation's awareness of the Carter case. They were able to generate positive stories in a wide range of national magazines, ranging from the liberal *New Republic* to the conservative *National Review*. Carter's case seemed to bypass ideology and go straight to the nation's collective heart and conscience.

A second celebrity of even greater notoriety joined the campaign in the spring of 1975. Muhammad Ali, the heavyweight champion of the world and an influential spokesman for black Americans, had become cochairman of the Hurricane Defense Fund. He was enlisted in the cause by Carolyn Kelley, a black bondswoman from Newark who had many contacts with the world of professional boxing who also shared Ali's devotion to Islam. On May 16, 1975, Ali announced in Las Vegas that he was dedicating his upcoming title defense to the fight to free Rubin "Hurricane" Carter.

A week after that victorious bout, in which Ali beat Ron Lyle, Lois organized a benefit dinner to raise money for Carter's defense fund. Ali appeared at the festivities, held in New York at the Blue Angel nightclub. Addressing the 250 individuals who had each contributed fifty dollars, Ali declared that the New Jersey judicial system is "too proud to admit they put the wrong man in jail for nine years. The people that convicted Hurricane Carter probably were doing what they thought was right at the time. But he needs a new trial."

By August 1975 the collection of celebrities supporting Carter had grown spectacularly. The group now included famous scholars from Ivy League campuses, entertainers, sports figures, and movie and television personalities, including Burt Reynolds, Dyan Cannon, Ellen Burstyn, Walt Frazier, Earl Monroe, Melba Moore, Johnny Cash, Harry Belafonte, Norman Mailer, Budd Schulberg, George Plimpton, and Claude Brown. Nearly all of these prominent figures became part of the eighty-two-member national committee known as the "Hurricane Trust Fund." The group planned a star-studded concert in Madison Square Garden in the fall to raise money for the Carter and Artis legal defense.

The first major public rally in support of Carter occurred on September 9, 1975, in Newark. Several thousand persons joined in a march led by Muhammad Ali to the steps of City Hall. Mayor Kenneth Gibson accompanied the marchers, declaring it Rubin Carter Day and renaming Newark's Central Avenue "Justice for Rubin Carter Avenue." Two weeks later a second rally was held in Newark, this one engineered by Carolyn

Kelley and her New Jersey Defense committee. Ms. Kelley had succeeded in collecting fifteen thousand signatures on a petition in support of a new trial. She also was planning her own elaborate celebrity-filled "entertainment marathon" to raise money for Carter's legal defense, but the event never took place.

In mid-October, Muhammad Ali returned to New Jersey to lead a rally in Trenton in front of the state capitol. Most of the crowd of 1,600 had been bussed down from Newark and Paterson to support their beleaguered hero. After a brief march through the city's streets, Ali, accompanied by the former heavyweight champion Joe Frazier, met briefly with Governor Brendan Byrne, requesting that he consider granting clemency. The governor then asked Ali what he thought of limited clemency rather than a full pardon.[20] Under such an arrangement, Carter and Artis could be released from prison while awaiting their retrial.

The publicity campaign organized on Carter's behalf was beginning to have an impact on New Jersey's political and judicial leaders. The willingness of the governor to meet with Ali and discuss the possibility of clemency was clear evidence of the movement's growing influence. Another example of its impact was the November 11 transfer of Carter from Trenton State to Clinton Correctional Institution in rural Hunterdon County, a minimum-security prison housing mostly female inmates. (It should also be noted that the transfer occurred one week after the State Supreme Court granted a direct appeal to Carter, bypassing the Appellate Division.)

By Halloween, Bob Dylan, with his Rolling Thunder Revue, was ready to begin a concert tour that would publicize Carter's plight even more dramatically, with Dylan singing the "Ballad of the Hurricane" before thousands in packed arenas and concert halls. On December 9 the tour performed for Carter and his fellow inmates at the Clinton prison. In addition to Dylan, the ninety-minute concert featured performances by Joan Baez, Roberta Flack, and Joni Mitchell.

The following evening, December 10, 1975, the troupe performed its emotional musical revue before twenty thousand enthusiastic supporters in Madison Square Garden in the highlight of the entire tour. The famous auditorium was filled with hundreds of prominent celebrities. As the concert drew to a close, one reporter wrote, "I have never experienced a more powerful performance by any artist on any stage." The final stop for Dylan's musical revue was Houston, Texas. There, in the Astrodome before forty thousand fans on January 25, 1976, Dylan joined with Stevie Wonder, Ringo Starr, and other musicians as they entertained the audience for seven hours. Despite the apparent success of the Houston concert, logistical and monetary problems developed, and the Rolling Thunder tour had to be abandoned.

THE HAWKINS REPORT—THE MYSTERY DEEPENS

The publicity campaign organized by Richard Solomon and George Lois had begun to grab the attention of key political figures in the state capital, long before Bob Dylan's Rolling Thunder Revue began its concert tour. The governor was especially eager to calm this gathering storm. It had been nearly one year since the recantation by Bello and Bradley had been announced on the front page of the *New York Times*. Governor Byrne appointed a state assemblyman, Eldridge Hawkins, the chairman of the assembly's Judiciary Committee, to conduct an investigation into the Carter case and to advise him on the matter of pardon or executive clemency. Shortly after Hawkins began his investigation, Governor Byrne announced that he would waive the normal ten-year eligibility requirement for pardon cases. Carter's attorneys, unsure whether they would formally request a pardon or commutation of sentence at this point, awaited the results of Hawkins's probe.

Hawkins initially received strong support from the governor and the state's attorney general; the latter ordered the Office of Criminal Justice to order the Passaic County prosecutor's office to cooperate with the Hawkins investigation by turning over to him all of the files on the case. Passaic County had a newly appointed prosecutor, Burrell Humphreys. Humphreys was a highly respected lawyer from South Jersey, untainted by past involvement in the case. He willingly turned over the complete files. When Hawkins went to Paterson to physically remove the material, he noticed that in addition to the files carefully packaged for him, there appeared to be some additional folders hidden behind the file cabinets. Although the police appeared reluctant to add these newly discovered files, Hawkins insisted that they be added to the original materials.

Initially, Hawkins believed he would be able to turn the report over to the governor in a few weeks, but as he began to pore over the documents, he realized that this would be impossible. Although pressured by Carter's supporters to produce an immediate report, Hawkins told them it would take additional time. Hawkins commented, "There are too many questions left unanswered if I turn the report in immediately. There is too much material to go through." He was also finding that the files were raising more questions than they were answering. Nervous about his safety and needing additional help in completing the investigation, Hawkins hired Prentiss Thompson, a former investigator in the Essex County prosecutor's office whom Hawkins trusted and respected.[21]

As Thompson and Hawkins searched more deeply into the case, it appeared that both defense and prosecution attorneys were trying to cover themselves. Thompson and Hawkins uncovered a great deal of information that had never been made public or presented to a grand jury. Despite the fact that these materials involved possible criminal activities on the part of key figures in the case, state officials decided to block their release and declined to investigate more thoroughly. As the investigation progressed, Hawkins discovered that Governor Byrne's early support began to wane.[22] Because Hawkins was charged with presenting his confidential findings directly to the governor, he became frustrated at his inability to get through to him.

Also troubling to Hawkins were a series of leaks to the press by someone in the governor's administration of sensitive material in his preliminary findings, turned over to Byrne on October 26. Hawkins indicated that his final report would be ready in two weeks. The governor continued to consider the option of executive clemency.

In early December, the defense attorneys informed the governor that their clients were withdrawing their application for a pardon because they wanted to have their "names cleared completely in the courts." They did request, however, that the governor grant them executive clemency so their clients could be temporarily released from prison until all judicial proceedings were completed.

On December 10, Hawkins submitted his report to Governor Byrne. Although unwilling to comment on the specific findings of the report, Hawkins said he believed that based on his inquiries Carter and Artis were entitled to a new trial on technical grounds. The governor said the report would be sent to the prosecution and defense attorneys. He also would be reviewing the report with New Jersey's attorney general, William Hyland, before making a final decision.

Within a week the contents of the report had been leaked to the press. It confirmed Hawkins's conclusion that Carter and Artis were not the shooters but were actually lookouts while two other men were inside the bar murdering the victims. Hawkins thought that the shootings were racially motivated, avenging the death of Roy Holloway, the black bar owner shot earlier that evening. The report also included several additional disclosures:

> • A woman victim in the Lafayette Grill killings who survived for a month before dying of gunshot wounds identified photographs of two other men—not Mr. Carter or Mr. Artis—as "looking similar" to the killers.
> • A woman who nine years earlier wrongly incriminated a Paterson man as one of the killers had now come forward to identify Mr. Carter and Mr. Artis as accomplices and two other men as the actual killers. This woman, who described herself as a friend of Mr. Carter, was questioned in 1966 by the police but her testimony was then considered unreliable.[23]

Some of the evidence uncovered by Hawkins was detrimental to the defense, such as a copy of a letter Carter sent to a witness, Ms. McGuire, asking if she and her mother would help him establish an alibi. On the positive side for the defense, Hawkins was able to obtain a copy of the seemingly exculpatory results of the lie detector test taken by Carter and Artis after they were arrested.

The most bizarre result of Hawkins's investigation was the reappearance of Annie Ruth Haggins, who was living in South Carolina at the time. Ms. Haggins had initially implicated another man, Roosevelt Davis, but she now told Hawkins that Carter and Artis were outside the bar while two other persons did the shootings inside the bar. She had remained silent for the past ten years out of fear of retaliation by Carter, an old flame. Hawkins had given the woman a lie detector test and even put her under hypnosis. He came away dubious about the accuracy of her recollections.[24]

Hawkins also spoke with Al Bello, who now offered a new version of what he saw at the Lafayette Bar and Grill on June 17, 1966. He told Hawkins that he was actually inside the bar when the murderers entered and barely escaped from the bar once the shooting began, hiding behind the body of one of the victims, Hazel Tanis. As he fled the scene, Bello spotted Carter and Artis outside the bar, apparently serving as lookouts.

The Hawkins report was criticized by both the prosecution and the defense. The prosecution remembered Ms. Haggins but had dismissed her because of her history of mental illness and alcoholism. Governor Byrne, still undecided about clemency, authorized the creation of a special Essex County Grand Jury to resolve the numerous questions raised by the Hawkins investigation.

Functioning primarily as a fact-finding body, the grand jury called Al Bello and Ruth Haggins, who repeated the same stories they had told Hawkins. The grand jury concluded that the testimony from these rather eccentric witnesses was not sufficiently reliable to justify the issuance of any further indictments. Hawkins was exhausted by the investigation. He soon stepped down from the state assembly, stating that the investigation had been the most frustrating event of his life.[25]

Even Hawkins was unable to emerge from this murky case without tarnish on his reputation. On December 4, 1975, Selwyn Raab reported in the *New York Times* that Artis claimed that Hawkins had offered to free him from his life sentence if he would admit he had been an accomplice to the murders. Artis refused the offer. Hawkins denied even making the proposition, but Jeffrey Fogel, who was at the meeting, substantiated Artis's account.

THE NEW JERSEY SUPREME COURT GRANTS A RETRIAL

It was now up to the state Supreme Court to decide if Carter and Artis should be granted a retrial. Oral arguments in the case were scheduled for January 12, 1976. The defense attorney, Myron Beldock, told the court that Carter and Artis were victims of a "massive, purposeful suppression of evidence" in their 1967 trial. Beldock argued that the Passaic County Prosecutor had also hidden from the defense and jury the fact that their office had made promises to two key witnesses (Bello and Bradley) in order to obtain their testimony, thereby preventing defense attorneys from being able to use this information in attacking Bello and Bradley's credibility.[26]

Both defense attorneys felt cautiously optimistic following the oral arguments. The recantations had seriously undermined the strongest element of the prosecution's case—the eyewitness identifications that were the state's only direct evidence linking Carter and Artis to the crime. Additionally, the suppression of the tapes from the Wayne police station, where Lieutenant DeSimone had made promises to Bello and Bradley, seemed to discredit the prosecution's earlier denial of any such deals at the initial trial.

Two months later, on March 18, 1976, the New Jersey Supreme Court rendered a unanimous decision granting Carter and Artis a retrial. The ruling held that the state knowingly allowed its two identification witnesses to falsely testify at the murder trial that no promises had been made to them (except for protection) by the prosecution in conjunction with the testimony. The record clearly showed that one witness (Bello) was told by Lieutenant DeSimone that he would "do everything in his power" to have the witness's parole transferred to another state so he could make a fresh start. The other witness, Bradley, was promised by DeSimone that he would inform every prosecutor's office in the state where there were pending charges against him of his having testified for the state in this murder case. Justice Mark Sullivan concluded that the state had suppressed exculpatory evidence in failing to disclose such matters to the defense.

The court was careful to add, however, that they were not overruling Judge Larner's decision rejecting the recantations as not being believable and "lacking the ring of truth." They thought that there was sufficient evidence to permit such a conclusion. Also, it would be unusual for an appellate court to intercede and declare the judgment of a trial judge to be so faulty as to warrant a reversal of his evaluation of the recantations. Questions of fact—such as whether the recantations or the original trial testimony are credible—are treated differently than issues of law in which the appellate court can point to applicable precedent or statutes to support their opinion. Justice Sullivan, writing for the majority, explained the unique position of the trial judge in determining the credibility of recantation testimony: a trial judge, he wrote,

> sees the witnesses, hears their testimony and has the feel of the case. Manner of expression, sincerity, candor and straightforwardness are just some of the intangibles available to the trial judge in evaluating the credibility of recantation testimony. A reviewing court, not having the same advantage, should ordinarily defer to the trial judge's finding on this sensitive issue as long as the proper criteria are used.[27]

After the decision was announced, the new Passaic County prosecutor, Burrell Humphreys, stated that his office would seek to retry both defendants. The defense attorneys were visibly disappointed, hoping that in light of the unanimous supreme court decision, the state would decide not to retry. Beldock and Steel issued a statement declaring that "the unjust conviction of Carter and Artis resulted from the suppression of evidence, deceit and perjury and we fail to see why they should have to go through the pain and anxiety of another trial."[28]

In a press conference from his Clinton prison cell, Rubin Carter, joined by the civil rights leader the Reverend Ralph D. Abernathy, showed a degree of satisfaction at the decision but was far from ecstatic. Carter said,

> I am satisfied that somebody is recognizing as I have recognized all the while, that I am here illegally—if I had my druthers I'd rather have a fair trial that's free from perjured testimony, that's free from manufactured evidence which put us here originally. I want everybody to know and understand that Rubin Carter and John Artis could not, would not commit that crime.[29]

5: The Second Trial
Part I

The decision by the Passaic County prosecutor to retry Carter and Artis following the New Jersey Supreme Court decision in February meant that a second trial would be held sometime during 1976, a decade after the Lafayette Bar and Grill massacre. It was not surprising, given the passage of time, that the retrial would involve many new participants, including entirely different prosecution and defense teams.

A NEW CAST OF CHARACTERS

Carter and Artis were now represented by Myron Beldock and Lewis Steel, respectively. Beldock and Steel replaced the state public defender in December 1974, following Judge Larner's refusal to grant a retrial. Beldock was a slight, sandy-haired attorney with an impressive history of successful criminal cases, including the highly publicized Whitmore case. His soft-spoken manner belied his intense commitment to his client's defense. He indicated years later that the Carter case totally preoccupied him for fourteen years. He admitted he was barely able to keep his small law firm (eight lawyers) going as he often worked on little or no sleep, seven days a week, burning out two associates who could not keep up with his manic pace.[1]

The other half of the defense team, Lewis Steel, matched Beldock's intensity but was more vocal and aggressive in espousing the defense position. A former civil rights attorney, he would react quickly and sharply to perceived injustices. As the trial proceeded, his fervor led to numerous shouting contests with the trial judge and threats of contempt citations. In a hostile environment such as the Passaic County Courthouse, Carter and Artis were fortunate to be defended by such stalwart, unyielding attorneys.

The prosecution team, also entirely new, was led by Burrell Humphreys, who was assisted by Ronald Marmo and John Goceljak, the only prosecutor to play a role in both trials. Humphreys was a quiet-spoken, scholarly, highly respected attorney. Originally from southern New Jersey, he had moved up to Wayne in the early 1960s. As a longtime liberal Democrat, Humphreys had been active as an attorney for the ACLU and various civil rights groups. In 1967 he represented several black community and religious groups in a case against the Paterson police department involving charges of brutality and discrimination. Humphreys was asked by Governor Brendan Byrne in 1975 to become Passaic County prosecutor. Byrne wanted Humphreys to straighten out the Paterson police, who were still plagued by corruption and a reputation for racial prejudice that bred tension with the city's black and Hispanic neighborhoods. Humphreys was reluctant to assume the position. He anticipated a difficult time with the local Democratic political machine since he was an outsider who had been a thorn in its side in the past. The governor nevertheless continued to pressure Humphreys until he finally agreed to the appointment.

Ronald Marmo provided critical assistance to Humphreys, arguing the Carter case before both the appellate division and the State Supreme Court as well as directing the Investigative Task Force for the second trial. Marmo had built an impressive record since joining the office seven years earlier (1968) and had recently been named chief trial counsel. Marmo, then only thirty-five years old, played an important role in the second trial and in all subsequent appeals. In contrast to Humphreys, who always seemed to be under control and relatively soft-spoken, Marmo was a high-energy, forceful assistant whose acerbic retorts toward the defense were among the emotional high points of the trial.

Humphreys selected county Detective Lieutenant Vincent DeSimone as his chief investigator. DeSimone had been deeply involved in the Lafayette Bar murder case since 6:00 A.M. on June 17, just three hours after the shootings. He had directed the initial investigation, personally interviewing Artis and Carter in the early morning hours following the murders. He later spoke with Bello and eventually engineered his taped confession at the Wayne police station on October 11, 1966. No one knew more about the case than DeSimone, but his appointment raised serious difficulties that the defense later exploited. DeSimone epitomized the tough cop who would go to any length to break a case. During a long career serving under seven different county prosecutors, DeSimone had been involved in several controversial incidents. During the 1950s his aggressive investigative tactics had been officially condemned by the federal district court in the Monks case, which involved the brutal slaying of a young Paterson girl on her way to church by fifteen-year-old William Monks. Monks's conviction was eventually overturned because of the detective's coercive interrogation.

DeSimone's relationship with the key prosecution witness Alfred Bello played a key role in the second trial and eventually provided the federal courts a focal point for their concluding decision in this case, twenty years after DeSimone first assumed control of the original investigation. His appearance on the witness stand—a gravelly-voiced, tough-looking cop, frustrated and angered by the defense team's lacerating cross-examination—became a hallmark of this protracted, bitterly contested case.

The second trial featured not only new lawyers but also a new judge, Bruno Leopizzi, a fairly recent appointment to the bench (1973) but a lifelong Paterson resident and a prominent litigator in the state for twenty years. Leopizzi gained statewide recognition for his successful defense in the Kavanaugh case, the most famous criminal case in Passaic County history before Carter and Artis came along. Ironically, Leopizzi's victory in the Kavanaugh case was based upon his ability to discredit the county prosecutors, denouncing their overzealous investigative efforts—charges raised frequently in the Carter case.

Leopizzi, like Humphreys, was reluctant to leave his private law practice, but Governor Cahill insisted that he be allowed to place Leopizzi's name before the State Senate to fill an emergency vacancy on the court. Leopizzi, who had not been active politically and was not aligned with either political party, thought his chances of appointment were slender, but after three other nominees were disqualified at the last moment, he was assured the position. A tough, apolitical judge, with a reputation for integrity and his own record of pitched battle with the county prosecutor's office, he seemed an ideal choice to preside over a highly contentious trial and to give the defense a fair chance to combat Humphreys, Marmo, and DeSimone.

BAIL HEARING AND A TASTE OF FREEDOM

Even before the State Supreme Court ordered a new trial in January 1976, Passaic County officials, particularly the prosecutor's office, had been under intense pressure because of the growing media and public outcry over the perceived injustices of the first trial. Once the state's highest court concluded that Carter and Artis had not received a fair trial and should be granted a retrial, state officials in Trenton began a lobbying campaign to force the Passaic County justice system to end the case. The county prosecutor had been encouraged by representatives of the attorney general's office to terminate the proceedings. Humphreys was relieved that Governor Byrne continued to support him, but Byrne soon launched the Eldridge Hawkins investigation to look into the case with the possibility of recommending a pardon by the governor.

Humphreys resolutely maintained his decision to retry the case despite the mounting pressure. The first order of business in the retrial was a bail hearing to determine the pretrial status of Carter and Artis. Both Humphreys and Judge Leopizzi were bombarded by calls from Trenton, some even rumored to be coming from the state's highest court, urging that Carter and Artis be immediately granted their pretrial freedom. Humphreys was so upset by the outside interference that he wrote a letter to the presiding judge criticizing the entire bail fiasco, which Leopizzi agreed to put into the record. At one point Humphreys threatened to file a protest, going public with his objections to the lobbying efforts. At this point officials in Trenton realized they had pushed too hard and backed off.

On March 19, Judge Leopizzi held a four-hour bail hearing in which he also established a modified gag order that barred all attorneys from discussing the case. During the hearing Muhammad Ali and a hundred supporters of the defendants waited outside the courtroom, jammed into a corridor. Humphreys argued that the defendants should be denied bail because of the heinous nature of the crime, but Judge Leopizzi established a fairly modest bond of twenty thousand dollars for Carter and fifteen thousand dollars for Artis.

The next day both defendants appeared before the judge and were granted their temporary freedom, emerging from behind prison walls for the first time in nine years. In an unusual twist, Carter, fearing reprisals from county police officers, phoned Chief Justice Hughes of the State Supreme Court and requested that he be transported from his prison cell in Clinton to Passaic County by the state police rather than Passaic County law-enforcement officers. The chief justice called Attorney General Hyland, who arranged a compromise whereby the state police followed the Passaic County sheriff's car as it transported Carter back to Paterson.[2]

On March 20 Carter and Artis appeared before Judge Leopizzi in a brief fifteen-minute bail hearing, during which their bond was posted and they were released. Carter was allowed to leave the state in order to help raise money for his legal defense. The trial date was set for June 6. As the hearing ended, Carter hugged his four sisters and then quietly exited the courthouse with Muhammad Ali. The pair drove away in a gray Cadillac to meet Carter's wife, Thelma, at the New York Hilton. John Artis quietly slipped away in another car with a group of his friends. The only bail restriction placed on the defendants was that they could only travel to New York or Florida, where Carter would be staying with a friend. Carter and Artis chose not to have a press conference following their release although Carter had given a telephone interview the previous day from the Clinton prison in which he declared:

> I'm going to get my head together. We are going to a place where I can feel safe and not worry about being locked in or locked down. I'm going to a place where the trees are green, the sky is blue, and there are no bars on the windows. A place where I can have a bath whenever I want, where I can eat what I want, where I can see and listen to the grass grow, and talk to my daughter and teach her not to make the mistakes that I did. That is what I call living after all these years in this hell.[3]

CAROLYN KELLEY AND HER ALLEGED ASSAULT

In a case filled with bizarre episodes, eccentric personalities, and inexplicable twists, the alleged assault of Carolyn Kelley by Rubin Carter remains one of the strangest. Ms. Kelley was a forty-one-year-old Newark bondswoman who had been the former head of the New Jersey Defense Committee for Carter. Although her fund-raising efforts were eventually superseded by those of George Lois and his better-known "Hurricane Defense Fund," she had provided the link to Muhammad Ali through her ties to the Muslim community. She had been campaigning since early 1975 on Carter's behalf, organizing strong support groups for him in several New Jersey cities. Kelley had recently expanded her efforts beyond the specifics of Carter's case to a nationwide campaign she called Freedom for All Forever, directed toward all individuals who had been wrongfully convicted of crimes.

On April 24, Carter and Kelley had been invited by Don King to come down to Landover, Maryland, to watch Ali fight in a title bout against Ron Lyle on April 29, 1975. According to Kelley, she was unable to stay in the Sheraton Hotel in Landover with Carter and the rest of his entourage because it was full. She was able, however, to obtain a room at a nearby Ramada Inn but needed to contact Carter in order to be able to pay for the room. After he reportedly screamed at her over the phone, she went to Carter's hotel room to try and work out the financial arrangements. Kelley stated that Carter invited her into the room and began laughing hysterically before hitting her in the face, knocking her down, and then kicking her in the back. She was carried to another hotel room by one of Carter's security men, Jerry Minik, who notified her son, Michael. Michael came to the hotel and took his mother to BWI Airport, where she boarded a flight for Newark the next day. Carter denied all of her allegations.

The entire incident did not become public knowledge until June 6, when Ms. Kelley told of her April 28 beating at a press conference from her bed at Crippled Children's Hospital in Newark. Ms. Kelley did not enter the hospital until nineteen days after the alleged beating. She also never notified Maryland authorities about her beating and had not pressed charges against Carter. She was unable to explain why the attack had occurred. Carter's attorneys issued a rebuttal to Kelley's charges, theorizing that she was angry and upset with Carter for not giving her financial assistance from his legal defense fund. Kelley had recently suffered severe personal and business losses. A spokesman for Myron Beldock, Carter's attorney, stated that Kelley was engaging in a smear campaign against Carter in order to extort badly needed money from him. She had been gradually excluded from the defense committee and the monies they were raising through concerts and rallies. Her own organizations and committees were about to force her into bankruptcy. Complicating the matter even further were rumors circulating linking Carter and Kelley romantically, fueling speculation that the incident arose over Carter's rejection of her amorous advances.

Within this swirl of accusations and counteraccusations, it became increasingly difficult to separate fact from fiction. Meanwhile, the Passaic County authorities were forced to try to unravel the complex incident because of its direct bearing on Carter's bail status. If Kelley's accusation was true, Carter would immediately lose his pretrial freedom and be returned to prison. Therefore, Passaic County Superior Court judge William Marchese scheduled a bail hearing on June 28, just three weeks after Ms. Kelley's bedside press conference announcing her beating at the hands of Hurricane Carter. (Marchese had temporarily replaced Judge Leopizzi, who had recused himself from the case because many years earlier he had served as an attorney for two of the witnesses in the 1967 trial. Both defense and prosecution attorneys rejected Leopizzi's fears and urged him to remain on the case as presiding judge.)

The hearing before Judge Marchese resembled an entire trial, lasting eleven days and involving thirty-three witnesses. The entire proceeding was conducted behind closed doors without the press or general public present. Despite its length and thoroughness, the hearing proved inconclusive.[4] They did, however, reveal a serious power struggle within the Carter camp between two factions: the biracial Hurricane Defense Committee (headed by George Lois, it had raised approximately $600,000) and the all-black Kelley group, then insolvent. Members of the Lois group, including Carter and his attorneys, emphasized that Kelley's accusation grew out of her being rejected both romantically and financially. Lois reported that most of the money raised had been spent on costly celebrity performers and that they had cleared only $104,000, $38,000 of which went for legal fees and out-of-pocket-expenses and $35,000 for bail for the two defendants.

Several inconsistencies in Ms. Kelley's medical records added to the overall confusion. Why did she wait seventeen days before going to the hospital if her condition was so serious? Several of Ms. Kelley's friends testified that when they visited her the next day, April 29, her face was badly swollen and she was suffering from fainting spells. A Newark doctor, George Stephens, visited her at her home and reported that she was in semiconscious condition with a stiff neck and badly swollen face and ordered her to a hospital. She did go to three different emergency rooms, but the doctors and nurses who attended to her at all three locations testified that they did not have any recollection of her appearing to have suffered a beating. Several did not remember her at all.

In view of the contradictory evidence, Judge Marchese decided to allow Carter to remain free on bail, but he was no longer permitted to leave New Jersey without the court's permission (with the exception of being allowed to visit with his attorneys in Manhattan). Judge Marchese acknowledged the various inconsistencies in Ms. Kelley's testimony but stated he was "convinced by a preponderance of the testimony that an incident did occur at that time (April 29) in Rubin Carter's room and that, in fact, Carolyn Kelley was struck by Rubin Carter."

Frustrated by the court's tepid response to her alleged beating and fearing possible reprisals by Carter, Carolyn Kelley finally filed a criminal complaint in Maryland as well as a civil suit for $1 million dollars. After an extensive investigation lasting two months, Maryland authorities announced on August 23, 1976, that they had not discovered sufficient evidence to substantiate Ms. Kelley's accusation, and the case was dropped. Chief Investigator Charles Kiess of the Maryland State's Attorney Office said the decision to press charges against Carter had been made on the basis of an affidavit filed by Ms. Kelley, on "medical testimony which did not substantiate her claims about an injury," as well as an investigation by his office.[5] (Without Maryland initiating criminal proceedings, the civil suit also disappeard by the end of the year.)

Was Carolyn Kelly a victim or simply a spurned lover? As with so many other questions raised in this case, there can be no definitive answer. One again finds a number of conflicting stories, told by individuals motivated in their testimony by such emotions as greed, love, or pride, but certainly not a strong desire to disclose the truth.

PRETRIAL MANEUVERS

In mid-April, just before the Carolyn Kelley fiasco and the ensuing bail-revocation hearing, Beldock and Steel went before Judge Leopizzi requesting a postponement of the trial, asserting that they could not be ready for the scheduled June 7 trial date. During the proceeding, which lasted an hour, there were several heated exchanges between the bench and bar, a preview of subsequent battles in the forthcoming trial. Beldock argued that he was having a difficult time locating missing witnesses because he had run out of money to pay for investigators. Leopizzi agreed to the defense attorney's request and rescheduled the trial for October 5, 1976.

During this delay both defense and prosecution attorneys engaged in a series of pretrial maneuvers designed to give themselves an advantage in the upcoming trial. The first issue to be resolved was the gag order imposed by Judge Leopizzi several months earlier. Leopizzi thought that the restriction of prejudicial comments by both sides would be the only way to make it possible to impanel an impartial jury. At the hearing granting a postponement of the trial date, Judge Leopizzi reaffirmed his original gag order.

In early July Judge Marchese, who had temporarily replaced Leopizzi, declared that Carter had violated the gag order when his supporters paraded in front of the Passaic County Courthouse. Carter's attorneys appealed the gag order violation to the appellate division of the New Jersey Superior Court, which agreed that the order should be overturned. This was a rather unexpected decision since the State Supreme Court in July rejected the defense request to lift the order which had been in effect since March 26, 1976. The appellate court's decision, issued on July 24, 1976, narrowly focused on the failure of Judge Leopizzi to establish clear evidence that public discussion would hinder efforts to have a fair trial.

The gag order was reinstituted on March 10 by Judge Marchese despite the appellate court decision, and defense attorneys quickly returned to challenge the judge's decision. Judges Leon Milmed and John Ard of the appellate court removed the gag order for a second time, declaring that "there is nothing in the record to show that pretrial publicity outside the confines of the courtroom would make it difficult to impanel an impartial jury or tend to prevent a fair trial."[6]

Both sides spent the month of August tracking down witnesses. Al Bello, the crucial witness whose eyewitness identification at the first trial and subsequent recantation was pivotal to the outcome of the retrial, had vanished from his home in Wanaque, New Jersey. He had recently completed a six-month jail term. The prosecution, which had identified Bello as a material witness, was uncertain how long he had been missing or where he was headed. Bello's father told authorities that he had not seen his son in three months. Finally, Humphreys announced that Bello had officially disappeared as of August 4. Three days later Bello was located in Albuquerque, New Mexico. Bello indicated that he would return to New Jersey and promised to respond to future prosecution subpoenas.

Arthur Bradley, Bello's partner in the burglary of the Ace Sheet Metal Company and also an eyewitness, had also vanished during the summer.

The main reason for his flight was his effort to elude Morris County authorities. He was being sought by the police for the attempted rape and assault of a young woman in Pequannock on May 21, 1976. Bradley, who had also recanted his testimony given at the first trial, was eventually located in Massachusetts but did not return for the retrial since neither side had much use for him given his lack of cooperation, poor health, and refusal to take a lie-detector test.

The third missing witness, also located during August, was William Hardney, Carter's former sparring partner, who had supposedly been with Carter at the Nite Spot and could serve as an alibi witness. He had not appeared in the original trial, hoping to avoid an outstanding New Jersey child support order. Both the prosecution and Senator Hawkins's investigator, Prentiss Thompson, were interested in tracking him down and learning exactly where he was on the evening of June 17, 1966, and in whose company. Thompson was the first to locate him at his home in suburban Maryland, outside of Washington, D.C., in October 1976. After an intense conversation with Thompson, Hardney went to see a local attorney. Meanwhile, Thompson visited the home of a federal district court judge, who granted a warrant for Hardney's arrest as a material witness. Thompson and several associates returned to Hardney's home. The federal judge agreed to extradite Hardney to New Jersey, where he would be needed for the upcoming trial.

By mid-August, Al Bello, the only remaining eyewitness to the Lafayette Bar slayings, was back in Paterson. Humphreys insisted that the only way he would use Bello was if he would submit to a lie-detector test. Humphreys was greatly troubled by Bello's history of perjury and his apparent willingness to tell the highest bidders whatever they wished to hear. Recently Bello had modified his recantation before the Hawkins investigation and Essex County Grand Jury, insisting that Carter and Artis were only accomplices, standing as lookouts outside the bar. According to one of his versions, Bello had been inside the bar when the shooting began and therefore was certain that Carter and Artis were not the killers. In late August Bello agreed to take the test, and polygraph experts were flown in from Chicago.

Humphreys was hopeful the tests would confirm Bello's original testimony given at the first trial where he testified to seeing the defendants running out of the bar and down the street carrying their weapons as they jumped into their getaway car. As we will learn later in this chapter, Bello gave Humphreys more than he could have ever wanted by the time he completed the polygraphs. It would prove to be a defining moment in leading to the ultimate outcome in this complex legal struggle. Humphreys felt confident that Bello's testimony, backed up by the polygraph tests, could convince the jury in the retrial that the recantations had been a lie and the original trial's identification the truth. (Humphreys even offered to have the polygraph experts give Carter a polygraph test in a private setting where no one but Beldock would learn the results, but the defense refused.)

As the trial date approached, Beldock and Steel became increasingly anxious about having to retry the case in Paterson. The pretrial publicity from the local papers, lingering bitterness over the first trial, and racial tensions prompted the defense attorneys to seek a change of venue. On September 2 they presented their request to Judge Charles Joelson, a Passaic County Superior Court judge in charge of the hearing. He told attorneys for both sides that he intended to read all 672 newspaper articles and stories submitted to him by the two groups of attorneys. Particularly troubling were a group of four editorials from the Paterson papers (the *Morning News* and the *Evening News*) that appeared to presuppose guilt. (Judge Joelson rejected an earlier defense motion to dismiss the indictments because the 1966 grand jury had allegedly excluded blacks.)

Nine days after hearing defense motions to change venue, Judge Joelson agreed that there had been enough prejudicial pretrial publicity to warrant moving the trial from Passaic County to the Hudson County Courthouse in Jersey City, approximately twenty miles southeast. Joelson stated that a "fair trial is not possible in Passaic County." After reviewing the pretrial newspaper coverage, he found that there had been "an incessant stream of publicity, permeated with prejudice to the defendants."[7] The judge selected Hudson County because he found the local news coverage there to be "balanced and unimpassioned." He also felt that the two counties (Hudson and Passaic) were demographically similar.

Nearly a decade after their initial arrests for the Lafayette murders, Carter and Artis began their retrial in Jersey City, October 12, 1976. Before the court could even begin to consider jury selection, Judge Marchese had to decide a number of complicated issues. In addition to the recantations from the original trial testimony, there was now Bello's repudiation of his recantation as well as an accusation against the prosecution for attempted bribery of a witness. The most bizarre problem awaiting the

judge was a mysterious witness for the prosecution who had been hypno-
tized in order to elicit more specific recollections of the night of the murder. Another unusual possibility was a series of switches of witnesses from
one side to the other. Several of Carter's alibi witnesses, including the two
women who had testified that he had driven them home at the time of the
shooting, and the former sparring partner who once gave Carter his Nite
Spot alibi, were all now scheduled to appear for the prosecution. Two
other important witnesses, one for the defense and one for the prosecution, had died: William Marins, the sole survivor of the shootings, and
John "Bucks" Royster, who was riding in Carter's car when it was first
stopped by Officer Capter. Finally, no one was sure whether the volatile
Ms. Kelley would cooperate with the prosecution or whether Arthur
Bradley would return as a defense witness. On October 14, Ms. Kelley indicated to the press that she was upset by the amount of pressure exerted
on her by Humphreys and his staff. She said she had been interviewed
two weeks earlier by four members of Humphreys's office who tried
to convince her to make incriminating statements concerning Carter's
ownership of a shotgun shortly before the Lafayette Bar shootings. She
even hinted that she was now willing to discuss the matter with Carter's
attorneys.[8]

JURY SELECTION

Although Judge William Marchese had been handling most of the pretrial proceedings in the retrial, both defense and prosecution requested
that the originally selected judge, Bruno Leopizzi, be brought back into
the case. Leopizzi had an outstanding reputation as a trial attorney and in
his time on the bench had impressed the legal community with his integrity and judgment. His negligible involvement with two of the minor
witnesses from the first trial was not viewed as sufficient grounds for rejecting his competent services in this difficult and highly publicized trial.

Leopizzi showed from his very first ruling that he would maintain tight
control over the case. The judge's first move was to exclude both the media and the general public from the jury-selection process. Neither defense nor prosecution lawyers objected to his decision. The judge had
already explained to the attorneys that he would personally question each
potential juror, although the attorneys could submit to him any questions
they wished him to ask a juror.

On October 22, Leopizzi had in hand one hundred questions from both sides. Thus far, 250 people had been excused for service for a variety of reasons, generally categorized as "personal hardships," but an additional 250 were available to be questioned. The selection process was conducted by the judge in his chambers. As a concluding note to this opening session, Judge Leopizzi reinstituted a gag order that restricted the defendants and all attorneys from commenting publicly on the case.

The voir dire selection of jurors took twelve days to complete as 130 potential panel members were questioned by Leopizzi. By November 5 the sixteen finalists had been selected—twelve jurors with four alternates, the alternates to be randomly chosen upon the completion of the trial. The group was composed of twelve men and four women, and two of the jurors were black. The jury was to be sequestered in a Hudson County hotel for the duration of the trial, a measure designed to remove the jurors from the intense media attention that would most likely surround the trial. Both sides used experts who could assist them in the selection of jurors who would be most sympathetic to their position. The prosecution hired a former Jersey City police officer who was familiar with the various county neighborhoods, while the defense used a team of jury experts from Columbia University who had recently written a book entitled *The Totalitarian Juror*.

There would be one more judicial decision made before the trial would commence. Judge Leopizzi wished to return to what he thought were the more comfortable surroundings in the new Passaic County Courthouse in Paterson. He also thought it would be easier for the jury to be bussed to Paterson rather than transport the Passaic County personnel back and forth each day. Assignment Judge Joelson (the chief judge for Passaic County) granted Leopizzi's request. The trial would begin on November 11 in the spacious sixth-floor courtroom of the county courthouse. Both Carter and Artis were upset by the decision. A frustrated Rubin Carter declared, "We were granted a change of venue from a hostile city (Paterson). . . . Jersey City was a much more amenable atmosphere. It's a very bad situation."[9]

OPENING STATEMENTS

On Thursday, November 11, the second trial began as defense and prosecution each presented their opening statements to the jury. However, before the jury was brought in, Judge Leopizzi ordered *New York Times* reporter Selwyn Raab to leave the courtroom. Raab had been deeply involved in the case for two years, playing an important role in obtaining the recantations from both Bello and Bradley. Leopizzi's ruling was also necessitated by the fact that Raab was listed as a possible witness. Once escorted outside the courtroom, Raab was served with a subpoena from the Passaic County prosecutor's office. The subpoena requested that he "produce all documents, memoranda, statements relating to your relationship and conversations with two defendants as well as Fred Hogan, an investigator for the defense." The defense indicated they would also be subpoenaing Raab in the near future. The subpoenas raised serious First-Amendment issues, and lawyers for the *New York Times* said later that evening that the newspaper and Raab would refuse to comply.

As the expectant jury was brought into the courtroom and settled into their soft leather seats, Judge Leopizzi solemnly addressed them. He cautioned the sixteen jurors that the opening statements about to be presented were merely outlines of what the attorneys hoped to prove during the trial and should not be thought of as evidence. He went on to instruct them, "You are the sole judge of the facts. I'll probably sound like a broken record when I tell you not to prejudge this case."[10]

The lead prosecutor, Burrell Humphreys, spoke first. He began his hour-long presentation with a gruesome, detailed description of the murders, indicating which victims were shot by each defendant and the types of injuries each victim suffered. He identified Carter and Artis as the assailants, stating, "The defendants came into that bar that morning with one purpose in mind, and that purpose was murder."[11] He next told the jury his two critical witnesses would be Patty Graham Valentine, who would identify Carter's automobile leaving the scene of the crime, and Al Bello, who would identify Carter and Artis coming out of the bar with the murder weapons and then driving away. Humphreys wasted no time in informing the jury of Bello's criminal record and his previous inconsistent statements, concluding with the caveat that "You will not admire Alfred Bello, and you may not even like him, but he was there and he was in a position to observe." He concluded with a promise to show the jury that Carter "had concocted a false story of his whereabouts" and with his lawyer had convinced several witnesses in the first trial to lie in order to produce an alibi for him.

Carter's attorney Myron Beldock spoke next, warning the jury in a soft voice that they would be facing a lengthy trial, echoing a similar prediction by the prosecutor. He devoted most of his opening statement to an acerbic depiction of the state's primary eyewitness, Al Bello, whom he termed an "incredible liar" and "a man who would sell his soul, a man who has sold his soul."

Lewis Steel, representing John Artis, spoke next, describing his client "as good a person as anyone in this courtroom." Steel noted Artis's exemplary record as a scholar-athlete and promised that Artis would testify, showing his truthful and courageous character to the jury. At the close of the day, Artis and Carter had distinctly contradictory appraisals of how much Paterson had changed in the ten years since their first trial. An optimistic John Artis told reporters, "It's a quite different setting, the whole aura is different. . . . We're almost out of racial strife, and with the economic decline, people have started to worry about each other. We've made more progress toward oneness."

Rubin Carter did not share his codefendant's benign reappraisal. He complained, "Nothing has changed. The prosecution is still committing crimes against the people."[12] It would be a month and a half before the judge and jury would confirm which defendant was closer to the truth.

THE PROSECUTION BEGINS TO PRESENT ITS CASE

The prosecution began its presentation of evidence by calling one of its two eyewitnesses, Patricia Graham Valentine. In June 1966, she was living in a small apartment above the bar with her boyfriend and young son. Ms. Valentine was now thirty-one years old, living in Florida, and working as a beautician. Lieutenant DeSimone had recently flown down to spend time with her in preparation for the retrial. Humphreys began his questioning of Ms. Valentine by having her recount the dramatic events of June 17, 1966, when she was awakened by gunfire (although at the time she thought it sounded like a door being slammed shut). Ms. Valentine then recounted how she looked out the window of her apartment and saw a white car with butterfly or triangular-shaped taillights pull away from the curb and speed down the street. After losing sight of the car, she went downstairs, where she discovered the victims in the bloody aftermath of the massacre. She explained how she went upstairs and called the police and then came down again to tend to Hazel Tanis before returning upstairs to call Hazel Tanis's boyfriend. The police had arrived by this point, and she gave them a description of the car. When Carter's car was brought back to the Lafayette Bar, she identified it as the car she had seen earlier.

At this point, Ms. Valentine began to add to her 1967 testimony by describing her trip to the Paterson police garage later that day. She noted for the first time that when Detective La Conte was escorting her toward the white car (Carter's) in the garage, she saw another policeman, Detective Emil DiRobbio, standing by the car, holding two bullets in his hand. Her amended testimony was helpful to the prosecution in their efforts to establish the exact time the ammunition was found in Carter's car. Her testimony also helped corroborate Detective DiRobbio's insistence that he found the ammunition the same day, June 17, thus countering suspicions that the police might have planted the shell and cartridge in Carter's car.

Lewis Steel, Artis's attorney, got the first shot at cross-examining Valentine, asking her why she never mentioned seeing Detective DiRobbio with the bullets and shotgun shell in any of her three previous accounts of that fateful day. She had no explanation other than that now she remembered it and that it had slipped her mind earlier.

When the cross-examination of Ms. Valentine continued the next day, November 13, 1976, additional contradictions emerged between her testimony in the first trial, at the November 1966 grand jury, and her most recent revelations. She had initially described Carter's car as a 1966 Dodge Monaco, a model whose taillights illuminate in the shape of two triangles across the rear of the car. She drew a likeness for the grand jury showing that the entire triangles had been filled with light. Rubin Carter's car, however, was a Dodge Polaro, which has a triangular-shaped aluminum decoration in the rear but conventional taillights with only the extreme portions at the widest part actually being lit.

As Ms. Valentine's testimony drew to a close, the defense believed it had raised several significant points that might diminish her credibility. She had been unable to give the color of the jackets worn by the men although Carter had been wearing a distinctive white jacket when he was stopped by the police. Additionally, she had initially only identified the background of the mystery car's license plate as dark rather than blue. It was not until four months later at the grand jury that she specified the color. Lastly, she had identified Carter's car at the first trial as being "similar" to the murderers', but nine years later, at the second trial, she had been able to improve her recollection to insist that she was certain they were the same.

Beldock and Steel's cross-examination of Patty Valentine appeared to expose an effort to upgrade her testimony in order to support the prosecution. The defense attorneys were prepared to attack Peggy Valentine even more aggressively, but they did not want to overplay their hand. It was obvious that despite her shaky testimony and transparent lies, the jurors and the audience in the courtroom did not wish to see her humiliated any further. Rather than continue to hammer away at Valentine's character, possibly creating a sympathetic figure in the eyes of the jury, Beldock and Lewis tried to create an image of a witness who had been carefully coached by Lieutenant DeSimone, tailoring her testimony to whatever was most beneficial to the prosecution's case.[13]

A VOICE FROM THE GRAVE

William Marins, the sole survivor of the Lafayette Bar shootings, died in 1973 of causes unrelated to his gunshot wounds. The chief trial counsel for the prosecution, Ron Marmo, read Marins's 1967 trial testimony to the jury on Monday, November 15. Marins had been sitting at the bar, drinking a beer, when he suddenly felt a sharp pain in his left eye. He turned toward the front door and saw "two tall colored men, one holding a sawed-off shotgun."

Myron Beldock, Carter's defense attorney, read Raymond Brown's cross-examination of Marins from the first trial. Brown showed that Marins had told a June 1966 grand jury that the two men who shot him were "light skinned Negroes, both about six feet tall." The one who was holding a shotgun was described by Marins as wearing a thin hat, clean shaven except for a pencil-thin mustache, and weighing about 190 pounds. During the cross-examination Marins repeated that both men were light-skinned Negroes about six feet tall. The importance of these descriptions was that they were so far off from accurately describing Carter, a stocky, muscular man who measures five feet seven inches and weighed about 160 pounds at the time. Carter was also very dark-skinned and, at the time of the shooting, had a very thick mustache as well as a goatee.

An even more significant aspect of Marins's testimony was his failure to identify Carter and Artis as the assailants when they were brought before him in the St. Joseph's Hospital emergency room. With the suspects standing at the foot of his bed, Detective Callahan asked Marins if these were the two men in the bar, and he indicated by shaking his head that they were not, even after Callahan repeated the question a second time. Prosecutors have downplayed the importance of Marins's failure to identify Carter and Artis because of his dazed condition in the hospital, but it nevertheless remains an important weakness in the prosecution's case. The defense hoped that Marins's testimony would have more impact at this trial than it had in the first one.

Interestingly, the prosecution had chosen to omit a final comment by William Marins that evening in the emergency room. When he indicated to Callahan for the second time that he could not identify the suspects, he stated he had trouble distinguishing black people because "all niggers look alike." Given the tense racial situation in Paterson, the prosecution decided it would be best to bury such a prejudicial and inflammatory comment.

ALFRED BELLO TAKES THE STAND AGAIN

There were two eyewitness identifications at the first trial, but only one was offered at the retrial. Arthur Bradley, who had identified only Carter at the second trial, was rejected by Humphreys because of his refusal to take a polygraph before testifying. Moreover, Bradley had been the first of the eyewitnesses to recant his 1967 trial identification of Carter, and, in contrast to Alfred Bello, he had adamantly stuck by his recantation. Humphreys categorized Bradley as a drug addict, continuing to live the life of a petty criminal. His unsavory reputation made him equally useless to the defense. If the prosecutors were to force him to testify, he would be an extremely hostile witness. The defense attorneys were also leery of Bradley because of his erratic behavior and persistent problems with the law. Either side would have a difficult time convincing him to leave Massachusetts.

Without Bradley the prosecution was left with only Al Bello, a witness whose constantly changing stories necessitated a "Wade" or "Stoval" hearing before Judge Leopizzi without the presence of the jury. This type of hearing is used by a judge in order to determine whether or not a witness's identification has been improperly suggested by the police or anyone else. It should be remembered that the primary reason the Supreme Court granted the retrial was because the prosecution had knowingly allowed its two identification witnesses—Bello and Bradley—to testify falsely at the first trial that no promises had been made to them in hopes of inducing the desired testimony. The tapes from the Wayne police station clearly showed discussions between Lieutenant DeSimone and the two witnesses in which offers of possible assistance were made.

On November 16, 1976, with the jury excused, Alfred Patrick Bello strode into the packed sixth-floor courtroom, prepared to present yet another version of the events he had observed in the early morning hours of June 17, 1966, at the Lafayette Bar. The prosecution hoped that Bello's performance would be good enough to convince Judge Leopizzi that he should be allowed to testify before the jury. The cocky thirty-three-year-old Bello was nattily attired in a dark blue suit and bright red cowboy boots. His testimony that day was marked by theatrical flourishes and coarse language. The spectators in the courtroom hung on his every word, frequently breaking into raucous laughter as when he brazenly stated at one point, "I am just here to state the facts." At another time, obviously set on entertaining his captive audience, he announced to Judge Leopizzi that the short muscular man he saw outside the bar "definitely wasn't Clark Gable." When tapes were played of his conversations with Joseph Miller and Melvin Ziem, his prospective partners in a forthcoming literary project, he casually laced his fingers behind his head and stared up at the courtroom ceiling.

Throughout the daylong hearing requested by the defense, Bello was forced to admit he had lied on numerous occasions to the police, Assemblyman Hawkins, an Essex County grand jury, and his own literary agents. In addition to creating a picture of Bello as an inveterate liar, the defense had also to convince the judge that the particular version of the events which Bello would be presenting to the jury during the retrial was the direct byproduct of improper police suggestions and promises made on October 11, 1966. On the other hand, the prosecution had to convince the jury that Bello's original testimony at the first trial was the only true version of what had taken place at the Lafayette Bar. Lieutenant DeSimone's taped conversations with Bello at the Wayne Police Station were only an effort to convince Bello to stick with that truthful account.

Beldock opened the hearing by playing the October 11 tapes, in which Lieutenant DeSimone was heard telling Bello that in exchange for "truthful" information, he would "do everything within my power . . . to have your parole transferred to another state." Bello then asked if his parole could be dropped entirely. DeSimone responded, "Well, that I can't promise. In other words, I'm taking this one step at a time."

Beldock next began to document Bello's series of lies and distortions. He first played a series of recently released taped conversations between Bello and his two literary agents, Miller and Ziem. Judge William Marchese, at an earlier pretrial hearing, had ordered the tapes to be sent to both the defense and the prosecution, which had had them for less than a week.

These tapes revealed Bello offering his agents a variety of possible scenarios to choose from, although they all place Bello inside the bar when the shooting occurred, saving his own life by going behind Hazel Tanis. The shooters were two black men he did not recognize. After the gunfire, the men fled, and Bello went out the door and saw Carter and Artis standing outside, probably serving as lookouts. The two shooters sped away in a black car while Carter and Artis followed quickly in a white one. Bello also comments that the October 11, 1966, tapes were rehearsed and designed to appear spontaneous but were in fact carefully planned a month earlier. Bello even went so far as to complain to Miller and Ziem that Lieutenant DeSimone had brainwashed and programmed him to give the desired responses. Following the playing of the Miller-Ziem tapes, Beldock questioned Bello, who explained that the tapes were supposed to be for a fictionalized story. Somehow their combined literary effort would produce the best scenario for creating a best-selling novel, capitalizing on Bello's notoriety from the Carter case.

Beldock next questioned Bello about statements he had made in a sworn affidavit before Assemblyman Eldridge Hawkins, who was investigating the case for Governor Byrne. Bello told Hawkins that there were two men besides Carter and Artis who did the shooting, while Carter and Artis waited outside. The story was similar to what Bello had told Miller and Ziem. Confronted with the Hawkins affidavit, Bello admitted that he said all of those things but that they were not true. Bello's explanation for his first deception was "I did not swear completely true to Assemblyman Hawkins. I wanted to get even with Passaic County [for not giving me the reward money they had promised me nine years earlier] and I also had these two guys [Miller and Ziem] on my back about the book. Most of the things I said were complete lies to avoid the issue."[14]

Bello also admitted that he had lied before a 1975 Essex County grand jury investigating several issues that had been raised during the Hawkins probe. Bello told the grand jury the same story he had presented to

Hawkins, identifying two others as the actual murderers. At the conclusion of his testimony, Bello stated that he realized he might get into some trouble in Newark over his lies before the grand jury but that all he cared about at the time was the money he hoped to make off the book.

The rest of the day was devoted to the testimony of several expert witnesses called by Beldock. They all attested to various physical and emotional problems plaguing Bello that might account for his unreliability as a witness; eye problems, medication he was taking, and excessive drinking on the night of the murders. As the day's testimony drew to a close, both the prosecution and the defense anxiously awaited Judge Leopizzi's decision the next morning as to whether Alfred Bello would be allowed one more chance to go before a jury and identify Rubin Carter and John Artis as the Lafayette Bar murderers.

The next day a disappointed defense team learned that Judge Leopizzi had decided to allow Bello to testify even though both his character and his credibility had been severely shaken in the hearings. In the judge's view, Bello's credibility was, in the end, a question for the jury to resolve for itself. Leopizzi did not believe that there was sufficient proof that the police had pressured or tricked Bello into identifying the defendants by certain inducements.

Thus, Bello was allowed to return to the witness stand and identify Carter and Artis as the two men who he saw coming out of the Lafayette Bar on June 17, 1966. He described how they came down the street toward him, Carter carrying the shotgun and Artis toting the pistol, and jumped into Carter's white car, speeding away into the night. Bello had now officially recanted his recantations of the fall of 1974. His testimony now was a reenactment of what he had said during the first trial.

Under Humphreys's direct examination, Bello went on to explain that after the white car left, he went into the bar and surveyed the scene, took money from the cash register, and then rejoined Bradley. He then returned to the bar and phoned the police. A half hour later, when the police returned to the scene with a white car containing Carter and Artis, Bello said he told the police it was the same car. He didn't identify Carter and Artis for three reasons: he feared involvement because of his own criminal activities that evening, he was on parole, and he feared reprisal by Carter's friends. Bello further explained that his recantation was the result of bribes and harassment from zealous Carter supporters.

As soon as Humphreys stepped down, Beldock began his cross-examination with a blistering attack on Bello's credibility, describing him as a compulsive liar whose testimony was worthless. The defense introduced the taped conversations between Bello and Lieutenant DeSimone at the Wayne police station. The tapes were characterized as "dripping with suggestibility, dripping with unfairness—it has been the butcher's thumb on the hand of justice."[15]

The next day, November 18, the defense resumed its dissection of Bello, a man they had already characterized as a compulsive liar and admitted perjurer. Beldock was able to force Bello to admit he had lied numerous times in sworn statements before several earlier proceedings related to the case: the Hawkins investigation, the resulting Essex County grand jury, and the 1974 recantation hearing. As the brutal cross-examination drew to a close, Beldock asked Bello if he had no shame, to which Bello replied simply, "No comment."

The next day, November 20, was Bello's final day on the witness stand, his chance to strike back at certain members of the defense team who had made his first two days on the witness stand so difficult. Bello defended his actions by accusing several members of the defense team of offering him bribes in exchange for his recanting his identification of Carter and Artis. He identified the investigator Fred Hogan, *New York Times* reporter Selwyn Raab, and the former television producer Hal Levinson as responsible for the numerous bribes.

Bello explained that, in 1973, Hogan, a former Monmouth County public defender investigator who had become Carter's agent, visited him in his Passaic County jail cell. Hogan told Bello he had money for him, which he could put into a bank account, available to him when he was released from jail. Bello said that Hogan also offered him a percentage of the profits from Carter's autobiography. Bello also learned from a fellow prisoner named Al Brown that he heard that Carter's family had raised a sizable sum ($27,000) for him (Bello). All of this money would be forthcoming, Bello explained, if he would go through with the recantations, exonerating the defendants.

Bello also testified that Hogan had told him he would soon be hearing from Raab and Levinson. Raab came to visit Bello after he was transferred to the Bergen County jail in Hackensack and supposedly offered him a job on the *Times*. Raab discussed how Bello should frame his recantation, being sure to clarify his inability to identify Carter.

All of the men accused by Bello immediately denied the accusations.

Ironically, Bello's allegations followed the previous day's courtroom reading of excerpts from Bello's October 1974 recantation hearing, at which he was asked if there were any promises or inducements or if anything was done to lead him to recant, to which he answered emphatically, "Nothing at all, sir."

Through a careful redirect examination by Humphreys, Bello explained his recantation as being the result of his anger at Lieutenant DeSimone and others for not having offered him more help in his recent problems. In June 1974 Bello had been sentenced to serve nine months in the county jail for burglary and now wanted DeSimone's help in getting transferred to an alcoholic treatment center. Bello became angry with DeSimone for failing to bring about his transfer and signed the recantations as a punishment. As Bello was being transferred to the Bergen County jail, he yelled out the bus window at a Paterson detective, "Tell DeSimone he can read about it (the recantation) in the *New York Times*."[16]

With his moment in the spotlight finished, Bello stepped down from the witness stand and swaggered out of the courtroom. Although he did not make another appearance during the trial, his tainted testimony and sordid behavior were pivotal to its outcome. Larner had declared that Bello's recantations lacked "the ring of truth."[17] Would the jurors reach the same conclusion?

6: The Second Trial
Part II

Al Bello's testimony, stretching over five days, brought much-needed comic relief to an otherwise somber and at times depressing criminal trial. On November 22, as Detective Donald La Conte took the stand, this interval of levity drew to a close. La Conte's testimony corroborated earlier testimony about two important issues. The first was the exact time when Detective DiRobbio discovered the ammunition from inside Carter's automobile. Both La Conte and Patty Valentine were needed to convince the jury that the bullets were found early on the morning of June 17. Like Patty Valentine, Detective La Conte had not addressed this issue during the first trial. The prosecution now needed further substantiation of DiRobbio's discovery because the defense had located the police department's property book, which indicated that the shells had not been officially recorded until five days later. Detective La Conte said he had met DiRobbio as he and Ms. Valentine were about to enter the police garage. DiRobbio was holding a shotgun shell and a bullet in his hand.

CORROBORATION

The second issue requiring Detective La Conte's corroboration was a series of meetings with Al Bello in which he eventually identified Carter and Artis as the murderers. La Conte actually had met several times with Bello prior to the latter's official statement on October 13, 1966. In late July 1966 La Conte said he ran into Bello at Frankie's Playpen, a Paterson nightclub. After recognizing each other, they began to converse. Bello

informed La Conte that he (Bello) had not disclosed to the police everything he knew about the shootings. Bello informed La Conte that another
person was with him the night of the shootings, eventually identifying
Arthur Dexter Bradley. Bradley, who Bello thought was in Massachusetts
avoiding prosecution for several armed robberies in New Jersey, was arrested on August 3, 1966, by the Paterson police. La Conte now had an
opportunity to verify Bello's story and questioned both men the same day.

The next meeting between Bello and La Conte was on October 3. La
Conte had been driving around Paterson and spotted Bello entering Joe
From's Tavern at 2:00 A.M. La Conte went into the bar and struck up a
conversation with Bello, who soon dropped a bombshell. Bello stated he
was scared and that he had been very nervous since the shooting, having
been threatened several times, once by a woman supposedly related to
Carter who warned him not to go to the police. Bello also worried about
the safety of his brother, who was confined in the state prison. He next
told the surprised detective, "You guys had the right man, and you let him
go."[1] La Conte asked who that was, and Bello answered Rubin Carter.

La Conte realized the importance of these revelations and told Bello that
they would have to go meet with Lieutenant DeSimone. Bello, who had had
several unpleasant run-ins with DeSimone, refused to talk to him, stating he
would deny everything. La Conte then arranged a meeting later that evening
with his boss, Captain Robert Mohl. This was acceptable to Bello, and the
three men met at 11:00 P.M. at the City Diner in Paterson, where Bello revealed all of the events surrounding the Lafayette Bar and Grill murders.

The officers planned to meet again with Bello a week later; this time
Lieutenant DeSimone would be present and a secret taping of their conversation would be made. On October 11 Bello was taken to the Wayne
police station, where he repeated the same story he had told Mohl and La
Conte previously at the City Diner as the hidden tape recorder captured
their conversation. The only embellishment was Bello's adding that he
had taken money from the cash register of the Lafayette Bar and Grill.

La Conte's testimony drew to a close with the defense cross-examination, which focused upon La Conte's failure to preserve any notes taken
during his conversations with Bello or his earlier observations of DiRobbio finding ammunition in Carter's car.

The next day Captain Robert Mohl took the witness stand to corroborate La Conte's testimony about his conversations with Bello on October
3 and 11. Mohl also admitted that no notes were taken by either man

during these critical conversations. Mohl supported La Conte in testifying that they had not pressured Bello into identifying Carter and Artis at their October 3 meeting. During Mohl's cross-examination by Beldock, the detective disclosed that they were aware of the attempted burglary on June 17 and had filed a report but that it had not made its way into the official police log until November. Mohl's simplistic yet puzzling explanation for the police department's failure to investigate the break-in was that "no one followed up the Ace Sheet Metal Company break-in because no one knew about it."

It is likely that the Paterson police finally made a formal entry of the attempted burglary in the official log book in order to muster some additional leverage in their efforts to compel Bello and Bradley to testify at the June 1967 murder trial. Possibly because both men did help connect Carter and Artis, neither was ever charged with the attempted burglary. Additionally, Bello was never charged with robbing the cash register of the bar, despite his admission. Detectives Mohl and La Conte disclosed that they wrote letters to the mayor of Paterson recommending that the city give Bello and Bradley the ten-thousand-dollar reward offered for information leading to the conviction of the killers. Unfortunately for Bello and Bradley, they never received any of the reward money, a fact that led to Bello's subsequent recantation of his original testimony.

Judge William Marchese testified after Mohl and La Conte. In June of 1974, he was scheduled to sentence Bello in another burglary and was visited by Lieutenant DeSimone. DeSimone told Marchese of Bello's key role in the Carter case. He asked the judge if he was considering sending Bello to the state prison, a requirement for sentences of over a year. DeSimone communicated a concern for Bello's safety in state prison because of the presence of Carter's friends in these institutions. A few days after DeSimone's visit, Marchese sentenced Bello to nine months in the Passaic County Jail, where it would be easier to protect him. Humphreys asked Marchese if he had altered Bello's sentence as a result of DeSimone's visit, to which he replied "Not at all," adding that this would have been his sentence even if DeSimone had never spoken to him.[2]

THE PROSECUTION CHALLENGES CARTER'S ALIBI WITNESSES

The defense in the second trial was hopeful that they had created a modicum of doubt in the minds of some jurors about Bello's eyewitness identification. In contrast to the first trial, at which both Bello and Bradley had come forward and clearly identified Carter and Artis as the murderers, the prosecution was now reduced to reliance upon the increasingly suspect Bello, with his zigzagging trail of conflicting accounts and his record of perjury. How could the jury continue to believe a man whose mendacity and greed were so transparent?

Given the tenuous nature of Bello's identification testimony, the prosecution realized that they would have to mount an aggressive campaign to discredit Carter's alibi witnesses. The prosecution was successful in convincing four of the alibi witnesses from the first trial to recant their earlier testimony. Ms. Cathy McGuire, Ms. Anna Mapes, and Welton Deary named Carter's former defense attorney, Raymond Brown, as the person who talked them into lying, whereas William Hardney stated that it was Carter himself who had asked him to lie.

Hardney was the first to testify. He recounted meeting with Carter at his Chatham training site in the summer of 1966, shortly after the shootings. They agreed that if Hardney was ever asked to verify Carter's whereabouts on the night of the murders, he was to say they were together at the Nite Spot and that he had seen Carter leave the bar around 2:15 A.M. with the two women and then return shortly thereafter. In December 1966, while Carter was awaiting trial, he again asked Hardney to testify, but by the spring of 1967, as the trial began, Hardney had left New Jersey and had moved to Washington, D.C. He could not return to testify because he was being sought on charges of nonsupport in the paternity of an illegitimate child.

In his cross-examination Beldock tried to show that Hardney had been under intense pressure to claim that Carter had influenced his original version of the events. In October 1976, a month before the second trial began, Hardney received several visits: first Prentiss Thompson, an investigator for Assemblyman Hawkins, and then several Passaic County law-enforcement officials, who came to his home at 1:00 A.M. and continued to visit him in his D.C. home for a week. They told Hardney and his wife that the other alibi witnesses had already recanted and that they would arrest them both for obstruction of justice if he did not admit that the Nite Spot alibi was a lie. After two hours of continuous interrogation, Hardney finally admitted that he had lied, never having seen Carter at the bar. At this point Hardney was arrested and taken into custody as a material witness. Escorted by a group of fifteen Maryland policemen, Hardney appeared before a federal judge who agreed to his extradition. He was next driven to a hotel in New Jersey, where he was detained for the three weeks leading up to his appearance in the trial.

Hardney had served a term of fifteen months in jail twenty years earlier on an assault charge and wanted desperately to avoid any more jail time. Was this reason enough to recant his earlier testimony, or had he actually lied for his friend Rubin Carter? Given the prosecution's pressures, one wonders if their recantation had any stronger "ring of truth" than Al Bello's change of heart before Judge Larner.

The second alibi witness to be challenged by the prosecution was Welton Deary. At the time of the retrial, Deary was a policeman for the Paterson Housing Authority, was a former friend of Carter's who testified at the first trial as having seen Carter at the Nite Spot between 2:00 and 2:15 A.M. in the company of Ms. Mapes and Ms. McGuire. Deary now told the court that he had seen Carter earlier at another bar, Ritchie's Hideaway, rather than the Nite Spot. Deary indicated that he had spoken with Carter's attorney, Raymond Brown, on May 20, 1967, at the Thunderbird Motel a month before the trial. Brown had asked him to say he was with Carter at the Nite Spot instead of Ritchie's and briefed him as to the exact time he was supposed to have been with Carter. Deary had followed Brown's instructions during the first trial, confirming Carter's presence at the Nite Sport around 2:15 A.M.

Beldock and Steel conjectured that Deary, like Hardney, had been pressured by the prosecution. They believed that his job with the city housing authority would have been jeopardized if he had not agreed to recant his initial testimony.[3]

Cathy McGuire and her mother, Anna Mapes Brown, were the final alibi witnesses to recant their testimony. Their testimony was critical if the defense was to sustain any chance of reestablishing a plausible alibi on the evening of the Lafayette shootings. Unfortunately, both women told the same story of going to the Thunderbird Motel in late May 1967, meeting with Raymond Brown, and being instructed to lie at Carter's upcoming trial. They were to say Carter had driven them home from the Nite Spot at approximately 2:15 A.M. Although they lived a short distance from the Nite Spot, it still would have been all but impossible for Carter to have driven them home and also to have committed the murders at the Lafayette Grill.

Ms. Brown (formerly Mapes) testified first, telling Humphreys that she "knew it was not true but wanted to help him out." She added that Brown "kept going on about time," trying to elicit the necessary statement from her, but when she testified at the first trial, she became confused, unsure whether all of this happened on June 17 or 18.

As Beldock cross-examined Anna Brown, her nervousness and confusion were apparent. She was unable to recall what had happened on the night of the murders, mixing up critical times and places. In closing, Beldock inquired if she really remembered what happened on June 17, 1966, to which she readily admitted "No, not really."[4] By the end of her testimony, she was crying and trembling, needing the support of the bailiffs to walk from the witness stand out of the courtroom.

The following day, Ms. Brown's daughter, Catherine McGuire, took the witness stand as the final alibi witness. She also told of being taken to the Thunderbird Motel. Brown asked for her cooperation in the upcoming trial. Carter had sent her a letter in April from his jail cell asking for her assistance in helping to provide him with an alibi for June 17. In her May meeting with Raymond Brown, Ms. McGuire had told him she had seen Carter at 1:00 A.M. on June 17, but after an extended conversation, she and Brown agreed to move the time that Carter drove them home to nearly 2:30 A.M. Somehow, the investigator Thompson was able to locate Carter's letter to her. Thompson confronted her with the letter on May 2, 1976, at which time Ms. McGuire admitted her role in the cover-up.

At the retrial, facing the prosecutor Ron Marmo, she admitted that her testimony at the first trial had been false and that all of her interaction with Carter had taken place an hour earlier than the time she had originally claimed. McGuire also stated that Carter had visited in July 1976, again asking for her help. This time she said she told him, "I wouldn't tell a lie. I said there were a lot of lies going at the other trial, and I wouldn't do it again."[5]

During cross-examination by Beldock, Ms. McGuire revealed that she was engaged to marry a Paterson police officer, but she rejected the suggestion that this circumstance had any effect on her testimony.

The combined impact of the testimony of the four alibi witnesses appeared to be significant. The defense had tried to show the jury the intense pressure to which these witnesses had been subjected by the prosecution. The defense also presented some new alibi witnesses who were not used in the first trial, but the prosecution had delivered a body blow to Carter's and Artis's chance for freedom.

Raymond Brown, who had been identified as the driving force behind the planned perjury, now faced the prospect of a hearing before the State Bar Ethics Committee. Shortly after the four alibi witnesses recanted, the committee's chairman, Robert Coun, commented on December 1 that he was aware of their testimony and would review the allegations. If he determined they were warranted, he would ask the State Supreme Court's Central Ethics Committee to conduct a hearing on the matter. Despite the seriousness of the charges and the publicity surrounding the case, the committee's investigation was unable to reach a definitive conclusion, and Brown was never sanctioned.

LIEUTENANT DESIMONE TAKES THE STAND

Detective Vincent DeSimone had spent most of his life as a police officer in Paterson and Passaic County. Alternately commanding respect and instilling fear, he had earned numerous citations for bravery but had also been tarred with charges of brutality. Catherine McGuire, the last person to testify, had stated at Carter's first trial that Lieutenant DeSimone said that "he would tear me limb from limb on the witness stand, if she did not tell the truth."[6]

Lieutenant DeSimone was an imposing figure: stocky, with thinning gray hair, black-framed glasses perched on a broken nose. He spoke authoritatively, in a deep, gravelly voice. He began his testimony by attempting to clarify exactly what he had promised Bello in exchange for his cooperation. DeSimone was aware that the jury had already heard his taped conversation with Bello at the Wayne police station in which he promised to help Bello in a pending case by having him transferred to a safer jail. During the prosecution's direct examination, DeSimone admitted he had promised to go before the grand jury if necessary to help Bello out of the attempted burglary charges if they were to materialize— which they never did. DeSimone explained that such promises were a common practice in enlisting the assistance of lesser criminals in order to convict the more serious ones.

DeSimone explained his policy by stating, "I would make a promise like this routinely, at any time, if I can solve the murder by not proceeding against an individual for a lesser crime. I would do it every day in the week. I would do it tomorrow again."[7] DeSimone was careful to add that at the time of his taped conversation with Bello (October 11, 1966), he did not even know that a break-in had occurred. (In cross-examination the defense disputed this point, presenting prior statements and departmental memorandums indicating that he did indeed have prior awareness of Bello and Bradley's attempted burglary.)

Humphreys next had DeSimone discuss his visit to Judge Marchese, when he requested that the judge consider Bello's help in the Carter-Artis trial in his sentencing decision. (Judge Marchese had already testified that he believed that this visit had no impact on his sentencing decision.) Humphreys ended his direct examination of the detective by focusing on subsequent instances of DeSimone providing legal assistance to Bello. DeSimone remembered having helped Bello with several drunk and disorderly cases in Paterson, Wayne, and Little Falls.

On cross-examination the defense reviewed the numerous instances of DeSimone's assistance to Bello. He admitted calling on magistrates to help Bello with his drunk and disorderly arrests as well as going to Judge Marchese in Bello's 1974 burglary conviction. On occasion, DeSimone admitted assisting Bello with nonlegal problems, such as getting him a "live-in job" at a country club as well as talking to one of Bello's employers about withheld wages.

Louis Steel was able to score points for the defense when he questioned DeSimone about statements he had made before a June 1966 grand jury. DeSimone declared at that time that the clothing worn by Carter and Artis on the night of the murders did not fit the descriptions of the killer's clothing he had received from witnesses. DeSimone went on to inform the grand jury, "With the time element, we feel it is almost impossible that these men could have changed clothes. Duck the weapons, yes; but change clothes, we feel is out."[8]

The courtroom had been uncomfortably overheated throughout Lieutenant DeSimone's lengthy testimony. He had sweated profusely, continually mopping his brow with paper towels. He did not waver under the relentless cross-examination, however, answering questions in a deep, gruff voice. As he stepped off the witness stand, broad shoulders erect, it was clear to everyone in the courtroom that he had no second thoughts about his testimony. The defense needed to portray DeSimone as a relentless investigator who had coerced Bello into identifying their clients and had then cemented this unholy alliance by coming to his defense on many subsequent occasions. But it did not appear that the jury had been upset or even disappointed by DeSimone's tactics.

SEARCHING FOR A MOTIVE: THE "RACIAL REVENGE" THEORY

Throughout the first trial the prosecution had failed to provide a specific motive for the Lafayette Bar murders, believing correctly that the eyewitness identifications by Valentine, Bello, and Bradley would be sufficient to obtain a conviction. Burrell Humphreys understood that given holes in his case—especially the recantations of Bello and Bradley—he would have to offer the jury a more tangible theory about motivation. Immediately after the murders detectives told reporters that in view of the open cash register and the money spilled over the bar and on the floor, robbery was the apparent motive. But they soon changed their minds as the investigation began to focus more narrowly on Carter and Artis. Police eventually concluded that they had exacted revenge for the murder of the black bar owner Roy Holloway by a former white owner, Frank Conforti. Holloway's son-in-law had become extremely agitated after the shooting, arousing a crowd of supporters outside the bar. Rawls drove down to the police station where Conforti had been taken and angrily insisted to the detectives in charge of the case that something had to be done. Because Rawls was friendly with Carter, the prosecution hypothesized that Carter was willing to avenge the death of his friend's father six hours later by shooting the four white victims at the Lafayette Bar.

With the jury removed from the courtroom, the prosecution and defense argued before Judge Leopizzi about the legality of introducing the "racial revenge" theory as a motive for the shootings. The defense argued that to introduce a racial motive would be highly prejudicial and would play upon the fear that already divided the races. Steel argued that there was no meaningful connection between Carter and Rawls. He accused Humphreys of introducing a racial angle into the trial, stating, "I can't conceive of a more emotional issue. They want to let a jury get hung up on the very thing that tears our society apart." Myron Beldock, Carter's attorney, added that Humphreys was simply trying to "stack inference upon inference to create a specter of racial killings and racism."[9] Humphreys responded to the defense criticism by declaring that he had sufficient proof to indicate that the shootings were racially inspired, "revenging the death of Roy Holloway." Humphreys told Judge Leopizzi that he would be able to show that the Lafayette murders were a retaliation for the earlier New Waltz Inn shooting. He would be able to link Eddie Rawls, the distraught son-in-law of the victim, to Rubin by showing that the men met two hours before the Lafayette shooting. Humphreys concluded his argument by declaring that

> if the state does not attempt to prove motive in this case, these defendants will have every right to argue to the jury, at the conclusion of the case, that motiveless murders do not occur. If we are precluded in this case from establishing motive, I think the defendants may well be able to escape with what they have done.

Throughout the discussion, tempers flared, particularly between Judge Leopizzi and the defense lawyers. The judge concluded that the prosecution had a right to establish a motive for the crime and listed seven areas of testimony where they had established a link between Rawls and Carter. Leopizzi went on to characterize as "nonsense" the charges of racism raised by the defense against Humphreys. He warned Beldock and Steel that he was not going to allow them to derail the trial with charges of racism.[10]

To no one's surprise, the next day the judge ruled in favor of the prosecution, allowing them to argue to the jury that the murders had been racially motivated. Leopizzi explained that the prosecution would be seriously handicapped if it were not allowed the opportunity to show a motive for the killings.[11]

Even after the decision was announced, an angry exchange erupted between Leopizzi and Steel. At one point Steel accused Leopizzi of trying to turn the trial into a "racial nightmare" by allowing the prosecution to try to prove the murders were racially inspired. The judge quickly responded to Steel's comments by terming them idiotic and citing Steel for contempt of court. As tempers cooled, Leopizzi eventually relented and dismissed the contempt charge.

PROSECUTION TESTIMONY BEGINS TO WIND DOWN

On December 4 the court held another of its Saturday sessions as the judge pushed to have the trial concluded by Christmas. The jurors had al-

ready been separated from their families for nearly four weeks, sequestered in a Jersey City hotel. The primary witness on Saturday was Detective Edward Callahan, who had been involved in several important
aspects of the case. It was Callahan who ran into the New Waltz Inn to
arrest Frank Conforti shortly after he had shot and killed Roy Holloway.
Callahan described the tense scene as he led Conforti out of the bar and
into a police car to be transported to headquarters. Callahan was also the
police officer who brought Carter and Artis to St. Joseph's Hospital to see
if William Marins could identify them. The officer stated that Marins had
a clear view of both men but failed to identify them. Callahan had also
visited Hazel Tanis in the hospital at a later date, shortly before she died
from her gunshot wounds. Hoping to obtain a description of the men
who had shot her, Callahan questioned her for a brief time but was unable to learn anything. He found her barely comprehensible: "She kept
rambling on, giving different descriptions all the time."[12]

As another indicator of the bizarre nature of this case, the prosecution
spent the weekend using a metal-detection expert to search Roy Holloway's grave at Fair Lawn Cemetery. They had received an anonymous
tip on Friday that the missing murder weapons had been buried there, but
despite an extensive search, nothing was recovered.

On Monday, December 6, the prosecution questioned William Johnson. Johnson had been with Eddie Rawls immediately after he learned of
the death of his father-in-law. He verified that Rawls had gone to the
Paterson detective bureau. He described Rawls as angry and excited. Detective Callahan had recently testified (on Saturday) that Rawls had
threatened that "if you don't do something about it (his father-in-law's
murder), we sure as hell will." Johnson had not heard any threats that
Rawls would take the law into his own hands. He thought that once they
had left police headquarters, Rawls had calmed down, satisfied that the
police had the suspect in custody and that he would be charged with murder. Johnson did acknowledge that after they returned to the Nite Spot
Holloway's murder was the general topic of conversation.

During his cross-examination by Lewis Steel, Johnson stated that he
had not heard Rawls ask anyone to go out and get revenge for him. Johnson told the court that he had seen Carter at the Nite Spot. He concluded
his testimony by telling Steel that neither he nor Rawls had discussed Holloway's murder with Carter. He had not seen Artis there at all.

DETECTIVE DIROBBIO AND THE MAGIC BULLETS

Detective DiRobbio took the stand again for the prosecution, testifying that the ammunition (a shotgun shell and two bullets) that he allegedly found in Carter's car the morning of the murders failed to match the ammunition recovered from the crime scene. The defense had challenged DiRobbio's fortuitous discovery of the shell and bullets, implying that the police had planted the evidence in Carter's car. It had already been determined that despite DiRobbio's claim to having located the ammunition that same day, the evidence was not recorded in the property book for another five days.

In an effort to support DiRobbio's version of his discovery of the ammunition, the prosecution presented Paul Alberta, a Paterson newspaper reporter who testified that he saw DiRobbio take both shells from Carter's car in the police garage. He remembered DiRobbio shouting "Holy cow, look at what I found," after recovering the shotgun shell from Carter's trunk. (Alberta also indicated that he saw DiRobbio go upstairs to record his discovery.) Alberta, like Patricia Valentine, had not testified at the first trial about viewing DiRobbio's finding of the shell. When Steel cross-examined Alberta, he asked the reporter why he had waited ten years before coming forward with a revelation that was so helpful to the prosecution.

THE PROSECUTION RESTS

On the next day, Wednesday, December 9, the prosecution concluded its case, which took twenty-three days and required forty witnesses. Two additional witnesses had been contemplated by the prosecution, but both had been scratched. The first was the enigmatic Annie Ruth Haggins. She appeared before Assemblyman Hawkins when he was conducting his 1975 investigation for Governor Byrne. Haggins told Hawkins she knew Carter and could place him at the Nite Spot. She also stated she had seen Carter throw the guns into the river after the shooting. The Paterson Police, acting on her testimony, immediately dredged the river at the location where the guns were supposed to have been tossed but found nothing. Ms. Haggins next appeared before the Essex County Grand Jury that grew out of the Hawkins investigation, where she repeated her story. When the Passaic County Prosecutor's office began preparation for the retrial, Chief Counsel Ron Marmo interviewed Haggins and concluded she was too unstable to put on the stand. They did bring in their polygraphers, Professor Leonard Harrelson and Dick Arthur, who spoke with her, but they also remained dubious. At one point the prosecution contemplated bringing in a psychologist to hypnotize Haggins because much of what she recounted occurred in her dreams. All things considered, Marmo and Humphrey were certain that Annie Ruth Haggins was simply not believable.

The prosecution had considered calling Carolyn Kelley but had thought better of it. She had been scheduled to appear a few days earlier, but Humphreys withdrew her name with the proviso that she would remain under subpoena by the state and could be called to testify at a later date as a rebuttal witness. Ms. Kelley had appeared before Judge Leopizzi on December 6 to determine if she could testify for the prosecution. It was a surprising request, given her recent accusations that the prosecution was forcing her to testify falsely against Carter. A week earlier, Kelley appeared before Passaic County assignment judge Charles Joelson in an unsuccessful attempt to quash her subpoena requiring her to appear for the prosecution. The proceeding lasted forty-three minutes and featured Kelley's accusation that Passaic County assistant prosecutor Martin Kayne had suborned perjury by asking her to sign a document they both knew to be false. The document purportedly to contain statements by Kelley indicating that she had knowledge that Carter had been searching for his missing shotguns on the night of the Lafayette Bar murders. The prosecutor's office said that Kelley had revealed to Kayne on September 29, 1976, that Neil Morrison, a friend of Carter's, had stolen Carter's shotgun from his Chatham training camp. Kelley said that Carter had caught up with Morrison and beaten him in order retrieve his weapon. Kayne denied Kelley's accusations, stating that to the best of his knowledge, Ms. Kelley's statement contained only truthful information.

As soon as the prosecution notified Judge Leopizzi that they had concluded their presentation of evidence, both defense attorneys immediately moved for dismissal of the murder charges. The motion, however, was denied by Judge Leopizzi. He ruled that "the prosecution has met its burden by presenting sufficient legal evidence for this case to proceed to the jury."[13] John Artis's attorney, Lewis Steel, argued the motion vehemently, believing that his client was just being dragged along because of his association with Carter. Steel pointed out there had been no direct identification of Artis as one of the gunmen. Judge Leopizzi appeared somewhat sympathetic to Artis's plight and agreed with Steel that "the evidence against Mr. Artis, comparatively speaking, is minimal, but there was enough evidence to warrant presentation to the jury." Leopizzi went so far as to state that if he (Leopizzi) had been on the case before the trial formally began, "I might have ordered a severance [a separate trial for Artis]."[14]

THE DEFENSE TAKES THE OFFENSIVE WITH AN ATTACK ON BELLO

Humphreys knew that he would be fighting an uphill battle in the re-trial. The recantations by two eyewitnesses and the upswing in popular support for Carter convinced Humphreys that he had only about a one-in-four chance of victory, but he believed that Carter was guilty, and he felt a responsibility to do his best job to convict him again. As Humphreys concluded his presentation of the state's case, he began to sense the chances of conviction were improving. True, Bello had been an embarrassment at times and Bradley was missing, but he had been able to develop a plausible motive, and Carter's alibi witnesses had been discredited. It was now time for Humphreys to learn what the defense had in store for him as they began to present their witnesses.

Steel and Beldock knew they were facing a difficult challenge, but if they could just convince one juror that the state had not proved Carter and Artis guilty beyond a reasonable doubt, they could achieve a hung jury and gain a mistrial. They hoped that the prosecution would then bow to public sentiment, decline to retry, and dismiss the charges against the defendants.

In criminal trials the defense need not present to the judge or jury an alternative explanation in opposition to the prosecution's theories. Victory for the defense is most commonly achieved by attacking the prosecution's case and poking enough holes in its arguments to convince the jury that guilt has not been proved *beyond a reasonable doubt*—a rather lofty standard, especially as applied to this trial.

The most obvious points of attack for the defense were the prosecution's key eyewitnesses, Patricia Graham Valentine and Alfred Bello. Bello was an especially enticing target. In his earlier testimony Bello appeared to be an opportunistic petty criminal with little regard for the truth. His demeanor on the stand, coupled with his confession of past perjuries, seemed to neutralize his impact on the case.

During Bello's earlier appearance for the prosecution, he had not only renounced his previous recantation but had also accused several defense witnesses of trying to bribe him into making the false recantation of his eyewitness identification. The *New York Times* reporter Selwyn Raab, the television producer Harold Levinson, and the former investigator Fred Hogan were the primary targets of Bello's accusations. The defense decided to begin its case by directly attacking Bello's slanderous charges.

Their first witness was Fred Hogan, who not only had been an investigator and long-time friend of Carter's, but had also served as his agent, working with Viking Press in publishing Carter's autobiography. Hogan had been instrumental in locating Arthur Bradley after the first trial and in convincing him to recant his eyewitness identification of Carter. Hogan, with the assistance of Raab and Levinson, was also able to track down Bello and convince him to admit that he had lied in the first trial when he identified Carter and Artis as the Lafayette Bar murderers.

Earlier in the second trial, Bello, appearing for the prosecution, testified that Hogan had offered him bribes or inducements to recant his identification of Carter and Artis. Bello said he was to receive a large sum of money derived from the profits of Carter's book, which would be placed in a special account for him. Hogan categorically denied Bello's allegations. Steel next asked Hogan if either Selwyn Raab, Hal Levinson, or Richard Solomon (an independent filmmaker who was familiar with the case) had made offers to Bello. Hogan answered that to his knowledge none of these men had made any kind of offer.

Ron Marmo, Humphreys's top assistant, handled Hogan's cross-examination. Marmo made several pointed inquiries into Hogan's financial activities while he was serving as Carter's agent. One rather suspicious transaction involved the timing of Hogan's cashing a five-thousand-dollar check (part of the ten-thousand-dollar royalty paid to Carter by Viking) a few days after he had met with Bello. Marmo also questioned Hogan about why he had not put any of the ten thousand dollars he received from Viking into a trust instead of cashing the checks.

Hogan weakened his credibility slightly when he returned to the witness stand the next day. Marmo had perceptively noticed Hogan referring to typewritten notes as he testified the preceding day, although he had not shared them with the prosecution, as required by New Jersey rules of discovery. Hogan's somewhat lame explanation was that his wife had typed up his recollection of his meeting with Bello after Hogan realized that he had discarded the original notes. In any event, the prosecution finally had a copy of the typed notes and was now able to discredit Hogan even further. The notes indicated that Bello would be willing to perjure himself and recant his identification if the price was right. The prosecution was drawn to one of the pages where the figure of twenty thousand dollars was drawn next to two question marks in the adjoining margin.

Judge Leopizzi was now faced with the complicated issue of what to do with the notes taken by Hogan, Raab, and Levinson during their interviews with Bello. They should have been turned over to the prosecution at a much earlier date, but the judge was now pressing to conclude the trial as soon as possible. His solution was first to exclude the jury and then to allow the prosecution to interview the witnesses who had withheld their notes before they could testify before the jury. Raab and Hogan had now turned over their notes to the prosecution, and Levinson was retrieving his notes from his home in Maryland.

THE DEFENSE PRESENTS NEW ALIBI WITNESSES

The next day, Saturday, December 11, the defense presented testimony from five new alibi witnesses. Their testimony was critical because the original alibi witnesses from the first trial—Hardney, Mapes, McGuire, and Deary—had all admitted lying on Carter's behalf after a meeting with his defense attorney, Raymond Brown.

The first of the new alibi witnesses was Merrit Wimberly. He had read about the trial and had returned voluntarily from Pasadena, California, to testify on Carter's behalf. He had been prepared to testify at the first trial, but somehow he was never called. A forty-one-year-old merchant marine who had grown up with Carter, Wimberly had spent a large part of the evening and early morning of the murder night with Carter and some other friends. Wimberly recounted that at 2:00 A.M. he was with Carter at the Nite Spot Tavern. He remembered that Carter left the bar at around 2:15 A.M. to drive Ms. McGuire and her mother home and then returned a few minutes later. Wimberly left the bar at 2:30 A.M. and recalled seeing Carter still there.

Wimberly also provided important assistance in reversing the damage caused by the earlier recantations of Deary and McGuire. Wimberly stated that when he was in Paterson last August, Deary told him that he was going to alter his testimony in order to protect his job as a patrolman in the Housing Authority. Deary informed him that Catherine McGuire was also going to change her testimony because she was about to marry a Paterson detective. Deary explained that there would be no legal penalty because the statute of limitations on perjury had just expired.

The next alibi witness was Elwood Tuck, the manager of the Nite Spot bar. Tall and muscular, Tuck had been the bartender and part owner of the Nite Spot. He had been a close friend of Carter's, serving as part of his boxing entourage on his travels around the country on several occasions. On the evening of the murders, Tuck remembered having seen Carter go in and out of his establishment several times. The last time he saw Carter was about 2:15 A.M., as he was locking up the back room of the bar. The prosecution tried to counter Tuck's authoritative testimony by noting that the Lafayette Bar was only a few blocks away, but it still appeared to be too tight a time frame to have allowed Carter to commit the murders.

The fourth witness of the day was George Andrews, a sixty-year-old lifelong Paterson resident who knew Carter from his days working as a trainer at the Lou Costello gym. He had even served in Carter's corner in his fight against Herschell Jacobs. Andrews's relevance to the Carter defense was his presence at the apartment of Annabelle Chandler on the night of the murders. Ms. Chandler was terminally ill, and as Andrews was going in to visit her, Carter, Neil Morrison, and Merrit Wimberly all exited the apartment. Andrews knew all three men and briefly exchanged pleasantries before entering Ms. Chandler's apartment. Ms. Chandler had earlier informed Carter that she thought Morrison had stolen his guns. From Andrews's description of this convivial group conversing outside Chandler's apartment, he saw no hostility between Carter and Morrison, who had continually denied knowing anything about the missing weapons.

Another member of the Nite Spot's bartending crew followed Chandler on the witness stand. Edward Allen, who was substituting for Eddie Rawls, corroborated Elwood Tuck's testimony by stating that he also remembered seeing Carter in their bar at 2:15 A.M.

Nathan Sermond, the final witness of the day, also testified about Carter's whereabouts that evening, although he had seen him two hours earlier at his club, La Petite. Sermond was Carter's "personal advisor" at the time of the murders, and the two arranged to meet to discuss some sparring arrangements for an upcoming fight in South America. He was supposed to meet Carter at La Petite at 10:00 P.M., but Carter did not appear till 11:00. Sermond remained there until 1:00 A.M., when Carter left with two other men. As Sermond completed his testimony, he and Carter shook hands and briefly chatted on his way out of the courtroom. It had been a long day of testimony, but Lewis Steel commented to reporters that he felt satisfied with the first complete day of defense testimony and thought they would be able to rest their case by the end of the week.

Court resumed on Monday with the defense presenting two witnesses whose testimony contradicted Bello's identification of Carter and Artis. Erwin Schankerelli was fifteen years old at the time of the murders, living on Lafayette Street one block from the bar. Schankerelli told the court that he was awakened suddenly on the morning of the shootings by a loud noise coming from the direction of the bar. Arising from bed, Schankerelli went to his living room window, where he saw two men running very fast north toward Ninth Avenue. He described both men as being colored. One was tall, wearing light-colored clothing and carrying in his right hand a long object that could have been a shotgun. The second man was shorter and dressed in dark clothing. After learning about the murders the next day, he told his mother what he had seen, but she told him to keep quiet and not get involved. Schankerelli was certain that Carter and Artis were not the two men he saw running down the street that morning.

Schankerelli obeyed his mother's warning and did not say anything at the time. Over the years he had forgotten about the incident, but when he read in the papers that a retrial was scheduled, he decided to call Myron Beldock and tell him what he had observed. Marmo, in his vigorous cross-examination, tried to undermine Schankerelli's testimony, but the witness doggedly stuck to his story.

The second defense witness that day was Ronald Ruggiero, a thirty-two-year-old former amateur boxer who also lived on Lafayette Street near the bar at the time of the murders. He was a friend of Carter's and had been in his car on several occasions. Ruggiero testified that he had heard shots from the bar just as he was about to go to bed. He looked out the window and observed a white car with two black men speed away from the scene of the crime. He next spotted Al Bello running away from the bar and then returning a short time later. By this time, Ruggiero heard the police arrive so he went downstairs to join the crowd beginning to gather outside the bar. A short time later, he noticed a caravan of police cars arriving with flashing lights, with Carter's car in the middle. He walked over to Carter and the police and spoke with them, informing them that Carter's car was not the getaway car. He told Carter, "It was a Chevy, wasn't it?" implying that the car he had seen earlier was a Chevrolet, not a Dodge Polaro as identified by Bello and Patty Valentine.

Ruggiero was taken to police headquarters, where he underwent further questioning. He later testified at the grand jury in late June 1966 and at the first trial. Marmo, during his cross-examination, was able to show that at Carter's first trial Ruggiero had said the getaway car looked "similar" in size and color to Carter's. Ruggiero, however, was now certain that it was not Carter's car and that he must have been confused at the first trial. He emphasized that his original statement to the police outside the Lafayette Bar was his "best recollection."

Ruggiero's testimony was also useful to the defense in contradicting the prosecution's attempt to establish racial revenge as a motive for the killings. Ruggiero, who is white, stated that black neighbors of his were regularly served at the Lafayette Bar by the bartender, James Oliver, thus contradicting the prosecution's portrait of strained relations between Oliver and the black customers he supposedly refused to serve. The testimony of Ruggiero and Schankerelli seemed to bolster the defense's strategy of discrediting the eyewitness testimony of Bello and Valentine.

SELWYN RAAB TAKES THE STAND

The next day, Tuesday, December 14, the *New York Times* reporter Selwyn Raab took the stand for the defense. The prosecution was eager to have the opportunity to cross-examine and perhaps discredit the *Times* reporter, who had written over fifty articles on the Carter case. Raab had probably been the most influential force in building sympathetic public support for Carter. He had remained a stalwart believer in Carter's innocence.

Initially it appeared that Raab intended to ignore the court's subpoena to testify about the Bello allegations, believing he was protected by the First Amendment and shield laws designed to protect the confidentiality of a reporter's sources. But Raab reconsidered his position and appeared in court voluntarily with his personal lawyer, Floyd Abrams.

Although the primary purpose of Raab's appearance was to refute Bello's bribery accusations, he began his testimony with a fairly detailed chronicling of his involvement in the case, which began in August 1973, when he was a television producer for WNET. He was approached at that time by Richard Solomon, a filmmaker and a member of the Carter-Artis Defense Committee. Solomon, accompanied by Fred Hogan, the attorney Michael Blacker, and the sportswriter Dave Anderson, were able to convince Raab to look into the case.

It was a another year before Raab, with the research assistance of Hal Levinson, also working at Channel Thirteen, was able to break the story. They first located Arthur Bradley, who recanted, and then found Bello, who was serving time in the Bergen County Jail. Raab visited Bello twice in jail and insisted that he had "never offered him a bribe, a job or anything else"[15] in return for talking. Raab declared that he had once given Bello ten dollars for canteen money (cigarettes), which he left with a guard to be credited to Bello's account. Under Humphreys's cross-examination, Raab stated that he had no recollection of Levinson or anyone else telling him that there was a problem with Bello wanting money.

Also taking the stand on Tuesday were Joseph J. Miller and Melvin Ziem. They had befriended Bello in the summer of 1975. Their relationship evolved into an economic enterprise designed to capitalize on Bello's notoriety from the Carter case. Miller, a real estate broker and Ziem, a furniture dealer, became Bello's literary agents, attempting to market his story to publishers and movie producers. They made tape recordings of Bello's various versions of what had occurred the night of the murders. Bello wanted their advice as to which of the numerous scenarios would be most marketable.

Miller testified that he did not believe any of the things Bello had told him. He told the court that he had never made any money from the tapes, despite efforts to market them. He eventually tore up his contract with Bello, who became upset, telling Miller that "he was going to recant the recant and throw me in the river with Selwyn Raab."[16] Ziem testified next, confirming most of Miller's statements. He added that Bello was also working on other possible story ideas, some involving his numerous criminal escapades, but they were unable to interest a ghostwriter taking on such a project.

ARTIS TESTIFIES, CARTER DECLINES

As the trial entered its final days, the defense had not yet resolved a critical strategic issue—whether or not Carter would testify, as he had (along with Artis) at the first trial. Pending that key decision, Carter's former attorney, Raymond Brown, took the witness stand in an attempt to refute charges that he had corruptly coached Carter's alibi witnesses in the first trial. Brown was vehement in his own defense, stating, "I didn't do it. I wouldn't do it, and if anyone says I did it, they are liars. I know it, they know it, and God knows it, and I hope this jury knows it."[17]

Brown went on to describe how Paterson police had intimidated the black community, singling out Detective DeSimone as a chronic harasser of potential defense witnesses. Brown concluded emotionally: "To my horror I had discovered that people in the community were hesitant to testify because they feared they would undergo the same kind of travesty and the same kind of crucifixion Rubin Carter had suffered."[18]

Brown's testimony had consumed the entire morning session, postponing Carter's decision to the afternoon. At 1:50 P.M. Myron Beldock rose and informed Judge Leopizzi that his client, Rubin Carter, would not testify. He then asked the judge to instruct the jury that it was Carter's right to decline to testify and that no adverse inferences should be drawn from his decision. Beldock later told reporters that the decision had been "an anguished one" and had not been reached until that morning. The key consideration was denying the prosecution the chance to cross-examine Carter about his criminal record, which included convictions for assault and theft. It was also likely that the prosecution would cull damaging quotations from Carter's autobiography that might sound violent and menacing.

Twenty minutes later John Artis—free of the taint of previous criminality and, indeed, a model citizen before the murder charge—had no such hesitation about testifying in his own defense. He took the witness stand and vehemently denied any involvement in the Lafayette Bar murders. His answers flowed calmly and smoothly as he reviewed his background and detailed his activities on the evening of June 17. His testimony spilled over into the next day, when he faced cross-examination. Artis declared to Ron Marmo, "I never fired any gun at anyone at any range."[19] Marmo relied heavily on Artis's 1966 grand jury testimony to try to develop the prosecution's racial revenge theory, but nothing clearly damaging was presented.

Artis's cross-examination lasted most of the morning. It was followed by a parade of character witnesses on Artis's behalf. Two of his professors from Glassboro State College, where he was taking courses while serving his time in prison, attested to his fine character and reputation for honesty. They were followed by Edward Migliaccio, Artis's high school track coach, who remembered him as "always respected by his peers" and possessing a "peaceful and nonviolent nature."[20]

The rest of the day was devoted to the prosecution's presentation of rebuttal testimony. Marmo's first witness was Ms. Leman Schankerelli, Erwin's stepmother. She stated that her stepson had recently informed her that he had not seen anything at all in the early morning hours of the murders. Erwin had initially told his natural mother in 1966 about having seen the killers, but she had since passed away. Ms. Schankerelli, who could barely speak English, admitted under cross-examination by Steel that it was possible that she hadn't understood exactly what her stepson had told her.

A second rebuttal witness, Evone Seldon, also had trouble sustaining her testimony. She told the court that she had seen Carter and Artis together on many occasions in numerous local bars, a contention that contradicted the defense's characterization of their relationship as a "casual acquaintanceship." Under Beldock's cross-examination, Ms. Seldon confirmed that she had been romantically involved with a Paterson police officer. When Beldock asked her where she worked, she refused to answer. When Judge Leopizzi directed her to answer and was also rebuffed, he was forced to consider striking her testimony from the record.

The next day the defense called its final witness: Harold Levinson, the reporter who had investigated the case with Selwyn Raab. Levinson denied that he had bribed either Al Bello or Arthur Bradley in order to obtain their recantations. During cross-examination, Humphreys elicited from Levinson an admission that his notes showed that Bello was interested in being paid for his altered testimony. Hogan had told Levinson that Bello told him that "If the price is right, I can cut Carter loose—ten thousand dollars or twenty thousand dollars."[21] Levinson was the trial's final witness, concluding thirty days of testimony.

SUMMATIONS

On Monday the jurors heard the defense and prosecution summations, which lasted a total of six hours. The defense went first, with Beldock leading off. He stressed the overwhelming reasonable doubt permeating nearly every aspect of the prosecution's case. The key witness in the state's case, Bello, was a compulsive liar who was willing to sell his testimony to the highest bidder. Beldock argued that "there is reasonable doubt upon reasonable doubt." He went on to explain how frustrating it had been for him to learn the truth: "At times, I've tried to question people as if I were trying to solve this case, and that's absurd. We can't solve this case—we don't know what happened. But there's more evidence of a robbery than of a racial killing."[22]

Beldock was especially appalled by the prosecution's efforts to apply their "racial revenge theory" to his client. He urged the jury to reject the state's depiction of Rubin Carter as a "mad racist killer" who indiscriminately set out to massacre white people in retaliation for the killing of Eddie Rawls's father-in-law. Beldock also emphasized the credibility of Carter's alibi witnesses and stressed that the alibi witnesses from the first trial who had recanted were under intense pressure to change their testimony.

Steel continued and elaborated Beldock's criticism of the Paterson police in his portion of the defense summation, directing his harshest criticism at Lieutenant DeSimone. Steel next moved on to Al Bello and his inability to tell the truth. He closed by reminding the jurors of their difficult and weighty responsibility: "Our history is not two hundred years ago. It is now in this courtroom, and you stand between us and our worst instincts. I ask you to be brave and you to be courageous, and you to understand that it is you who guard all of our freedoms and no one else. Thank you."

The prosecution began their summation in the afternoon. Humphreys described his case as being like six "strands of evidence" that formed a "rope strong enough to bring the two murderers to justice." He then described the six strands: (1) the identification of Carter's auto; (2) the identification of the defendants by Bello; (3) the location where Carter and Artis were arrested; (4) the racial revenge motive; (5) the effort by the defense to construct a false alibi; and (6) the alleged discovery of the cartridge and shotgun shell in Carter's car. Humphreys concluded his three-hour speech with a reminder

that the jury must not forget the victims—James Oliver, Fred Nauyoks, and Hazel Tanis. They cry out to you from the grave for justice, for justice for the killers that put them there. . . . In many ways the American jury system is the custodian of all we hold dear in this country because you represent justice. We are counting on you. I don't think you will let us down.[23]

Exhausted by his lengthy oration, Humphreys returned to his chair and slumped down, turning to his assistant, John Goceljak, and telling him in a whisper that he believed their chances of victory were fifty-fifty. He had revised his prediction from the beginning of the trial, when he pessimistically thought he only had a one-in-four chance of success. He felt satisfied with what he and his staff had accomplished during the retrial.

THE JURY DECIDES!

Judge Leopizzi began his charge to the jury shortly after 9:00 A.M. on Tuesday morning December 21. If the jury was able to decide the case in less than three days, they would be home by Christmas, as he had initially promised. By 11:45 A.M. the jury was ready to retire to begin their deliberations. The defendants were cautiously optimistic. John Artis told reporters, "If they (the jurors) deal with facts, I have a chance. I'll be going home free, with all this behind me." Carter was more cautious, although the day before he had said, "I feel good. I feel confident. I feel strong. . . . We do not have the vivid racial disorders we had ten years ago. People were scared. People can look at things more objectively now than they could ten years ago."

A little before 9:00 P.M., guards and court attendants were seen scurrying in and out of the courtroom. It appeared that the jury verdict was near. The jury reentered the courtroom at 9:02. The forewoman, Ms. Helen T. LaRocca, rose and in a soft, barely audible voice told Judge Leopizzi that they had found Carter and Artis guilty of all charges. The word "guilty" seemed to float in suspension until a woman's voice cried out "No!" piercing stunned silence and triggering emotional outbursts of weeping and sobbing among the defendants' family and friends.

The judge then asked each juror to affirm the verdict for all three murders as Carter and Artis sat frozen in disbelief. The jurors spoke in hushed tones with one another as the judge prepared to dismiss them. The sole black juror remained seated, tears streaking his dispirited face. The judge thanked the jurors for their service and then sternly warned them not to speak to anyone, especially reporters, about their deliberations. The jurors quickly exited through a side door of the courthouse and were taken by a van and station wagon to the Holiday Inn in North Bergen, where they had lived throughout the trial. Court bailiffs escorted them to their rooms as they gathered their belongings and set off for their homes in time to celebrate the holidays.

Judge Leopizzi's concern over the welfare of the jurors as well as the sanctity of the judicial process may have influenced his decision to bar the media from speaking with the jurors. Leopizzi warned the press as well as courtroom spectators not to attempt to contact the jurors in hopes of discussing the case. The judge delivered his admonition to the media even before the verdict was returned, threatening contempt citations for any attempted violations of his order.

Leopizzi refused defense requests to allow the defendants to continue their pretrial freedom while awaiting the sentencing, scheduled for February 2. He promised the attorneys that he would reconsider their bail application at that time, after receiving probation reports on both men.

The defense attorneys announced at a press conference following the verdict they would appeal. Both attorneys stated that the introduction of the racial motive guaranteed guilty verdicts for their clients. Lewis Steel commented, "It's hard to say I'm surprised; I'm hurt and I'm sad."[24] Steel had hoped that the jury would see through the racial demagogy of the prosecutors.

A triumphant but emotionally drained Burrell Humphreys stepped outside the courthouse, where he was immediately blinded by spotlights and besieged by reporters. Carefully controlling his emotions, the Passaic County prosecutor delivered the following brief comment: "In my judgment, the American jury system is the greatest instrument of justice in human creation. The contest between the American jury system and Madison Avenue is no contest."[25]

7: Postscripts and Sideshows

In a press conference at the Passaic County Courthouse in Paterson on the day after they were convicted of the Lafayette Bar murders for a second time, Rubin Carter and John Artis said they were "shocked" by the guilty verdict.

Carter's comments that day veered from despair to hope. He began by stating that he was still optimistic, believing that there were several viable issues upon which to base an appeal, but he also acknowledged the depressing reality that he no longer had his freedom. Carter also said that he was prepared to fight for a third trial "no matter how long it may take, no matter how hard it may be." Although he voiced no hostility toward Judge Leopizzi, he described the second trial as simply "a rerun." The only objectionable part of the retrial was the prosecution's use of the racial revenge motive, an issue that the prosecution had avoided at the first trial in the racially charged atmosphere of those times.

Artis added, "It's like walking in a tunnel that keeps going around and around in circles. You think you're at the end and then you find that you're back at the beginning. It's really appalling."[1]

In a reaction to Judge Leopizzi's unusual order forbidding reporters from talking to the jurors, Harvey Fisher, a reporter for the *Elizabeth Journal* and president of the New Jersey Chapter of Sigma Delta Chi, a national journalism organization, protested to the chief justice of the New Jersey Supreme Court, asking the court to

> provide some guidelines to Judge Leopizzi and other judges. . . . What Judge Leopizzi did represents a raw attempt at prior restraint. I know

nothing in the Court rules that gives him such power. I know nothing that says jurors cannot speak to reporters at the conclusion of a trial, if the jurors are so willing. More importantly, there is nothing more onerous than the specter of a judge hanging a jail threat over the heads of news people exercising their constitutional rights.[2]

Governor Brendan Byrne, who had been a cautious supporter of Carter and Artis in 1975 following the recantations and unanimous Supreme Court decision ordering a second trial, issued a statement informing Carter that he should not expect a grant of clemency. The governor added that a pardon was also unlikely, stating to the press that, "What Carter wanted was a new trial, and he got what he was after."[3] The governor's withdrawal of support came only one year after he had ordered the state legislator Eldridge Hawkins to look into the Carter case. The second conviction, however, had fatally damaged Carter's political support from influential politicians in Trenton.

The next day, Thursday, December 23, Judge Leopizzi denied requests from both defendants to be set free on bail pending their sentencing. The judge, however, did move up their sentencing date from February 6 to January 26, at which time Carter and Artis could file appeals and ask for a reconsideration of the bail decision. Carter's attorney, Myron Beldock, notified the court that no action had been taken by the state against Alfred Bello and that he could not understand how Bello could remain free after admitting to perjury, taking part in an attempted burglary, and stealing money from the Lafayette Bar's cash register on the night of the murders.

Addressing criticism on his posttrial gag order on jurors, Judge Leopizzi stated that he knew that the order was unenforceable but that he was merely trying to assist the jurors in adjusting "to home life after the trauma of the trial." Leopizzi still forbade the defense attorneys and their agents from conducting interviews with the jurors.

The next week the Passaic County prosecutor declared that he and his office were preparing a report for the state attorney general on "possible criminal conduct on the part of various people other than the defendants." Prosecutor Humphreys said the report would be accompanied by "transcripts of pertinent testimony at the trial." He expected to confer with the attorney general's office in the near future on "the advisability of further criminal investigation or prosecution."

Humphreys planned to focus his report on three problem areas. The first involved the recantations and how they were obtained. Accusations

were made at the trial concerning attempted bribery of Al Bello by Fred
Hogan, the public defender investigator; Selwyn Raab, the *New York
Times* reporter; and Harold Levinson, a television reporter-producer. The
three men had visited Bello in jail and, according to the allegations, had
offered bribes or other inducements in order to obtain his recantation.

The second area of Humphreys's inquiry would focus on the former
Carter defense attorney Raymond Brown and his role in inducing four
alibi witnesses to lie for Carter during the first trial. All four witnesses recanted their original testimony during the second trial. The four had been
with Carter at the Nite Spot Tavern around the time of the Lafayette Grill
shootings.

The third and final area of investigation was the consideration of perjury charges against Bello, who had recanted his 1967 trial testimony identifying Carter and Artis as the men who emerged from the bar carrying
weapons and came toward him. In the second trial, Bello renounced his recantation and proceeded to identify the defendants a second time. Complicating the situation even more, Bello had also perjured himself before an
Essex County grand jury and in an affidavit given to Eldridge Hawkins.
Bello's numerous versions placed him both inside and outside the bar.

SENTENCING IMPOSED

Judge Leopizzi sentenced Rubin Carter and John Artis to life terms, the
same sentences they had received following their first trial a decade
earlier. As before, Artis received a relatively lighter sentence based on the
belief that Carter had initiated the crime and that Artis had literally been
along for the ride. Artis's life sentences would run concurrently, and he
would be eligible for parole around 1981. Carter, whose life sentences ran
consecutively, would not be eligible for parole until 1996. Both men had
already served nine years of their original sentence, which would count
toward their eligibility for parole.

Before the sentences were imposed by Judge Leopizzi, both defendants
were given an opportunity to address the court. Carter spoke first, pro-
claiming his innocence for nearly fifty minutes. He said that "the only
evidence is that two black people did the crime, but contrary to some
opinions, your Honor, all black people do not look alike." Artis also emphasized the important role played by racial prejudice. He was angered
by his being depicted as a "barbaric animal, a sadistic murderer who

could cold-bloodedly kill three people. . . . I don't know how I can come in here and be judged by fourteen whites and two elderly blacks who don't know history—who don't realize that you don't have to conform just because of color."[4]

Earlier in the day, after several hours of rancorous debate, the judge had denied defense motions to set aside the verdict or grant them a new trial. In assessing Carter's background, the judge found too "little evidence that he made any sincere attempt to rehabilitate himself." His probation report was characterized by the judge as being "totally unfavorable."[5] In reviewing John Artis's potential for rehabilitation, Leopizzi adopted a more favorable attitude, stating, "It's gratifying to find a defendant who had tried so hard as Mr. Artis to rehabilitate himself by pursuing every opportunity made available to him as a prisoner." The judge concluded by admitting that he had "no choice, distasteful as it may be, except to sentence him to a life term."[6]

On April 24, 1977, Rubin Carter and John Artis requested that judge Leopizzi grant them indigence status so that they would be able to appeal their case. State appellate courts require trial transcripts, and the two defendants declared that they did not have sufficient funds to pay the necessary ten thousand dollars for the twelve-thousand-page document. Although Carter and Artis had both been defended by private attorneys rather than a public defender, their lawyers stated that they had been defending both men on a pro bono basis and had not been paid since December 1975. Their lawyers asserted that without the financial assistance to purchase the transcripts, the two attorneys would be unable to continue to represent the defendants. The prosecutor's office opposed the granting of the funds, insisting on a more thorough investigation into what happened to all of the money raised by the Carter Defense Funds (which had been succeeded by a new organization, Freedom for All Forever).

The defense presented records to show that the new organization had assets of $6,900 but also unpaid bills totaling $18,400. The earlier defense fund groups were able to raise $141,000 at their celebrity concert at Madison Square Garden with Bob Dylan as the headliner in December 1975, but they lost $45,700 at the second concert the next month in the Houston Astrodome. Legal expenses and administrative costs consumed most of the returns from the first concert. Two months after receiving the request, Judge Leopizzi granted the defense indigence status and agreed to have the state pay for the transcripts.

Ten months after sentencing, the defendants were back in their respective prisons. Their attorneys continued to work on their appeal, hoping for a third trial. Artis was at Leesburg, where he continued to cooperate with authorities. Within four years of possible parole, he had returned to his academic studies at Glassboro State College, hoping to complete his degree in business administration.

Carter, on the other hand, remained bitter and defiant as he continued to fight for his freedom, refusing to give up hope. In contrast to the halcyon days of 1975, following Bello's recantation and the granting of a new trial by the New Jersey Supreme Court, Carter now faced a lonely and prolonged struggle.

The implacable Carter continued to isolate himself from the prison regimen, refusing to work or wear prison garb. Food was brought to Carter by a friend, Thom Falick. The twenty-five-pound monthly supply of food consisted mostly of canned soups and vegetables that he warmed up and ate in his cell. Carter argued that following prison rules would be tantamount to admitting his guilt.

On November 27, 1977, in an interview with the *Newark Star-Ledger*, Carter explained,

> My work is to get out of jail. It would be totally insane for me to help my keepers. There's nothing in here that could possibly be beneficial to me. I don't get involved with guards or inmates. I do not go to the yard, to the mess hall, or the movies. I do my talking on the typewriter to people who can help me. My job is to remain a complete observer of this prison . . . this death trap.[7]

He continued, "I'm still fighting and fighting hard to get out of here (Trenton State Prison). If I felt for a moment it was hopeless I'd be out of here in a moment. . . . Sure I'm bitter but I'm not a madman. I don't have saliva dripping from my mouth. It is intelligent for me to be angry. Damn right I'm angry at what has been done to me." As Carter reflected over his retrial, he commented, "It was a deliberate frame-up; an appeal to the basest emotion which is racism. The thing that really irks me is that I know the Passaic County authorities know I did not commit a crime. They know I haven't killed anybody."[8]

Carter continued to maintain sporadic contact with his attorney, Myron Beldock, who was filing an appeal emphasizing the prosecution's use of the racial-revenge theory. This theory, argued Beldock, linked Carter and Artis to the crime only because of their race and the race of the victims. The defense would also argue that Judge Leopizzi had erred in allowing Bello to testify, given his numerous admissions of perjury.

In the months following the conclusion of the second trial, as both sides began to contemplate their appellate strategies, they first engaged in a review of the legal battle they had just completed. Prosecutor Burrell Humphreys was openly critical of the defense strategy at a press conference following the trial. He thought they erred in constructing a theory that "everybody was persecuting them." He explained that, "The best way to try a case is to stress reasonable doubt, and not antagonize the court, heap abuse on the prosecutor, and try to convince everybody the police are out to get you.

What bothered Humphreys the most about Beldock and Steel was what he perceived to be their overriding concern with being able to make money off the case, through future profits from books and movies Humphreys explained to reporters that they "had to make a decision on whether they wanted to win, or whether they wanted to win in a manner designed to produce books. If they were acquitted on the basis of reasonable doubt, would that make much of a movie?" Humphreys believed that this mentality was the primary reason why Lewis Steel decided not to seek a severance and have his client, John Arts, tried separately. It was clear from the beginning of the case that the preponderance of the evidence was against Carter. Carter, because of his notoriety and violent past, was the primary focus of the prosecution. Humphreys indicated that if Artis would have pleaded guilty before the second trial the prosecution would not have been opposed to allowing him to be released based on the nine years he had already served. Of course, if Artis had done this he would have had to implicate Carter as well, assuring the prosecution of victory. Artis understood all of the repercussions and not only refused to plead guilty, but also to sever himself from Carter, an action that would have sealed Carter's fate.

Myron Beldock saw Bello as the key to the trial. Early in the case he thought there was a possibility of winning by convincing at least one juror of Carter's innocence so he could at least come up with a hung jury. He thought Bello's credibility was so weak that at least one or two jurors were not likely to believe him. As the trial progressed, however, Beldock began to realize he had underestimated the racial tensions, prejudice, and animosity toward Carter and his attorneys. Here were two slick Jewish lawyers from New York who were accusing the good people of Paterson of being racists.

In the middle of his summation, Beldock knew that he had lost the case. A few minutes earlier when Humphreys gave his concluding address to the jury, he could see the close bond between them. As Humphreys explained the "racial revenge theory," Beldock observed several jurors quietly nodding their heads in approval. when Beldock rose to present his closing argument, he sensed the enmity of the jurors; the cold hard stares instead of the friendly nods that Humphreys had received.[9]

Beldock found the trial to be a frustrating experience. He and Steel both sensed that they were in an "us against them" situation. One of Beldock's most vivid memories of the entire trial was going into downtown Paterson for dinner while waiting for the jury to arrive at a decision, and feeling hatred in the eyes of the locals in the restaurant.[10] Newspaper coverage of the trial paralleled the adversarial struggle between defense and prosecution. The *New York Times*, with one of their top investigative reporters, Selwyn Raab, accused of bribing a prosecution witness, was clearly supportive of defense efforts and critical of prosecution excesses. The Paterson papers, the *Morning Call* and *Evening News*, continued their unabashed support of the police and prosecution. It was almost as if they had a vested interest in assuring the conviction of Carter and Artis. Leaks to the local newspapers were frequent and sometimes erroneous — such as one story declaring that Carter had failed his lie detector test in 1966.

Lewis Steel, Artis's attorney, shared all of the sentiments expressed by Beldock but was especially upset over the judge's inability to maintain his impartiality. Steel was surprised by what he thought was the judge's intemperate behavior during the trial, having observed him on several previous occasions in which he found him to be decent and fair. He remembered being especially impressed at a sentencing hearing where the judge showed empathy for both the victim and the defendant. Steel disclosed in an interview with the author that beginning with his first motion to change venue, Leopizzi appeared to take this and nearly all future motions as a personal affront and a direct challenge to his authority. Particularly when the judge was forced to decide in favor of the defense, Steel sensed that the judge became even angrier.[11]

Judge Leopizzi was keenly aware of the tension existing between himself and the defense attorneys. Leopizzi told the author that he had made a conscious effort not to play into the defense's hands by making arbitrary rulings against them. He pointed out at least twenty instances during the trial where he had ruled in their favor although his efforts did not seem to appease them or noticeably reduce tension during the trial. The judge thought the defense was attempting to try the case before the media, using the *New York Times* to develop support for their clients. Leopizzi respected Beldock, although he felt his real strength was in drafting appeals rather than litigating. He admitted that Steel occasionally annoyed him, giving too many emotional speeches and carelessly shooting from the hip. Leopizzi was also uncomfortable with the entourage of additional defense lawyers, which included such prominent figures as Leon Friedman and William Kunstler, who was there to defend Carolyn Kelley.

The most difficult problem for Judge Leopizzi during the trial was trying to ensure that the proceedings would not turn into a circus. He brought the trial back to Paterson with the Hudson County jurors, primarily because he believed he could keep a firmer grip over the proceedings in a more familiar setting, working with his own courtroom personnel. Once the court convened each day, no one else was allowed into the courtroom. He thought he had been fairly effective in preventing the situation from getting out of hand.

In an objective assessment of the second trial, the credibility of both defense and prosecution witnesses is the most puzzling aspect of this case. Turning first to the key prosecution witness Al Bello, it is difficult to imagine that at least one or more jurors did not have sufficient doubt about the veracity of his critical testimony. Bello's admitted perjury, his multiplicity of contradictory stories, and his suspect motives would seem to raise reasonable doubts for most individuals.

Of course, the defense also had its puzzling group of recanting alibi witnesses who discredited Carter's efforts to place himself at the Nite Spot during the time of the shootings. The defense did, however, explain why several of these recanting witnesses might have been pressured into changing their testimony by Lieutenant DeSimone and other members of the Prosecutorial Task Force. Additionally, the defense team offered a new group of witnesses that also placed Carter at the Nite Spot at the critical hour.

Like so many issues in this case, the alibi question appears to be impossible to resolve conclusively with so many conflicting stories from such a large group of witnesses. By the time the prosecution and defense concluded their direct and cross-examinations of their respective witnesses, it was a stand-off, without a credible witness remaining. There were so many additional important issues which were equally unresolved—for example, the discovery of the shotgun shell and bullet in Carter's automobile or Patricia Valentine's identification of the getaway car—that it is hard to believe that not a single juror had sufficient doubt to vote against conviction. These issues will be discussed again more thoroughly in the concluding chapter.

THE ADAMO JURY MISCONDUCT HEARING, MAY 1979

The defense team of Beldock, Steel, and Friedman filed their appeal with the New Jersey Superior Court's Appellate Division in early 1978. Before the Appellate Division could take action, John Adamo, an alternate juror at the 1976 retrial, telephoned Judge Leopizzi on October 2, 1978, and requested a meeting with him regarding an important matter related to the trial. Leopizzi met with Adamo, a tower operator from North Bergen in Hudson County, three days later. Adamo told the judge that he was concerned about the possible misconduct of certain jurors who had participated in the trial. Before hearing the allegations, Leopizzi notified the assignment judge of this new development and summoned a court stenographer in order to place Adamo's accusations on the record. The judge was troubled by the serious nature of Adamo's charges against the other jurors, realizing that if they were true they could serve as the basis for granting Carter and Artis a new trial. That afternoon Adamo recounted his story of jury misconduct, and the following morning, October 6, 1978, Leopizzi telephoned Beldock, Steel, and Humphreys and asked them to appear in court that same day. All of the attorneys arrived promptly, and the judge provided them with a transcript of Adamo's interview. After reading the transcript and learning of the serious allegations, the defense attorneys brought a motion before the Appellate Division (which technically had jurisdiction since the appeal had already been filed), seeking a hearing at which they could question all of the jurors who had sat at the 1976 trial. Approximately three weeks later the Appellate Division denied the defense motion. Beldock and Steel next appealed to the New Jersey Supreme Court, which, three weeks later, also denied their request.

The defense, having exhausted their state remedies, turned to the federal district court, where it filed a petition for a writ of habeas corpus in oral argument before Judge Stern on January 29 and 30, 1979. The district court decided to retain jurisdiction over the habeas corpus petition but also ruled that the trial court should determine the scope and procedures to be followed in a hearing on the jury misconduct allegations. On February 21, 1979, the state Appellate Division ordered the hearing to be remanded to the trial court and provided specific instructions. The hearing was to be held in camera (closed to the public) within thirty days of the court order, and initially only the three specifically accused jurors, Guy Alario, John Armellino, and George Demetriades, would be questioned (in addition to Adamo), although the trial judge retained the authority to summon additional jurors as he deemed necessary.

Finally, on March 12, 1979, the juror interrogation began, with Judge Leopizzi questioning each juror. After this phase was completed, the lawyers would have the opportunity to submit additional questions for the court to consider for further inquiry of the jurors. Each juror would be provided with transcripts of Adamo's allegations before testifying. The questioning stretched out to three days because of additional allegations by Adamo that necessitated calling another juror, Edward Fischer, to come forward and respond to the new charges.

On March 2 defense attorneys presented motions requesting Judge Leopizzi to recuse himself from the proceedings and to open them up to the public. The judge denied both motions, which permitted for the oral argument stage to begin. It continued through April, convening on only four separate days. On May 1 the judge concluded the hearings and began to work on his decision, which was issued on May 31. In a carefully worded fifty-one-page opinion, Judge Leopizzi rejected all of the allegations of juror misconduct and found Adamo not to be credible.

Adamo initially made four allegations attributing improper conduct by jurors Alario, Armellino, and Demetriades. (Six additional allegations were added during the hearing, which were also rejected by Leopizzi.) The following are the allegations as presented in the judge's ruling:

(1) That Alario had informed Adamo that the defendant Rubin Carter had failed a lie detector test. Alario received this information from his wife prior to being sequestered as a juror.

(2) That Armellino, possibly along with several other jurors and one or

more jury guards, made jokes by using the Italian word *melanzana*. This word, literally meaning eggplant, could conceivably be interpreted as a derogatory term for black people.

(3) That both Armellino and Demetriades had prejudged the trial near its outset. These two jurors had stated that they no longer needed to listen to further testimony because they already had made up their minds.

(4) That one of the jury guards, while having dinner at the Holiday Inn where the jurors were sequestered, told of an incident concerning an unrelated holdup in Paterson allegedly perpetrated by black people. This guard stated that because of a legal technicality, "those guys got off" and that Carter and Artis, who he called "those bastards," would also achieve the same result.

The essence of Judge Leopizzi's decision is found in this simple statement: "This Court's inescapable conclusion is that Adamo's allegations of jury misconduct are not believable and must be totally rejected." He was troubled by the tenor of Adamo's charges, which he found to involve "mere feelings rather than specific examples." Leopizzi was skeptical not only of the validity of Adamo's accusations but also questioned his motivation in bringing them before the court.

Adamo first raised his allegations in an interview with Barbara Haekja, a former member of the defense team and an investigator with the National Jury Project. The judge thought that Ms. Haekja had manipulated Adamo, playing off of his desire to "resurface center stage as a key witness." Adamo was frustrated by being selected as one of the four alternate jurors and not being permitted to take part in the final deliberations. Leopizzi believed that Adamo's inflated ego had been bruised by his dismissal from the proceedings. Encouraged by Ms. Haejka, Adamo, he believed, had constructed a scenario that exaggerated all of the incidents out of proportion.

As expected, the defense lawyers were upset with the judge's conclusions. They found Adamo to be "a strong and believable witness and should be commended rather than condemned for coming forward and exposing misconduct in the jury process."[12] The Adamo jury-misconduct decision was now added to the other arguments raised by the defense team as it prepared their brief for the Appellate Division. Only two days earlier they had faced the three-judge court during oral arguments that focused primarily on the prosecution's use of the "racial revenge theory."

It could be expected that the Appellate Division would soon hear arguments challenging Leopizzi's jury misconduct hearing and an explosive new issue that would be at the heart of the defense case for the next ten years: the discovery of the results of a set of polygraphs given to Al Bello before the prosecution permitted him to testify at the second trial.

THE BELLO POLYGRAPH RESULTS, MAY 1978

As noted earlier, Humphreys was deeply troubled by Al Bello's credibility as an eyewitness. Bello, following his 1974 recantations, had gone on to give several additional versions of what he had witnessed at the Lafayette Bar, and as the retrial was about to commence, he notified the prosecution that he was prepared to renounce the recantations. Humphreys desperately needed to know the truth and concluded that he would give Bello a lie-detector test. Humphreys selected a highly recommended polygrapher from Chicago, Dr. Leonard Harrelson, and told him to find out what exactly had happened that night at the Lafayette Grill. He told Harrelson he wanted an unbiased test and "let the chips fill where they may."

On August 7, 1976, Harrelson came to New Jersey and tested Bello in order to conclusively determine which of his versions was true. Although Humphreys hoped Bello's testimony would validate his 1967 trial testimony, which placed Bello outside the bar during the shooting, Harrelson concluded that Bello was telling the truth when he said he was *in the bar* during the shooting. Shortly after the tests were concluded, on the same day, Harrelson gave an oral report of his findings to Passaic County assistant prosecutor Martin Kayne and Lieutenant DeSimone. DeSimone was visibly upset when he heard Harrelson's conclusions, realizing their disastrous implications for the prosecution's case. He told Harrelson that his conclusion was impossible because Bello could not have been inside the bar at the time of the shooting.

A few days later, on April 11, the polygrapher repeated his conclusions by telephone to Humphreys. This phone conversation was followed two weeks later by a written report filed with the prosecution's office. The report summarized the analyst's conclusions that "After careful analysis of [Bello's] polygraphs, it is the opinion of the examiner that [Bello's] 196[7] testimony at the trial was true and the statement recanting his original statement is not true." Unfortunately, the conclusion created a serious discrepancy with what Bello had actually stated at the 1967 trial, which was that he had been out on the street at the time of the shooting. This version of his location was also repeated in Bello's oral reports to the prosecutor and police.

One explanation for the discrepancy was Harrelson's failure to actually read Bello's 1967 testimony. He had been told only that Bello had identified Carter and Artis in 1967, and thus his polygraph examination supported the general veracity of that identification. Harrelson, however, did not know that Bello's 1967 testimony clearly placed himself out on the street. Thus, Harrelson was unaware that the polygraphs contradicted this aspect of Bello's 1967 testimony.

The prosecution shared the April 24 final written report with the defense, choosing not to notify their adversaries of the earlier oral report that had Bello testifying truthfully to his being "inside the bar" and that Carter and Artis had not been the shooters. By the time of the retrial, the prosecution was able to have Bello renounce his recantations and place himself once again outside the bar, observing Carter and Artis leaving the scene—testimony which the prosecution was pleased to declare was consistent with Bello's 1967 identification. No evidence of Harrelson's polygraph examination was introduced at the trial, thereby keeping the defense in the dark about Bello's polygraphs and Harrelson's conclusions reported orally on April 7 and 11, 1976.

Humphreys was now convinced that Bello's original, "on the street" version was the truth. In September Humphreys brought in a second polygrapher, Richard Arthur, to again confirm that Bello's 1967 testimony was accurate and that his recantation seven years later was a lie, generated by Bello's anger at Detective DeSimone's failure to assist him in his recent conviction as well as his inability to come through with the reward money. As Bello met with Humphreys in late September to prepare for the second trial scheduled for the next month, he was told of the results of Arthur's recent polygraph exam as well as Harrelson's final written report. Bello reassured the prosecution that he would renounce his recantations and stick with his original first trial testimony, premised on his "on the street, outside the bar" identification of Carter and Artis.

Beldock, in his preparation for the appeal, began to grow suspicious of the Bello polygraphs, but was unable to pinpoint what was amiss. On a hunch, he decided to call Harrelson and talk to him in greater detail about the exact results. He was aided by rumors that Bello's initial polygraph with Harrelson indicated that he had not seen Carter or Artis inside the bar and they were therefore not the murderers.

A second fortuitous break for Beldock occurred just before he was about to call Harrelson, who he expected would not be very cooperative. Beldock was speaking with John McNally—a long-time investigator for his law firm and former FBI agent—who informed him he was an acquaintance of Harrelson's and that he could use his name. Beldock called Harrelson immediately, dropping McNally's name and to his surprise, was invited out to Chicago to discuss the polygraphs.[13]

Harrelson spoke candidly with Beldock, disclosing that he had determined that Bello was being truthful when he gave his "in the bar" version. Even though Bello testified at the second trial that he was on the street when he saw the two defendants, the defense now had a statement from the prosecution's own polygrapher that he was convinced that Bello was telling him the truth when he stated he was inside the bar during the shooting and the defendants were not the shooters but were instead waiting outside.

Unfortunately for the defense lawyers, they had not learned of Harrelson's oral report at the time of the second trial. But now that report could provide a devastating rebuttal to Bello's credibility as a witness. Also, because the prosecution had purposefully chosen to suppress this information and not to share it with the defense, they had provided a clear constitutional foundation for reversal.

The constitutional basis was a 1963 U.S. Supreme Court decision, *Brady v. Maryland* (373 U.S. 83[1963]). In the *Brady* case, the prosecution withheld a statement by Brady's codefendant. The Supreme Court held that Brady required as a matter of due process that the prosecution turn over factual evidence that is favorable to the defense when the evidence is material to guilt or punishment. A *Brady* violation can occur even if the prosecutor acted without a malicious motive in suppressing the evidence.

The defense team quickly incorporated this new information into its appellate brief. They would have to convince the Appellate Division that the prosecution knowingly suppressed the contradictory results of the Bello polygraph with Harrelson and show that this new information was material evidence favorable to the defense and would have contributed significantly toward granting them a new trial.

APPELLATE DIVISION AFFIRMS CONVICTION, MAY 1979

On May 30, 1979, at exactly the same time that Beldock and Steel were awaiting the results of Judge Leopizzi's hearing on allegations of jury misconduct, the Appellate Division, represented by Judges Matthews, Kale, and Milmed, heard oral arguments on the broader question of whether the defendants should be granted a new trial based on a wide array of issues raised by the defense, including the recently raised *Brady* violation. Less than a month later, on June 27, Judge Matthews, writing a fifty-eight-page opinion for a unanimous court, affirmed the convictions.

Matthews methodically discussed and rejected each of the fourteen points raised by the defense. After a thorough presentation of the facts covering twelve of the fifty-eight pages of the opinion, he first rejected the defense's position that the prosecution's use of the racial-revenge theory and the evidence introduced in its support was so prejudicial that the trial judge erred in admitting any evidence relating to it. Judge Matthews found that the trial judge has discretion to determine whether a theory has probative value as opposed to prejudicial value. The court found that Judge Leopizzi's choice of probative value was not a mistaken exercise of his discretionary power, which must be broadly interpreted.

The next point argued by the defense was that the State should not have been permitted to present Alfred Bello as a witness because they knew he had perjured himself numerous times in the past and had also committed two other crimes on the night of the murders. The court ruled that the defense failed to indicate an applicable rule of evidence precluding his testimony, and therefore he was properly allowed to testify. The degree to which his testimony is to be believed is a question for the jury to decide.

The third point pertained to the Harrelson polygraph test. The judge discounted the defense's ascription of deceitful intent, finding that Harrelson was simply confused because he had not read the 1967 testimony. Matthews next reviewed the defense complaint that prosecutorial misconduct had "infected the entire proceedings requiring that the court reverse the conviction and dismiss the indictment." Matthews, writing in concurrence with the other two appellate judges, systematically moved through the remaining eleven points raised by the defense, rejecting one after another. The opinion concludes with a complete endorsement of Judge Leopizzi's decision on the issues raised by John Adamo's allegations of jury misconduct. They agreed with Leopizzi's rejection of Adamo's allegations.

It was a resounding defeat for the defense. The Appellate Division's unanimous opinion had decisively rejected all of the defense's arguments, leaving no hint of any possible weakness in the prosecution's case or in Judge Leopizzi's handling of the trial or even his posttrial juror misconduct hearing. Beldock knew, however, that the New Jersey Supreme Court was likely to be more sympathetic to several of the defense's major arguments such as the *Brady* violation and the prejudicial nature of the racial revenge theory. It had only been three years since they had voted unanimously to overturn Judge Larner and grant Carter and Artis a retrial. Even more significant, the basis for the court's earlier decision was the failure of the prosecution to share tapes of conversations between Bello and Detective DeSimone indicating that assistance would be given to Bello in exchange for his identification of Carter and Artis. Maybe the current court would take an equally hard look at the prosecution's continued tendency to suppress evidence that might be useful to the defense.

NEW JERSEY SUPREME COURT REMANDS CASE BACK TO LEOPIZZI FOR EVIDENTIARY HEARINGS, MARCH 1981

In a *per curiam* decision (this is a decision by the entire court without a detailed opinion by any members of the court) handed down on March 3, 1981, the New Jersey Supreme Court focused its attention primarily on the interpretation and use of Bello's polygraph examination oral report from Harrelson to Humphreys. It concluded that in order for the court to reach an appropriate decision, it needed to have a more complete record presented for their deliberation of the issue. Therefore, it remanded the case back to the trial court for Judge Leopizzi to conduct an evidentiary hearing on the issues raised. The justices ordered the hearing to be conducted as soon as possible, "on an expedited basis." The State Supreme Court would retain jurisdiction of the case, rendering its final decision after receiving the results of the trial court's evidentiary hearing.

The court clarified its position by stating,

> Our concern at this juncture is whether a new trial is warranted on either of two grounds. The first inquiry is whether the prosecution withheld material evidence favorable to the defendant, thereby violating the

rule developed in *Brady v. Maryland* 373 U.S. 83 (1963). If a *Brady* violation is not established, there nevertheless remains the question whether the evidence accumulated since the trial, taken together with the facts to be developed at the hearing on remand satisfies the test for a retrial based on newly discovered evidence.

EVIDENTIARY HEARING BEFORE JUDGE LEOPIZZI

The New Jersey Supreme Court order was disappointing to the defense attorneys. It not only meant that the appellate process would drag on even longer without resolution, but also that they would be back in Paterson before their old nemesis, asking him to perform the most unlikely task of reversing himself. Nevertheless, they would have to go through the motions in order to build the foundation for a strong case on their inevitable appeal back to the State Supreme Court. Before accepting their fate, the defense attorneys filed a motion asking Judge Leopizzi to disqualify himself from presiding over the hearing. The judge heard all parties on the motion on March 30, 1981. As expected, the motion was denied. The evidentiary hearing would begin in his Paterson courtroom on May 18, just six weeks away.

The hearings lasted three weeks and resulted in fourteen volumes of transcripts. Judge Leopizzi's eighty-page opinion concluded that the defense failed to show that the prosecution had intentionally misrepresented the results of Professor Harrelson's polygraph test on Alfred Bello or attempted to manipulate and dictate the contents of Harrelson's final report. On the last page of his opinion, Judge Leopizzi succinctly stated the result of his inquiry; "On the basis of the remand evidentiary hearing, the record as a whole, and all other relevant and material evidence disclosed since the trial, I find that no new trial is warranted under *Brady v. Maryland,* nor under the newly discovered evidence approach."[14]

The judge's opinion contained detailed findings that would be helpful to both the prosecution and the defense as they prepared to meet again before the New Jersey Supreme Court in just eight months. Leopizzi found that although the prosecution had technically failed to turn over information pertaining to Harrelson's oral report to the defense, the failure was justified under the unique circumstances.

The hearings also revealed through the testimony of Chief Assistant Prosecutor Kayne that after Harrelson administered the test to Bello on

August 4, he told Chief DeSimone that Bello had been in the bar at the time of the shootings. Prosecutor Humphreys was informed by his staff of Harrelson's conclusions, and he discussed the matter with Harrelson in a lengthy telephone conversation. The prosecution claimed that this oral report was so preliminary and tentative as to be beyond the scope of discovery. Although Judge Leopizzi accepted the prosecution's position, future appellate courts would take a more critical posture.

Harrelson testified at the hearing that he did not at any time indicate that his oral report was preliminary or that he was unsure of the accuracy of its results. Judge Leopizzi accepted the prosecution's contention that the written report presented by Harrelson was in good faith, accurate and complete, and that it superseded any prior oral statements concerning the Bello polygraph.

PRISON LIFE FOR CARTER AND ARTIS

Despite the persistent struggles continuing after the 1976 retrial, the five years following their second conviction meant simply a return to their lonely, drawn-out prison existence. John Artis continued to be a model prisoner at Jamesburg, taking additional college courses at Glassboro State. Artis, however, had contracted Buerger's disease, a rare circulatory illness that resulted in the amputation of several toes and fingers. When he appeared for his parole hearing in December, 1981, having served the minimum fifteen years, his release was granted as much for treating his serious illness as for his excellent prison record.

Carter meanwhile had also suffered physical problems. The prison doctor's clumsy surgery on his detached retina resulted in an infection that soon caused total blindness in the eye. His other eye became strained and was barely functioning. Carter had retreated into the confines of his cell, refusing to participate in any aspect of the prison's regimen. A further blow was the news that his wife, Mae Thelma, had filed for divorce.

At the same time that Artis was appearing at his parole hearing (December 5, 1981), Carter was facing another serious crisis. He had been charged with inciting a riot and, after an abbreviated kangaroo court, had been transferred to the Vroom Building, the Psychiatric Hospital for the Criminally Insane in Trenton—possibly the only place more horrible than his current location. The sentence to be served at Vroom would be fifteen days in the hole and one year in its readjustment unit as well as the loss of 365 days' commutation time—time counted toward his parole date.

This had happened to Carter once before, in 1974, and after serving ninety-two days in Vroom's isolation wing, he was able to gain his release by a federal court. After serving the difficult fifteen days in solitary, Carter was moved to a relatively better part of the facility, where he was placed in an isolated, sterile cell within what prison officials euphemistically termed the "reduced mobility unit." Unexpectedly and without explanation, Carter was informed that his sentence for what the prison authorities stated was his failure to "stand for the count" had been reduced from a year to only ninety days. He was returned to Trenton State, where he would serve out the remaining ninety days in the isolation unit, "the management control unit."[15] His time in isolation passed, and Carter was returned to the prison's general population. Somehow the original charges of inciting a riot, which warranted his being thrown into the psychiatric unit's most deplorable isolation unit, had been transformed into simply a severe punishment for failure to sound off when the prison attendance was being taken. No explanation has ever been given for the incident. Carter had survived another round of adversity and now anxiously awaited news from his lawyers on the progress of their appeal, which had finally reached the New Jersey Supreme Court. On approximately the same date that Carter was returned to the prison's general population, he learned that his attorneys were also in Trenton, delivering their oral argument before the State Supreme Court.

8: The Appellate Labyrinth with a Federal Resolution

It had been six years since Rubin Carter's retrial. A frustrated Carter, sitting in his Trenton State Prison cell, knew that his attorneys were about to finally extricate his case from the grasp of Judge Leopizzi and the Passaic County justice system. Carter's lawyers had recently appealed his case to the New Jersey Supreme Court, and they were hopeful that the state's highest judicial tribunal would be receptive to their position since the defense's only legal victory had occurred at this very same court when it authorized the retrial.

The defense would be facing a new adversary. Burrell Humphreys had just stepped down as county prosecutor to become a superior court judge. The new county prosecutor, Joseph Falcone, selected his top assistants, Ronald Marmo and John Goceljak, to handle the latest Carter appeal.

John Artis, after serving nearly fifteen years, had just been granted parole and would attend the oral arguments scheduled for March 9, 1982. Although enjoying his freedom, he nevertheless wanted his name cleared, telling reporters that the conviction "is still pertinent to my life and to my name." Artis, who had moved back to Paterson and was working for a travel agency, stated that he would "gladly go through another trial if it served to clear my name." [1]

The defense concentrated on two major issues during the oral argument before the State Supreme Court. Of primary importance was their argument charging that the prosecution had committed a *Brady* violation in suppressing the results of an oral report made by Professor Harrelson following his polygraph examination of Al Bello. Justice Robert Clifford repeatedly questioned the prosecutors as to why the defense was not given a full account of Bello's polygraph results. It appeared that at least one justice was sympathetic to the defense position.

The second issue raised by the defense was that the prosecution had improperly appealed to racial prejudice during their trial by arguing that the killings were motivated by racial revenge. Chief Justice Robert Wilentz seemed persuaded by this argument as he questioned the prosecution on the propriety of using the racial-revenge motive in a way that implied that an angry black man would simply be willing to go out and murder any four white people in retaliation for the earlier killing of a black man.

In their brief opportunity to respond (the oral argument phase allowed only fifteen minutes for each side), the prosecution answered that the polygraph evidence was neither improperly nor deliberately withheld from the defense. Additionally, they argued that the confusion surrounding Bello's statements was just one more contradictory piece of information regarding his testimony and would not have changed the outcome of the trial.

A DISAPPOINTING DECISION

The defense team felt cautiously optimistic. The two justices most vocal during the oral argument clearly supported their position. If they could just pick up two of the remaining five justices, they could eke out a narrow victory. Unfortunately for Carter and Artis, when the supreme court finally handed down its decision ten weeks later on August 17, 1982, Clifford and Wilentz were able to convince only one additional justice, Mark Sullivan, to join with their position. Thus, in a tantalizingly close decision, the New Jersey Supreme Court, by a four-to-three vote, rejected the defense motion for a new trial.

Justice Sidney Schreiber wrote the sixty-page majority opinion for the court. He was joined by Justices Alan Handler, Stewart Pollock, and, suprisingly, Morris Pashman, who usually voted in accordance with Chief Justice Wilentz in defendant-rights cases of this type.

Schreiber's opinion focused on three points: first, the oral report made by Harrelson was not the type of information or evidence that would be likely to change a jury's verdict. The prosecution had not deliberately withheld the information. Bello had lied on so many occasions that this additional prevarication would not have made any difference in the outcome of the trial; therefore no *Brady* violation could have occurred. Second, there was a considerable amount of additional circumstantial evidence to convict the defendants. The identification of Carter's automobile by Patricia Valentine and the discovery of a shotgun shell and bullet in Carter's car were examples of such damaging evidence. Third, it was permissible for the prosecution to try and prove the slayings were racially motivated, done in retaliation for the murder of a black bartender earlier that evening. The prosecution's use of the racial-revenge theory was not designed to arouse latent racial hostility. The prosecution needs to be given fairly wide latitude in constructing a motive in a criminal case, and the racial-revenge theory fell within acceptable boundaries. Schreiber explained his reasoning on the third point by writing, "Defense counsels err when they insist that the state's theory impermissibly casts all blacks as being motivated to seek retribution when a black person is murdered by a white person. There is no place in the courtroom for any such labeling."[2]

The consistent theme of Schreiber's majority opinion was to give the benefit of the doubt to the prosecution's arguments and the trial judge's findings. The justice's conclusions regarding the questionable polygraph results are another example of this approach: "We (the Court) accept the trial court's findings that the oral report was not preliminary and that the defense failed to prove that the prosecution intentionally misrepresented the results of the polygraph test or attempted to manipulate Harrelson and dictate the contents of his final report."[3]

A strongly worded dissenting opinion, written by Justice Clifford, surprisingly concentrated solely on the *Brady* violation, omitting any mention of the prosecution's use of the racial-revenge theory. Clifford argued persuasively that the defense could have greatly benefited from Harrelson's oral report. First, the defense could have attacked Bello's credibility in a more devastating fashion than any other evidence in the case would have permitted. Second, the defense would have been able to attack Lieutenant DeSimone (who had died the past year), who, it appeared, had confronted Bello with Harrelson's written report endorsing the "on the street" version and had "turned him around"(i.e., convinced him to renounce his recantation and agree to testify in the retrial that his original 1967 version was the truth). It was quite plausible that the defense could have convinced the jury that DeSimone had been instrumental in concealing the polygrapher's conclusion that Bello was actually in the bar. Third, the defense could have argued that Bello's testimony on any point was utterly worthless by showing how he could confound the two polygraphers (Harrelson and Arthur) on the very same issue giving directly contradictory evidence that both found truthful.

Clifford concludes that as a result of this added information, "Never before could defendants argue so persuasively that Bello was in all respects a complete unvarnished liar, utterly incapable of speaking the truth."[4] As a result of all of the previously stated reasons, Clifford forcefully wrote that "a more egregious *Brady* violation than the one presented by this case is difficult to imagine." He found it irrelevant whether the prosecution withheld this evidence purposefully or not. The magnitude of their error was so costly to the defense as to deprive them of due process and therefore required a reversal of the defendants' convictions.

One surprising aspect of the court's decision was the failure of the chief justice to articulate his specific reasons for joining in the dissent. Wilentz had been very vocal during the oral argument, challenging the prosecution's use of the racial-revenge theory. Nevertheless, he chose to join in the dissent without writing a separate opinion discussing the unconstitutionality of the theory. Since Clifford's dissent dealt only with the *Brady* violation, it would have appeared natural for Wilentz to focus on the racial-revenge question. A possible explanation given confidentially by a member of the press was that it had been rumored that Wilentz had promised a fourth justice, one who had been on the verge of voting to reverse the conviction, that if Wilentz would drop a discussion of the rather controversial racial question, he would vote with him. Unfortunately, the justice changed his mind and decided at the last second to reject the defendants' appeal. A frustrated Wilentz decided to honor his promise not to discuss the racial-revenge motive even though the other justice changed sides.

Carter and Artis had come agonizingly close to victory. Despite public statements indicating his intention to continue to maintain a confident outlook, Carter was deeply depressed. It would be almost a year before he would regain his commitment to active participation in his attorney's efforts to appeal the case at the federal level. Carter's attorney, Myron Beldock, released a statement to the press indicating his extreme disappointment in the court's decision but added positively a strong belief that the federal courts would adopt the dissenting opinion written by Clifford and supported by Wilentz and Sullivan. Beldock concluded by stating "we are convinced that this case was contaminated by prosecutorial misconduct from the beginning to the end. We therefore will continue the struggle as long as necessary to obtain justice for Rubin Carter and John Artis."[5]

CANADIANS TO THE RESCUE

One of the most fascinating aspects of the entire Rubin Carter case was the involvement of a group of Canadians and a young boy from Brooklyn. Their contribution to Carter's emotional well-being and to his legal struggle in the federal courts was immeasurable. They organized a comprehensive legal-support unit that provided critical assistance to Carter's lawyers; the Canadians' relocation to New Jersey allowed them to offer sustained emotional support to Carter at a critical juncture in his life.

The Canadians were a group of friends who had first met when they all were students at the University of Toronto in the sixties. Like many other students of this period, they were concerned social activists, opposed to the U.S. involvement in Vietnam and angered by what they regarded as the oppressive actions sometimes taken by government and business. Ironically, they became successful entrepreneurs operating a highly profitable fabric and fashion import business.

The group used its profits to benefit worthy causes and devoted itself to a variety of philanthropic enterprises. By 1979 it was in need of a new money-making project to finance its good deeds and began experimenting with developing a gadget designed to save gas. While visiting the Brooklyn, New York, laboratory of the Environmental Protection Agency in order to test their new invention, they met Lesra Martin, a young black teenager. Lesra lived with his large family in the Bushwick section of Brooklyn. One day after work the Canadians drove Lesra home and saw the impoverished, desolate neighborhood in which he lived. The group of Canadians was led by Sam Chaiton from Toronto and Terry Swinton from Montreal but also included their friends Kathy, Lisa, Michael, Mary, Marty, and Gus.

After returning to Canada following their summer of research in Brooklyn, the group decided that it would like to do something for Lesra and invited him to visit them in Canada in September 1979. They were captivated by him and asked his father, Earl Martin, if they could help with his education and permit him to move up to Toronto and stay with them. They were surprised to see how readily the Martins were willing to provide Lesra with this unique educational opportunity. Lesra seemed to blossom under their tutelage, spurred on by his burgeoning intellectual curiosity.

The group was concerned that since Lesra was living in an all-white Toronto community, it would be important for him to continue to learn about his African-American heritage. They encouraged him to learn as much as possible about his roots. The following summer (1980) at a book sale, Lesra purchased a copy of Carter's 1974 autobiography, *The Sixteenth Round*. He quickly devoured the book and wanted to learn more about Carter. He returned with his friends to the local library and was shocked to learn that Carter was still in prison, after losing his second trial in 1976, serving consecutive life prison terms.

The Canadian group, seeing Lesra's strong feelings toward Carter, encouraged him to write his new hero. On September 20, 1980, Lesra mailed his first letter to Carter. He thanked Carter for helping him to better understand his older brother, who had served time in a New York prison, and praised him for the lesson in courage. The Canadians also sent a letter of their own, including a money order so Carter could purchase stamps for the return letters that they hoped would come soon. In mid-October Lesra finally received a reply. He and Carter began a regular correspondence during the subsequent months. Eventually, they arranged for Lesra to visit Carter in Trenton around Christmas, and in February 1981 the entire group came down to see "The Hurricane."

Lesra and the Canadians continued their close relationship with Carter throughout the next year. Their hopes rose once the case was argued before the State Supreme Court in June of 1982, but their spirits took a nosedive when the conviction was upheld.[6] Slowly, the Canadians and Carter began to rally and turned their attention to the planned federal appeal by the defense team, which had now added Leon Friedman, a distinguished law professor and nationally recognized expert on federal appellate procedures.

THE CARUSO FILES

One of the most intriguing figures in the entire Lafayette Bar and Grill murder case was Richard Caruso. He had volunteered to serve as an investigator on the Carter-Artis Task Force in 1976. The task force was nominally directed by Burrell Humphreys, but Lieutenant DeSimone was responsible for its day-to-day operation, maintaining tight control over its direction. Its purpose was to provide the Passaic County Prosecutor's Office with a careful examination of the evidence before beginning the second trial. Caruso had served for only three months on the task force, resigning to join the Essex County Prosecutor's Office.

Caruso's name first gained the attention of the defense team in 1981, during a remand hearing on Bello's polygraph, where it was rumored that Caruso was rather upset over the conduct of the task force and might be willing to discuss his perceptions of their performance. Harold Cassidy, who had been working with the defense since 1977, was able to contact Caruso and arrange a meeting. Caruso was nervous about disclosing inside information from the task force, fearing it might have some effect on his future plans to practice law. Nevertheless, Caruso continued to see Cassidy a number of times, telling the lawyer in increasing detail his impressions of the task force and its questionable pursuit of the truth. Caruso thought the investigation was actually conducted on two levels. The first level was the public investigation, which was a sham, designed to placate critics and reassure the general public. The second level was a behind-the-scenes inquiry directed by Lieutenant DeSimone in which no notes were to be taken. Caruso believed that DeSimone's efforts were geared toward withholding damaging evidence as well as controlling witnesses. Most of Caruso's conclusions were based on a combination of personal observations, overheard conversations, and office gossip during his brief three months with the task force.

One aspect of Caruso's disclosures that was especially tantalizing to the defense was a rumor concerning Bello's polygraph with Leonard Harrelson. Caruso's information indicated that Bello had initially "flunked" the polygraph by convincing Harrelson that he was in the bar when the shooting occurred, thereby exculpating Carter and Artis by placing them outside the bar. The subsequent written report by Harrelson to the prosecution revised this earlier version, placing Bello outside the bar, in conformity with his 1967 trial testimony.

As Caruso related his experiences on the task force to Cassidy, he held a thick folder containing notes that he had taken despite stern warnings from DeSimone to the contrary. The defense lawyers were anxious to glance at Caruso's notes, hoping to gain information that might show other prosecutorial transgressions and efforts to conceal evidence favorable to the defense. Beldock drove out to Caruso's home in Lakewood, New Jersey. The two men spoke for an hour and, as the meeting drew to a close, Caruso turned the file over to Beldock. The file was approximately one hundred pages, containing handwritten as well as typed notes. After a perusal of the entire folder, Beldock returned the notes to Caruso for safe-keeping.[7]

It was now obvious to the defense that Richard Caruso's files contained a wide-ranging treasure trove of information. Not only did his file contain his own observations of DeSimone and the task force's investigation, but it also had Prentiss Thompson's invaluable research, obtained during his work for Assemblyman Hawkings at the request of the governor. Thompson's investigation uncovered previously missing police notes as well as his own intensive probing. Included within the police files was what appeared to be a portion of Lieutenant DeSimone's missing notes dating as far back as the summer of 1966.

Caruso came forward in 1981 at the request of the defense with his critical file to the remand hearing being conducted by Judge Leopizzi. Beldock now had an opportunity to introduce evidence derived from the "Caruso files" that would show that the prosecution had suppressed Harrelson's oral report of Bello's polygraph that placed the witness inside the bar along with other examples of prosecutorial misconduct. Judge Leopizzi, however, was not impressed by Caruso's testimony or the potential importance of his files. The judge ruled that the Caruso file was not directly related to the polygraph issue and blocked a defense motion to open the file. Leopizzi did respond favorably to the defense's request to seal and impound the file. Beldock also asked for the file to be unsealed, inspected, and copied, but this request was denied. The defense appealed this decision to the State Supreme Court, but in August 1982, when the court affirmed the convictions, they failed to rule on the Caruso material.

The defense team doggedly repetitioned the supreme court to release the Caruso file, and finally, in the fall of 1983, its request was granted.

The court's decision also jump-started Carter back into action as he and the Canadians began a rejuvenated effort to assist Beldock, Steel, and Friedman as they prepared to enter the federal arena.

On Tuesday, November 1, 1983, the defense team returned to the Passaic County Courthouse with a new motion seeking a new trial, claiming critical evidence had been withheld during the 1976 retrial. The defense specifically requested a November 18 hearing to show the court newly discovered evidence that was improperly kept from the defense and to request a new trial. Their motion specified that this new information was derived from files kept by Caruso. This information, much of which had been uncovered during the 1976 reinvestigation prior to the second trial, was not shared with the defense lawyers, as is the custom under state court rules of discovery. Many of the issues involved in this new motion were not directly dealt with in the 1982 State Supreme Court decision, according to Beldock, because the Caruso information was still under Leopizzi's lock and key.[8]

Judge Leopizzi, still technically responsible for the case, received the defense motions for a new trial. On January 20, 1984, Leopizzi denied the motion after reviewing the new evidence uncovered by the Caruso files and subsequent information uncovered by defense investigators. The defense investigators were assisted by the Canadians, who had now sent half of their Toronto-based group down to New Jersey. They were strategically located near Bordentown, shuttling between Trenton State Prison and New York to coordinate with Carter and the defense attorneys.

This combination of dedicated lawyers, Canadian friends, and now Carter himself carefully scrutinized the Caruso files, uncovering exciting new areas of inquiry.[9] The Canadians, who eventually wrote a book about their experiences working on the Carter case, *Lazarus and the Hurricane,* described their "painstaking scrutiny" of the Caruso and Thompson documents as "uncovering a pot of gold."

The first and possibly most important question raised by the Caruso files and Thompson report relates to the testimony of Patty Valentine, the only remaining prosecution eyewitness with the exception of the badly tainted Al Bello. Valentine, whose testimony at both trials was largely unchallenged, was responsible for identifying the white getaway car from her window. Later, when Carter was returned to the Lafayette Bar, she again identified his car as being the same as the one she had spotted earlier from her window. She also contributed to the second trial by stating that she had seen Detective DiRobbio discover a shotgun shell inside Carter's car at the police garage on June 17.

Until Prentiss Thompson began his thorough investigation in 1975, guided by the newly discovered original police notes, even the defense had assumed that Patty Valentine's testimony was fairly accurate. For the first time the defense team had the benefit of Thompson's penetrating analysis, which directly challenged Valentine's credibility. Valentine had always maintained that she had been alone the night of the shooting, having fallen asleep in front of the television around 10:00 P.M., after putting her child to bed. Yet Thompson's research uncovered a new cast of characters who had spent the evening partying with Ms. Valentine until one in the morning. The festivities took place next door, at the home of Avery and Louise Cockersham of 257 Lafayette Street. A woman identified only as Sandy, who had never previously been mentioned, went over to the Cockershams' that evening with Patty. Subsequently, it was learned that Sandy was Patty's roommate. Valentine returned to her apartment around one in the morning while Sandy left an hour later. A little later, as the Cockershams were about to go to bed, they heard gunfire. Avery Cockersham glanced out the window and saw people running down the street.

Thompson had interviewed Louise Cockersham in 1976. She had subsequently divorced Avery, who had been suffering from a brain tumor and was confined to a North Carolina hospital. Although Avery was unable to speak and died shortly, his new wife, Fanida, told Thompson that her husband had told her he had seen two men running from the bar following the gunshots and that they were not Carter or Artis. Louise Cockersham encouraged Thompson to speak with Sandy because "she saw more than any of us and told Pat (Valentine) not to mention her name to the police." Both Sandy and Patty were eventually located by Thompson, but they were uncooperative.

Thompson also found Patty's boyfriend, Steve, who Louise Cockersham thought had come over to her apartment that same evening. Steve told Thompson he was unsure of his whereabouts that specific night, stating suspiciously that he "might have a mental block about the evening." The investigator recorded his impression of Steve as being "anxious, evasive, and afraid," contradicting himself in many ways and was very concerned to know what Patty Valentine had said. Steve concluded his discussion with Thompson by stating that he thought Patty's other boyfriend and a woman named Ruth may have also been over at Patty's apartment later that evening.[10]

On the basis of his review of Thompson's notes and his own careful analysis of Patty Valentine's testimony at both trials, Richard Caruso grew increasingly suspicious, believing that there was a strong likelihood that she had not been alone when the shootings occurred but had been partying with her married boyfriend (Steve) and probably several others. Caruso's investigation also found additional pieces of evidence that conflicted with Patty Valentine's original testimony. His review of physical evidence at the scene of the crime—the location of tire marks, for example—convinced him that she could not have clearly viewed the getaway car from her window as she had testified. Caruso also noted that Valentine had moved down to Florida sometime after the first trial and somehow had been able to purchase a home despite being unemployed and apparently insolvent. He documented that DeSimone had met with her in Florida, going over her testimony for the upcoming retrial.

At the same time that Caruso was discovering several interesting leads concerning the questionable testimony of Patty Valentine, he was becoming increasingly frustrated by the direction the task force was taking, forcing him to abandon these new areas of inquiry. The person responsible for reining him in and keeping the task force investigators in line was DeSimone. It was obvious that DeSimone, handpicked by Humphreys, wanted to use the task force strictly for the purpose of convicting Carter and Artis in their second trial. Despite its supposed directive to conduct an open-ended investigation, it was clearly a single-minded enterprise designed to assist the prosecution and undermine the defense. After three frustrating months on the task force, Caruso resigned, threatening to expose what was going on if he were not removed from the case.[11]

The Caruso file, which contained important elements of the Thompson report, was an exciting starting point for the reenergized defense team. Despite the temporary setback of Judge Leopizzi's expected denial of their motion for a new trial based primarily on the Caruso file, the defense attorneys, along with Carter and his Canadian allies, were ready to begin a rigorous reinvestigation of the *entire* case, reviewing the original police documents in light of the Caruso and Thompson reports. Most of this tedious work was done by Carter and the Canadians as they pored over the massive amount of new information and mountains of material accumulated through discovery at both of the trials. Beldock, using his law assistants, began to turn over the documents, which were copied by the Canadians and then passed on to Carter.

Although the defense team found much of DeSimone's original notes to be "misleading, uninformative, and unintelligible,"[12] they nevertheless were able to use the prism of Caruso and Thompson's analysis to decipher the notes and develop many interesting new leads to pursue. Beldock and Carter soon discovered several unexplored and possibly fruitful avenues of investigation. Although most of what was uncovered failed to conclusively prove Carter's innocence, it did raise serious doubt about his guilt and undermined the credibility of several prosecution witnesses in both trials.

One of the most puzzling, yet potentially explosive discoveries was the presence of a mysterious cabdriver who had been at the Nite Spot Tavern at the time of the Lafayette Bar murders and supposedly had seen Carter outside the bar. There had long been rumors about such a shadowy figure, but it was not until a white cabdriver picked up Rubin's cousin, Edward Carter, that the enigmatic figure actually emerged. The cabdriver told Edward that he knew his cousin was innocent but had not previously come forward because of fear of police reprisals. Ed notified Carter, who immediately called his attorney, Myron Beldock. Beldock arranged to go with Ed and attempt to get a statement from the cabdriver. They arranged a meeting at the Meadowlands Hilton, but the cabby failed to show. A few days later, April 4, 1984, Ed Carter observed the cab company waiting for the mystery driver to come on duty. He hailed the nervous cabbie, who drove to Eighteenth and Grove, the location of the Nite Spot, at which point Beldock and his assistant Herb Bell jumped into the cab. The driver never denied the rumored story but was very concerned about protecting himself and his family. Beldock gave his card to the nervous cabbie after failing to convince him to come forward, hoping he might have a change of heart, but apparently he remained steadfast in his anonymity, still troubled by possible future recriminations.

Another significant new question raised by the research was the exact time of the shooting. It had been assumed from the initial police investigation—and confirmed at the first trial—that the murders had taken place at 2:30 A.M. Caruso's notes indicate that it was possible that the shooting might have occurred earlier, thereby confirming Carter's alibi. As with so many critical elements in this case, the police tape recorder that monitors all incoming calls and could have verified the exact time at which the police were notified had mysteriously broken down that evening and failed to record the night's calls. The telephone operator's log, which was supposed to provide a record of customer contact, had not been signed by the operator on duty, Jean Wall, but had been initialed by her supervisor, Lenor Harkinson. The defense group was suspicious of the initials and brought in the Canadian handwriting expert Linda Pitney. After extensive review of several documents written by Lieutenant DeSimone and compared with Harkinson's initials over the telephone log, Ms. Pitney concluded not only that it was a forgery but that Lieutenant DeSimone was the culprit. Efforts to locate Ms. Harkinson proved futile. The forgery issue was never revealed because the defense lawyers were about to make an important tactical decision that would negate the significance of the Caruso and Thompson disclosures.

MANEUVERING INTO THE FEDERAL COURTS

Carter, his Canadian friends, his lawyer, and a team of investigators had been working assiduously for ten months, following leads developing from the Caruso evidence as well as original police records. Their most recent court battle had been an unsuccessful effort to have Judge Leopizzi grant their motion for a new trial based on the Caruso materials. The defense attorneys (Beldock, Steel, and Friedman) decided it was now time for a strategy meeting, which was convened at Rahway State Prison on November 14, 1984, so Carter could participate. Beldock spoke first, bringing the other attorneys up to date on the newly discovered results of the investigation by Carter and the Canadians. Next came a discussion of what would be their next legal move.

The attorneys were eager to move their case from the unfriendly confines of the New Jersey courts and into the more receptive federal courts, but they were first required to exhaust all available remedies at the state level. They had done this satisfactorily with regard to their unsuccessful appeal to the New Jersey Supreme Court based on their belief that (1) the Bello polygraph results had been suppressed in violation of the *Brady* rule and (2) the prosecution's use of the racial-revenge motive theory violated the defendant's constitutional rights. But the discovery of the Caruso file had opened up many new avenues to challenge the prosecution. They had presented a motion to Judge Leopizzi (state law requires that such motions must be first reviewed by the trial judge) requesting a new trial based on the suppression of the Caruso evidence.

The quandary now facing the attorneys was that if they tried to press the issue of the suppression of the Caruso evidence, they might be mired in the New Jersey justice system several more years before they could exhaust all state remedies and move into the federal system. They remembered that it had taken them six years to move from the second trial to the State Supreme Court.

The defense attorneys were aware of the inhospitable attitude of the New Jersey justice system. In the eighteen years since Carter and Artis had been indicted, they had been unsuccessful in every trial, every hearing motion, and every appeal, with the sole exception of their 1976 State Supreme Court victory granting them a retrial. Moving at a faster pace would probably mean jettisoning the Caruso evidence and basing their appeal on the two issues on which they had already lost at the New Jersey Supreme Court: the *Brady* violation and the unconstitutionality of the racial-revenge theory. Time was running out.

Leon Friedman, a professor of law at Hofstra University and an expert on federal appellate procedure, came up with a creative, somewhat risky compromise position that would focus mainly on the two issues from the State Supreme Court appeal but would introduce the federal court to the Caruso evidence. He realized that ultimately the Caruso evidence and its suppression would have to be eliminated from their appeal, but if it was mentioned in their brief seeking a writ of habeas corpus, the federal district court judge hearing their case would be briefly exposed to the evidence. Beldock and Steel enthusiastically endorsed Friedman's plan.

Friedman was not overly concerned with losing the Caruso material because he believed that the Bello polygraph and racial-revenge issues were strong enough to guarantee success in the federal courts. Ever since they had lost the close decision at the New Jersey Supreme Court, he had been eager to move into the federal system. It would have been nice to have the supplemental Caruso issue, but it was not important enough to justify slowing them down for another year or two. Friedman further explained his position by declaring,

> We should submit the habeas corpus petition now. These things take a
> couple of months to process. By the time a federal court is ready to hear

our petition, we'll either have been technically exhausted on the Caruso
issue because they'll have denied us in the state or we'll argue that we are
exhausted because we have no real state remedy, the corrective process
in the state is so deficient as to render futile any further effort to obtain
relief.[13]

Friedman returned to Manhattan ready to begin writing Carter's petition for a writ of habeas corpus in order to advance to the federal system.
(Technically a writ of habeas corpus simply means court proceedings to
be held in order to discharge a prisoner in unlawful custody.) The only
way people can move from the jurisdiction of the state courts into that of
the federal system is to satisfy the following two critical requirements:
(1) They must have satisfactorily exhausted all of the state remedies, and
(2) they must be able to show that their conviction was the result of a violation of a right guaranteed under the federal Constitution. Friedman's
petition had to address and satisfy both of these federal requirements before the federal district court would begin to evaluate the case on its
merits.

Friedman was confident that his two leading issues developed in their
unsuccessful State Supreme Court appeal would provide a solid basis for
granting the writ. The defense team argued that it was imperative that
they stress the due-process violations related to both the *Brady* violation
and the use of the racial-revenge theory. No opportunities were to be
missed. They reasoned that they would write the petition as an educational brief for a judge who would be viewing this complex case for the
first time. Nothing could be taken for granted.

Beldock and Friedman worked on the first draft, exchanging comments
before showing it to Carter and soliciting his input. At fifty-four pages, it
was an unusually long and comprehensive petition, covering twelve
separate grounds for reversal, the final one being the Caruso issue. Although the question of the illegal suppression of the Caruso evidence was
still before the New Jersey courts, having only been ruled on by trial
Judge Leopizzi, the defense argued that it should be reviewed by the federal courts as having been realistically exhausted because of the inordi-
nate delays and futility of their prior appeals. Artis filed a separate
petition of seventeen pages. Lewis Steel, his attorney, incorporated all of
Carter's issues as well as three more, specific to Artis's case. After a careful review of the petition by Carter and all of the attorneys, the petition

was filed with the federal district court in Newark, New Jersey, on February 13, 1985.

JUDGE SAROKIN AND THE FEDERAL DISTRICT COURT

On February 14 the defense attorneys learned that the federal district court had accepted their petition. Through the court's random assignment procedure, the case was given to Judge Lee Sarokin, appointed to the bench by President Carter in 1979. Sarokin was born and raised in New Jersey. He received his undergraduate education at Dartmouth College, earning a law degree in 1953 from Harvard Law School. After graduation Sarokin practiced civil litigation in Newark for twenty-five years, staying on the fringe of Democratic party politics, choosing not to run for political office but contributing to selective campaigns. In 1978 he increased his level of partisan activity by becoming the Democratic party finance chairman for Bill Bradley's successful run for the United States Senate. The next year a vacancy opened on the federal district court in New Jersey, and with the strong support of Senator Bradley, President Jimmy Carter nominated Sarokin, who was readily confirmed.

Beldock and Friedman were pleased with the assignment of Judge Sarokin. Although a member of the federal bench for only a little over five years, he had already established a reputation as a strong civil libertarian and dedicated defender of the rights of individuals against governmental abuse. He was characterized as a "soft-spoken, genteel man with a sharp sense of humor and a strong feeling for the underdog."[14]

On February 20, Judge Sarokin ordered the state of New Jersey to respond to Carter's petition by March 31. The state's Appellate Division sprang into action, scheduling oral arguments for their still-pending appeal of Judge Leopizzi's rejection of their motion on the Caruso evidence. The case had been dormant for over a year. It was obvious that the prosecution wanted to keep the case in New Jersey for as long as possible and was nervous about its chances in the federal judicial system.

The defense attorneys, meanwhile, had their own problems. They acknowledged that they would have a difficult time convincing Judge Sarokin that they had satisfactorily exhausted state remedies as long as the petition on the Caruso evidence still lingered within the New Jersey appellate courts. After a series of contentious discussions among Beldock, Steel, Carter, and Friedman, the lawyers finally decided to drop the

Caruso issue from their federal petition. Beldock, a trial attorney, was most reluctant to lose the evidence from Caruso, but Carter and Friedman convinced him that it would not be worth the inevitable delay. Eighteen years had already been spent slogging through the New Jersey justice system, and Carter could not endure another series of setbacks and delays.

When the Passaic County prosecutor's office finally responded to the Carter-Artis petition, it focused only on the Caruso evidence, charging that the defense had failed to exhaust all state remedies on this issue. The defense countered with a motion for summary judgment, which in essence meant that their issues were so clear and persuasive that there would be no need for laborious and time-consuming hearings. Instead the case should be decided on its merits after briefs were filed and oral arguments heard. The defense realized that it would have to respond to the prosecution's charge concerning its failure to exhaust the Caruso issue. The federal rules were clear that one could not consider a petition compounded of issues that had exhausted state remedies and those that had not.

Friedman understood that even though they had lost on the Caruso issue and would not be able to use any of the important material in that document, it would not be a total loss. Judge Sarokin would still have had to read most of the critical information from the file that Friedman had woven into the body of his "Memorandum Regarding the Exhaustion of State Remedies." Thus, even though Sarokin technically could not consider the Caruso material once Friedman had requested during the oral argument that the Caruso issue be removed from consideration by the court, the judge would have already had an opportunity to read it in the brief, before the oral argument. The situation was clearly analogous to a jury that hears improper damaging statements during a trial and is told by the judge (following an objection by one of the attorneys) to disregard what it has just heard. It is difficult to imagine anyone really blocking out the misdirected information—judges included. Friedman was hopeful that at least a residue from the Caruso evidence would lodge in the judge's unconscious.

The oral argument for the motion for summary judgment was held on Friday, July 26, 1985. John Goceljak, the first assistant prosecutor for Passaic County, would argue the case for the state. Leon Friedman would argue for the defense, although Beldock and Steel would add a few comments at the conclusion of his address. (Also joining the defense team was Ed Graves, a young attorney at the Beldock law firm who had done a large amount of leg work in the final preparation of their briefs.) The impressive, massive courtroom was somber as Professor Friedman began to deliver his address, which would last approximately an hour and a half. There were no reporters and only a few spectators. The scene was in sharp contrast with the chaotic atmosphere surrounding the first two trials in the Passaic County Courthouse.

Friedman first informed the court that the defense was amending its petition and would be deleting the unexhausted Caruso claim, the only issue that had been addressed by the prosecution. He next informed the court that the defense was now prepared to argue the merits of the case. The prosecution had little choice but to accept the exhaustion issue and to begin to debate the substance of the petition.

Friedman began his formal oral argument by first attacking the state's use of the racial-revenge motive, which he claimed was a violation of Carter's and Artis's constitutional rights under the Fourteenth Amendment's equal protection and due-process clauses. Friedman emphasized the prosecution's inability to present any evidence that confirmed that the defendants hated white people or why the Lafayette Bar was an appropriate target for an enraged black person. At no point was the prosecution able to show any personal motive for why these two specific defendants would become involved in the murder of whites anywhere. Friedman next discussed the significance of the prosecution's suppression of Bello's polygraph and why it qualified as a violation of the *Brady* rule.

Following a short break, John Goceljak presented the state's position. He initially tried to minimize the prosecution's use of the racial-revenge theory, but Judge Sarokin aggressively pressed him on this issue until he finally admitted "that there was nothing either Mr. Carter or Mr. Artis said that would support this motive."[15] The prosecutor had an equally difficult time with the *Brady* issue and appeared relieved when the judge allowed him to sit down. Sarokin noted that because of summer vacations and other complications, he would allow the prosecution until August 30 to file its brief and relevant transcripts. The defense would then be given until September 9 to file a reply brief. A ruling could be expected sometime in the fall.

The defense team felt optimistic following the oral argument. They quickly called an expectant Carter to give him the good news. They clearly felt positive vibes emanating from the judge. His sharply focused questioning of John Goceljak indicated that the judge had accepted most of the defense position related to the unconstitutionality of the racial-revenge theory as well as the illegal suppression of Harrelson's oral report on Bello's polygraph. It would be another three and a half months, however, before they would learn if their optimism was warranted.

The weeks dragged by, but finally the nervous lawyers were notified by Judge Sarokin's office to report to his chambers at 9:30 A.M. on Thursday, November 17, 1985. Ed Graves and Lewis Steel nervously waited outside the judge's inner sanctum for an hour and a half before being admitted and learning of the judge's decision. Within a few minutes the two attorneys ran out into the hall, where they excitedly met several members of the Canadian group, screaming, "We did it! We won! We won!" Graves immediately raced to the phone, where he reached an expectant Rubin Carter and conveyed the wonderful news.

Other members of the Carter defense team were soon notified, and a joyous, tearful celebration began from the Manhattan law offices of Myron Beldock to the Rahway State Prison and all the way to Toronto, where Lesra Martin and other members of the Canadian group had been waiting nervously.

Judge Sarokin agreed with both of the defense's two basic arguments. He held in his seventy-page opinion that the state had violated the due-process rights of the defendants, improperly appealing to racial prejudice during their trial by arguing that the killings were motivated by racial revenge. Additionally, he found that the state had violated requirements of the *Brady* rule by failing to disclose results of a lie-detector test given by the state to a key eyewitness. Sarokin explained that "the extensive record [of the case] clearly demonstrates that petitioner's convictions were predicated upon an appeal to racism rather than reason and concealment rather than disclosure."[16]

He further argued that "the jury was permitted to draw inferences of guilt based solely upon the race of the petitioners but yet was denied information which may have supported their claim of innocence." Sarokin concluded his opinion with the simple statement that were it not for these grave constitutional violations, the guilty verdict of the jury might well have been otherwise. The judge then ordered a retrial but stated his hope "that justice and compassion will prevail. . . . The killings that led to the petitioners' indictment and conviction occurred nearly twenty years ago, and to try and retry such conflicting events, further aggravated by dim memories, does not appear to serve the interests of justice."[17]

Judge Sarokin's compassionate words fell on deaf ears as the prosecution returned to court the next day to notify the judge of its intention to file an appeal and would oppose Carter's release. Thus, on November 8, one day after his joyous celebration over the judge's decision, the defense and prosecution were back in court for a contentious bail hearing to determine if Carter would actually have any immediate benefits from the previous day's ruling. A motorcade of federal marshals had transported Carter from Rahway State Prison to the Federal Courthouse in Newark. Carter, wearing sunglasses and a sheepskin coat, was hustled into the courthouse, past a large crowd of news reporters and television crews.

Because Sarokin was now officially notified that the state would be filing an appeal, the judge would have to resolve the question of whether Carter should be granted his freedom while the appeal was pending. Ronald Marmo, speaking for the prosecution, argued against his release, claiming that Carter's violent, dangerous nature rendered him a threat to society. He alluded to his continued violence in prison, although when pressed by the judge, he was unable to provide any meaningful examples in the last twelve years. When Marmo cited psychiatric reports affirming Carter's violent personality, they turned out to be dated from 1957, twenty-eight years earlier.

After Beldock countered the prosecution's arguments, Judge Sarokin announced that he would retire to his chambers for approximately fifteen minutes to review any additional documents either side wished to submit on the release issue. He took nearly an hour to complete his evaluation of the material, as Carter and his attorneys anxiously awaited his return. When he finally resumed the bench, he announced that his decision would be brief. He determined that nothing the prosecution offered convinced him that Carter posed a threat to society. He went on to explain that

in the face of the conclusions reached, in my opinion, and the injustices found, I cannot permit Mr. Carter to spend another day or even an hour in prison, particularly considering that he has spent almost twenty years in confinement based upon a conviction which I have found so constitutionally faulty. . . . There is no evidence before me now which would permit me to conclude that society will be harmed by his immediate release. . . . Human decency mandates his immediate release.[18]

Sarokin freed Carter on his own recognizance without having to post a cash bond, with the only condition being that he notify the state of his residence. The packed courtroom erupted as the spectators rushed to embrace each other as well as Carter and his attorneys.

Carter decided not to address the media until he was sure the case was officially terminated and all appeals completed. He slipped quietly out of the courthouse through a back door. Carter's attorney Myron Beldock was willing to address the media in a brief press conference on the courthouse steps. He commented that there should never have been a case against Carter or Artis from the beginning. He characterized the prosecution efforts as creating

> a case of passion and prejudice that was wrong from the beginning. . . .
> There is so much pressure on the police to arrest, and on prosecutors to
> prosecute and convict someone for a crime, that fairness and objectivity
> are swept aside, and all efforts are focused on making and often distort-
> ing evidence to fit the theory. . . . The defendant becomes the victim of
> this blind push to get a result.[19]

Not everyone was happy about Judge Sarokin's decision to release Carter. The *North Jersey News* reported that many people in the Paterson community were angry over the judge's ruling, expressing both anger and surprise at the unexpected turn of events. Passaic County sheriff Edwin Englehardt, a Paterson police commissioner at the time of the murders, stated, "There is something wrong with the system. I think it's falling apart. He was convicted by two different juries and just because one man, one judge, says he should be free, he gets out."[20] Other members of the Paterson law-enforcement community echoed Englehardt's sentiments, but in the black working-class neighborhood near the site of the shooting, nearly all of those interviewed expressed joy over Carter's release. The racial divide over the decision was obvious. Paterson's racial chasm was as wide as it had been twenty years earlier, on the night of the shootings.

POSTTRIAL MANEUVERS FOLLOWING THE DECISION

Carter deeply wished to travel to Canada and spend time with Lesra and his other friends in Toronto, but Judge Sarokin denied his request. A month later, on December 19, the Passaic County prosecutors made official their intention to appeal by filing legal briefs with the Federal Third Circuit Court of Appeals in Philadelphia. They also formally challenged Sarokin's decision to release Carter, stating, "For almost thirty years, Rubin Carter has presented a profile of violence, dangerousness, and extreme hostility. There is nothing to suggest that this well-entrenched disposition and behavior should be any different now."[21]

Exactly one month later a Third Circuit Appeals Panel upheld Sarokin's initial bail decision granting Carter freedom during the appeal. The appellate panel explained that the only issue was whether Carter would appear at future proceedings, and the prosecutors, they held, had failed to address this question, focusing only on their persistent evaluation of him as a dangerous and potentially violent person.

Nearly four months later (early May 1986) the prosecutor returned to Judge Sarokin in the hopes of convincing him to reverse his bail order by showing him new evidence related to Carter's alleged predilection to violence. The wide range of materials included excerpts from Carter's autobiography as well as earlier psychiatric evaluations. Ron Marmo, representing the county prosecutor's office, argued that the court needed to review the new material in order to correct some factual errors that were made at the initial bail hearing with regard to the defendant's background. Judge Sarokin characterized the prosecution's efforts to bring in the new evidence as "ludicrous and totally without legal justification."

Throughout the next fourteen months (April 1986–June 1987) the prosecutors continued their relentless effort to bring in new material before the appellate court panel, hoping to widen their avenue of attack. Federal appellate rules are fairly clear and very restrictive on such efforts to develop new issues and present new evidence. The prosecution, despite its persistence, was consistently unsuccessful, bouncing back and forth between the federal district court in Newark and the circuit court of appeals in Philadelphia while challenging decisions from both courts until they finally appeared for oral argument in Philadelphia on June 22, 1987, when the prosecutors faced the third circuit panel of Chief Judge John Gibbons, Judge Ruggero Aldisert, and Judge Joseph E. Weiss.

CIRCUIT COURT AFFIRMS

Ron Marmo represented the Passaic County prosecutor's office. Speaking within the tight fifteen-minute time limit, Marmo described the heinous crime as an assassination of three innocent people, only briefly addressing the motive for the shooting. He argued that the state had presented "a considerable amount of evidence" on the racial-revenge theory that fit both defendants. The judges quizzed Marmo on the racial motive, repeatedly asking him what specific evidence indicated that Carter and Artis were prone to racial hatred and violent revenge.

Leon Friedman and Lewis Steel next spoke for their respective clients. The fifteen-minute time limit restricted their presentations, which were also punctuated with questions from the panel of judges. Most of the discussion centered on the racial-revenge theory. It did not seem that the three judges were as receptive to the defense position as Judge Sarokin had been, but overall the defense team remained cautiously optimistic.

The lawyers for both sides had to wait only two months to learn of the circuit court's decision. On August 22, 1987, Judge Ruggero Aldisert delivered a unanimous circuit court opinion affirming Judge Sarokin's decision to overturn the convictions of Carter and Artis. Judge Aldisert based his opinion on only the *Brady* violation, choosing to reject the racial-revenge theory and its constitutional implications. Aldisert noted that the prosecution used the Bello polygraphs to sway the testimony of their key witness (Bello) and that the lack of that information deprived Carter and his attorneys of the right to attempt to discredit Bello's testimony.

The judge commented that the defense could have argued that Bello was such a malleable witness that he would have testified to either version (on the street vs. in the bar), depending upon what he was told the polygraph tests showed. This information could have dramatically changed the outcome of the case. The twenty-two-page decision also dismissed the prosecutor's appeal against Artis because his name was never mentioned in their notice of appeal. In essence, the appellate court found that the suppression of the polygraph results was material and sufficiently important to satisfy the *Brady* disclosure allegation. Therefore, even without the racial revenge issue, the *Brady* violation was reason enough to overturn Carter's conviction.[22]

THE FINAL ROUND—THE U.S. SUPREME COURT

The defense had won round two in their struggle within the federal judicial system, and now there was only one round remaining—the U.S. Supreme Court. On November 12, 1987, the prosecution filed its "Petition for Certiorari" requesting that the nation's highest court hear their appeal. The defense regrouped one final time as Professor Friedman wrote the majority of their "Brief in Opposition." It was filed with the Supreme Court on December 14. In order for the Court to grant certiorari and hear an appeal, four of the nine justices had to be willing to hear the case. If an appellant cannot convince four justices to hear his/her appeal, it is denied without any reason being given and the lower court decision is thereby affirmed. Although the defense would have liked a Christmas present of the Court's denying certiorari, they had to wait until January 11, 1988, to learn that the state's appeal had been refused.

The prosecution still had the option of deciding to try the case a third time. Acting County Prosecutor John Goceljak said, after learning of the Supreme Court decision, that his office "will have to assess the option and decide whether to retry the case or allow the indictment to be dismissed." Fortunately for all concerned, it took the Passaic County prosecutors only one month to decide not to retry either Carter or Artis. On February 19, 1988, the office filed a motion in the county superior court to have the original 1966 three-count indictment against both defendants dismissed. The next week Judge Ralph Martin formally dismissed the indictments, following the prosecutor's motion.

AFTERMATH

The twenty-two year struggle was seemingly over. Unfortunately, it was not that simple for John Artis, who learned of their Supreme Court victory while confined in his cell in Northern State Penitentiary in Newark, where he was serving a six-year sentence in an unrelated drug case. Even though Artis had been granted parole six years earlier, his life had been dogged by misfortune. He had contracted Buerger's disease, a rare circulatory ailment, while in prison and had been forced to have some of his toes and fingers amputated. Artis was in frequent pain and discomfort from the disease, and the only thing that seemed to alleviate the pain was smoking marijuana—a remedy currently associated with cancer patients and now used in several states for that specific purpose. Artis was arrested in April 1986 along with twelve other individuals as part of a Passaic County drug ring. In June he plea-bargained to one charge of conspiracy to distribute cocaine and one count of possession of a stolen handgun. Because Artis had already served eighteen months of his sentence by the time the prosecutor's office dismissed all charges against him for the 1966 Lafayette Bar murders, his attorney was eventually able to have him released from prison a few months later. He now lives in Newport News, Virginia, where he counsels troubled youths and lives with his wife, whom he met while attending college during his first term in prison. He frequently lectures young people about the lessons learned from his near-fatal experience with the justice system. Understandably, Artis remains bitter, commenting in 1988 when the prosecutor's office finally dismissed the indictments, "I'm not happy. I'm relieved but I'm not happy. I'm not grateful or appreciative for this action by Passaic County. . . . It has taken twenty-one years to bring it about. From the moment this nightmare began, I told the truth."

Carter had emerged from his ordeal in prison in only slightly better physical condition than Artis. He had lost his sight in one eye, and the other was weak, but he had kept himself in excellent physical condition with a rigorous exercise regimen. His mind had also remained sharp and active, flourishing during the last five years as he, the Canadians, and his attorneys worked together on the countless appeals.

The weekend following the official dismissal of all indictments in late February 1988, Carter joined the Beldock family for a celebration at their Manhattan home. Over forty people attended the joyous affair, including the Canadians, lawyers, investigators, paralegals, and support staff who had all worked so hard and for so long in Rubin's behalf. The legal effort had been mind-boggling, encompassing over eleven thousand hours of legal work in just Beldock's firm alone. Beldock and associates had spent $100,000 in direct out-of-pocket expenses. It was estimated that the fees for all of the lawyers would have come close to 5 million dollars.

On the last day of February, Carter finally broke his silence and held a press conference that was reported in the *New York Times* by Selwyn Raab. Carter triumphantly announced that after twenty-two years, the longest conceivable fight imaginable, he had finally won—the sixteenth round was finally over. He remarked in wonderment at how his life had hurtled from the pinnacle of being a championship prizefighter to the depths of becoming a "reviled triple murderer thrown into prison for twenty-two years, finally climaxing with his current legal victory—How do *you* try to make sense out of that, because I'll be damned if I can! It is just too much."

Carter next discussed several conclusions he had reached about the American criminal justice system based on his more than two decades of legal struggles, fighting for his very survival. He was first critical of the death penalty and its potential for executing an innocent person. Second, he wanted everyone to know that the prisons were not country clubs where inmates are coddled. The public must understand the horrors found inside penal institutions and realize that these brutal, inhumane conditions are totally ineffective in eliminating crime. This can only be done by concentrating society's energies upon the vast causes of crime: poverty, drugs, illiteracy, unemployment, and racism. He also criticized the overly broad discretionary powers granted to prosecutors with too little accountability and pointed to the need for more effective federal review of state criminal court procedures.

Carter devoted a lengthy portion of his comments to Judge Sarokin, whom he praised for his clarity, wisdom, understanding, and, above all, his courage. Carter said that "he (Sarokin) had the courage to face squarely an issue that the state courts for nineteen years had side-stepped—and that is that the poison of racism had permeated the state's entire case." He closed his press conference by answering the question which he anticipates will invariably be raised by anyone reading about his case: "Rubin, are you bitter?":

And in answer to that I will say: after all that's been said and done—the fact that the most productive years of my life between the ages of twenty-nine and fifty, have been stolen; the fact that I was deprived of seeing my children grow up—wouldn't you think I would have a right to be bitter? Wouldn't anyone under those circumstances have a right to be bitter? In fact, it would be very *easy* to be bitter. But it has never been my nature, or my lot, to do things the easy way. If I have learned nothing else in my life, I've learned that bitterness only consumes the vessel that contains it. And for me to permit bitterness to control or to infect my life in any way whatsoever, would be to allow those who imprisoned me to take even more than the twenty-two years they've already taken. Now,

that would make me an accomplice to their crime—and if anyone be-
lieves that I'm going to fall for that . . . then they are green enough to
stick in the ground and grow!
Thank you.[23]

Not long after the press conference, Rubin Carter left the United States
to live with his Canadian friends in Toronto. He was divorced from his
wife and had not seen his children in nearly twenty years. On a happier
note, he had fallen in love with one of the Canadian women who had
been working on his appeal, and they were soon married. Carter has been
actively concerned with prisoners' rights and the travesty of wrongly convicted defendants. He writes and lectures widely. He is the chairman of
the Toronto-based Association in Defense of the Wrongly Accused. A recent speaking engagement found him addressing a National Conference
on Wrongful Convictions and the Death Penalty at the Northwestern
University School of Law in Chicago.

In early March 1988, the *Newark Star-Ledger* sent a reporter to Paterson to see what if any legacy of the Carter case lingered on in that beleaguered community. Carter himself was asked by the author of the article,
Karl Johnson, if he had any plans to return to Paterson now that his name
had been cleared. Carter's first response was a hearty laugh, but he
quickly replied emphatically, "I would not go back to Paterson under any
circumstances, at any time, for any purpose." Paradoxically, when the
daughter of one of the slain victims in the Lafayette Bar shootings, Hazel
Tanis, was asked the same question by the reporter, Barbara Minces
replied, "I hate Paterson. I hate even driving by on Route 80. I never go to
Paterson if I don't have to."[24]

What is the legacy of this perpetually divided city, split along the fault
lines of class and race? Does Paterson hold such a virulent strain of animosity as to drive out many of its former denizens? Did the tragedy of
Rubin Carter, John Artis, and the victims of the Lafayette Bar shooting
teach the city nothing about compassion and tolerance?

9: Final Judgment

Throughout the two years that I was working on this book, whenever someone found out I was writing on the "Hurricane" Carter case, I was invariably asked if I thought he was guilty. My stock answer was that if I had been a juror I would have voted to acquit because the prosecution had failed to prove his guilt beyond a reasonable doubt. As I progressed more deeply into the project, gathering more reliable information, I became increasingly certain that both juries had erred in their decision to convict Carter and Artis. Reviewing court documents, police reports, and newspaper accounts and conducting numerous interviews, I became convinced that there were serious weaknesses in the prosecution's case. I cannot, of course, say conclusively that they are innocent because I was not in the Lafayette Bar that night. Only Carter, Artis, the four victims, and perhaps Al Bello can definitively attest to what actually happened that evening. The greatest puzzlement in my final assessment of this case is how two separate juries (totaling twenty-four jurors) could conclude in less than six hours of deliberation at each of the two trials that the defendants were guilty beyond a reasonable doubt.

As one looks back over the barely credible and often contradictory evidence presented by both sides, it seems that there are still more questions than answers at the conclusion of this perplexing case. The following are examples of a few of the more puzzling issues in this case that have never been resolved: (1) Exactly who was with Patty Valentine the night of the murders, and what did she and her friends see outside her window? (2) What did Al Bello actually see and was he inside or outside the bar at the time of the shooting? (3) Who was in the mysterious first car spotted by Sergeant Capter as it sped toward Route 4 on the ramp to New York City? (4) When did Detective DiRobbio find the bullet and shotgun shell in Carter's car? (5) What role did Lieutenant DeSimone play, if any, in getting Professor Harrelson to change his findings in his written report? (6) Did Carter actually hit Carolyn Kelley in a Maryland motel just before the second trial? (7) What type of pressure was applied by the prosecution to coerce Carter's alibi witnesses to recant their testimony?

These unanswered questions, when combined with all of the contradictory testimony, generate such a fog of confusion and uncertainty that it is difficult to believe that the jurors as well as the Passaic County prosecutors were so certain of the defendants' guilt. Some of the blame can be laid at the feet of the defense, particularly in the first trial. Nearly all of the attempts by the defense to construct a credible explanation for Carter's whereabouts in the early morning hours of June 17, 1966, ended in failure. The alibi witnesses were discredited at the second trial. It would have been beneficial to the defense had they developed an alternative explanation for the murders. The defense is under no obligation to provide a different explanation for the crime—the prosecution has the clear burden of proof—but it might have shifted the spotlight away from the defendants a few degrees and allowed the jury to ponder some alternatives to Carter and Artis. A final difficulty facing the defense was Carter's violent past and criminal record. In contrast to Artis, it was conceivable to the white jurors who dominated the jury that a person with Carter's past history of violence might be capable of shooting four people if he was sufficiently angered. The Paterson newspapers persistently portrayed Carter as a dangerous person. They quoted comments made by Carter in the 1960s reflecting his willingness to use violent means against the white power structure.

EVALUATING THE EVIDENCE

Notwithstanding the weaknesses in the defense's case, the critical factor in considering the defendants' guilt is the evidence presented by the prosecution. Was the prosecution able to develop a strong enough case to eliminate any reasonable doubt from the mind of an impartial jury?

The first issue to discuss is the prosecution's insistence on using Al Bello's eyewitness identification in both trials. Actually, they had little choice, since without his testimony placing Carter and Artis outside the bar just after the shooting, carrying weapons, the state would have to rely entirely upon unimpressive circumstantial evidence. Even a conviction-bent jury would likely have been stymied without Bello's eyewitness account.

But why would a member of the jury have believed Bello, given his notoriously drastic zigs and zags? At times he appeared willing to sell a particular version of what he observed to the highest bidder. For the first four months following the murders, Bello, supposedly out of fear of reprisal, refused to say anything. In October he was convinced by Lieutenant DeSimone and other police officers to come forward and identify Carter and Artis.

Seven years later Bello recanted the original version, stating that he actually did not see Carter and Artis coming out of the bar that night. Speculation abounds about his change of tune, ranging from accusations that members of the defense bribed him to Bello's anger at Lieutenant DeSimone for not helping him with his more recent legal problems to DeSimone's failure to pay him his share of the reward money. In 1975 Bello told an investigator for Governor Brendan Byrne, under oath, that he was actually in the bar when the shootings occurred and that Carter and Artis were not the murderers. He did, however, see them later outside the bar, possibly serving as lookouts. Seeing the possibility of exploiting his role in the case, Bello signed on with two supposed literary agents (Melvin Ziem and Joseph Miller) and provided them with at least four additional variations of his role in the Lafayette Bar shooting so that they could help him select the scenario that would be the most lucrative in terms of future book and movie deals.

Given Bello's record of spectacular mendacity, why was the Passaic County prosecutor still willing to rely on his latest version of the events of June 17, 1966? This is an especially valid concern given the fact that the prosecutor knew the results of Harrelson's polygraph, which convinced Harrelson that Bello was telling the truth when he stated that he was *inside* the bar at the time of the shooting while Carter and Artis were outside.

Having Bello testify at the second trial indicated to the jury that the prosecution believed Bello's original version placing himself outside the bar. The defense attacked Bello relentlessly during cross-examination, and although they showed him to be a criminal and liar, they never really cracked his bravado on the witness stand. Other prosecution witnesses

Arthur Bradley and Patty Valentine also showed a tendency to shade the truth and, along with Bello, were manipulated and coerced by Lieutenant DeSimone.

A second puzzling aspect of the case was the presence of John Artis. Artis was only twenty years old at the time of his arrest, a recent high school graduate about to enter college. He was an honor student, star athlete, regular member of his church's choir, and had no prior criminal record either as a juvenile or as an adult. Moreover, Carter and Artis barely knew each other, having met socially on only two or three prior occasions. Why, then, would Artis, ten years younger than Carter, join up with a person he barely knew to drive across town and shoot four people? There was absolutely nothing in John Artis's brief life indicating a single instance of antisocial or violent behavior. What could have provoked this mild-mannered young man to suddenly join a casual acquaintance in committing such a heinous act?

Artis had been drinking excessively that evening, which is why he requested a ride home in the first place. When he and Carter were stopped by the police for the second time and were brought back to the Lafayette Bar, the police noticed that he was so drunk that he was barely able to stand up, leaning against the car for support. Could such a person in such a condition have run into the Lafayette Bar only fifteen minutes earlier, accurately shot three people, and then run down the street to escape in the manner described by Bello? The prosecution has linked Carter and Artis as partners in the Lafayette shooting. They were arrested together in Carter's car shortly after the murders. Yet, Artis's presence in this violent crime makes no sense. And thus, if logic and common sense clearly point suspicion away from Artis, then Carter must also be rejected as a suspect.

A third piece of evidence that undermines the prosecution's case is the failure of the two surviving victims to identify the defendants. Both victims also gave physical descriptions of their assailants that did not correspond to Carter and Artis. William Marins, who was shot in the head but survived, and Hazel Tanis, who was shot in the stomach and lived for a few weeks, both described the pair of shooters as tall, slender, light-skinned black men with thin mustaches. Although the description partially fits Artis, it doesn't come close to describing Carter, who is only five feet, seven inches tall, with a stocky, muscular build, and is dark-skinned. This was the description given by the victims to the police at the scene of the crime and at the hospital. Additionally, Carter and Artis were brought by the police to the hospital that same day for Marins to have the chance to identify his assailants. Although in obvious pain, Marins was able to clearly indicate to Officer La Conte that these were not the men who had just shot him. The prosecution subsequently tried to downplay Marins's failure to identify the men, arguing that his physical condition impeded the accuracy of his judgment, but it can be assumed that if he would have identified Carter and Artis, his physical condition would not have been noted.

In any murder case, it is usually critical for the prosecution to establish a motive. In this case there was none. In the weeks following the shooting, the police and prosecutors were quoted in local newspapers as concluding that robbery was the motive. Soon, however, robbery was dismissed as a reason for the crime. In fact, the cash register's drawer was open, but other than the twenty or so dollars stolen by Bello before he called the police, most of the money was either in the drawer or scattered on top of the bar. The prosecution chose not to discuss a motive in the first trial because there was no convincing reason available; it was confident that with Bello and Bradley's eyewitness testimony, there was no need to establish a motive in order to obtain a conviction.

In the second trial, however, following the recantations of the two eyewitnesses, the prosecution found it necessary to support Bello's shaky testimony with a clear reason why Carter and Artis decided to commit this crime. Humphreys and his staff developed what they termed the racial-revenge theory. They argued that Carter and Artis had been enraged by the shooting of a black bartender earlier the same evening and sought out a white bar owner to kill, thereby avenging the earlier crime. Not only are there serious flaws in trying to apply this theory to the facts of this case, but, as pointed out by Federal Judge Lee Sarokin, its use by the prosecution violated the Fourteenth Amendment due-process and equal-protection rights of the defendants.

The major weakness in the prosecution's efforts to utilize the racial-revenge theory was in its failure to apply the theory specifically to Carter and Artis and to the murder victims, especially the bartender, James Oliver. Although a crowd gathered outside of Roy Holloway's bar after he was slain, no direct evidence was even presented at the trial linking Carter and Artis to this scene or describing how the two defendants were so outraged that they indicated they wanted to revenge his death. Carter did know Holloway's son-in-law, who told him about the crime, but that weak linkage is the extent of any direct evidence. It is also important to understand that there was no effort made by the prosecution to explain why the Lafayette Bar was targeted by the defendants. The bar itself was not a very likely candidate for a racial retaliation. It was located in an integrated neighborhood on the edge of the black community, and it frequently served black customers without incident. As a matter of fact, one of the last persons served by Oliver was Louise Cockersham, a black woman who lived next to the bar.

Because the police focused so narrowly on the two suspects to the exclusion of any other possible suspects, they failed to pursue any alternative leads. One plausible theory that was noted in several confidential interviews was that the shootings might have grown out of the illegal bookmaking activities known to have been taking place in the bar. Supposedly James Oliver was the target of the shooters whereas the other victims were eliminated to silence them. Oliver, it was rumored, had failed to pay protection money to the organized-crime group controlling gambling operations in Paterson. After several warnings, they could have chosen to make a bloody example of his transgressions. A similar rumor had Oliver being shot because he was thought to be skimming money off the top of the bar's gambling profits. Both gambling-related theories have more intuitive appeal than the wispy racial-revenge motive.

A fifth weakness is that the police department's single-minded focus on Carter and Artis affected the thoroughness of their investigation. Like the O. J. Simpson case, in which a sloppy police investigation contributed to his acquittal and was likely related to the department's strong assumption of his guilt, the investigative work at the crime scene by the Paterson police was careless and tainted. There was no effort made to dust for fingerprints, nor were the defendants given a paraffin test to see if they had recently fired a gun. Even though such tests are not always conclusive, they nevertheless could have provided some guidance on whether or not the investigation was proceeding in the right direction. The result of the police investigation failed to provide a single piece of physical evidence that contributed to the solution of the murders.

The question of establishing Carter's whereabouts at the time of the shootings is another weak element in the prosecution's case and emerges as one of the most perplexing of the several unanswered questions in the case. In their attempt to weaken the eyewitness testimony of Bello and Bradley in the first trial, defense attorneys introduced a group of alibi witnesses who swore they had seen Carter at the Nite Spot Tavern around the time of the murders. The most critical were two women (Ms. McGuire and Ms. Mapes-Brown) who supposedly were being driven home by Carter at the time the shootings occurred. If the jury had believed them instead of Bello, the defendants should have been acquitted.

The alibi question reemerged during the second trial, although under a different set of circumstances and with a slightly different cast of witnesses. The prosecution, after an intense investigation of the previous alibi witnesses, was able to convince three of them to recant their earlier testimony. They stated that Carter had pressured them into lying for him in the first trial with the knowing assistance of his lawyer, Raymond Brown. The new defense team of Beldock and Steel tried to show how Mapes, McGuire, and Hardney had all been coerced by aggressive police and prosecutors into recanting their earlier testimony out of fear of reprisals against themselves or their spouses. Although the new defense attorneys were never able to resurrect the testimony of McGuire, Mapes, and Hardney, they were able to uncover a new group of witnesses for the second trial who were willing to place Carter back at the Nite Spot at the time of the murders.

What can we conclude from these conflicting accounts of Carter's whereabouts in the early morning hours of June 17, 1966? Certainly not a clear understanding of where Carter was at 2:30 A.M. We are left with the constantly changing testimony of Al Bello and the equally inconsistent stories of a group of alibi witnesses. This evidentiary standoff may not prove Carter's innocence, but, remembering the prosecution's strong burden of proof, it certainly raises reasonable doubt.

The Caruso files uncovered just prior to the second trial by the defense was never used even in the appeals but do contain many fragmentary pieces of information that might have shed some much-needed light on many of the unresolved issues recently discussed. Investigator Caruso's notes indicate original police reports uncovering many fascinating avenues that needed to be explored. Caruso's notes also suggest a more expansive and obtrusive role for Lieutenant DeSimone, linking him to possible tampering with evidence and attempts to misdirect defense investigators. How accurate and believable are the Caruso notes? Was he a hero or simply a spurned employee? Again, no conclusive judgments can be made.

The cumulative effect of this analysis of the prosecution's case points not only to many unresolved questions but also to a failure to satisfy their heavy burden of proof to convince the jury of the defendants' guilt beyond a reasonable doubt. Why did both juries conclude just the opposite and choose to convict? This is a most difficult question to answer, especially since the jurors have uniformly remained silent as ordered by the judges. It is likely that social pressure played a significant part in their decision—they knew that only a conviction would be acceptable to their family and friends and the rest of the white middle-class segment of Paterson.

CRITIQUE OF THE ADVERSARY SYSTEM

In hotly contested cases like Carter's, in which the search for the truth falls victim to the legal combatants' deadly struggle for victory, the inherent weakness of the adversary system becomes all too apparent. The basic premise of the adversary system is that the best way to learn the truth and thereby arrive at a just decision is to allow the attorneys for each side in the dispute to argue their client's case before a judge and/or jury. The judge sits in the middle of this struggle, acting as a neutral arbiter and ensuring that due process of law and proper legal procedures are followed. The system rests on the somewhat naive assumption that both sides will start out with fairly equal legal capabilities, neither one having undue advantage.

I believe it is reasonable to conclude that the adversary system is seriously flawed because both of its major assumptions—equal combatants and a viable search for the truth—are fallacious. After twenty-five years of studying and observing the criminal courts, I am convinced that the adversary system has failed to reach its lofty goals and has evolved into a brutal legal struggle between two opposing sides, each seeking victory for its side rather than engaging in an altruistic search for the truth. This is especially true in criminal cases, where the prosecution seeks to convict the defendant by convincing the judge or jury that he or she is guilty beyond a reasonable doubt. The prosecution presents as much evidence as possible while discrediting the defense. The essence of the defense strategy is to poke holes in the prosecution's case so that a sufficient number of questions are raised in the mind of judge or jury, who will then presumably conclude that the prosecution failed to remove that reasonable doubt. Discovering the truth and achieving a just result are often forgotten ideals in this legal struggle. The New York attorney Martin Erdmann, when asked about the lawyer's responsibility to be honest, replied, "My only responsibility is to my client. . . . I have nothing to do with justice. Justice is not even part of the equation."[1]

In reviewing the professional conduct of the legal adversaries in the Carter-Artis trials, it is clear that both the prosecution and the defense wished to keep certain damaging truths from emerging. They were committed to their clients' best interests, even if this meant abandoning a meaningful search for the truth. One can observe this preoccupation with their clients' best interests, even before the trial has begun, in the selection of a jury. Rather than trying to choose an impartial cross-section of the community, both prosecution and defense do everything possible to ensure that the jury will be composed of individuals who will be favorably disposed toward their side of the case.

As the Carter trial began, the prosecutors rigidly followed the lead of the Paterson police in relying upon dubious eyewitnesses, career criminals who recanted their testimony only to subsequently renounce the recantation. Police investigators promised financial and legal rewards to these men while they conveniently suffered a loss of memory concerning their written reports that somehow vanished and then resurfaced later at a more propitious time. Other pieces of evidence magically appeared (the shotgun shell in Carter's car), while polygraph examinations disappeared into thin air. The defense was hardly committed to the truth since all of their alibi witnesses from the first trial wound up recanting their testimony. A secret midnight meeting at the Thunderbird Motel to coordinate their testimony nearly had Carter's defense attorney investigated by the Bar Association on charges of suborning perjury. Throughout both trials, confusion and chicanery became the legal strategies of both sides as the defense attempted to save its clients from lifetime imprisonment while the prosecution tried to protect the community while also saving face.

Is there an alternative to the adversary system? Can reforms be implemented to limit the more egregious actions by legal counsel in protecting clients' interests? Realistically, very little can be done to remedy this problem short of scrapping the entire system and rebuilding it more along the lines of the European inquisitorial system, which joins the prosecutor and judge together in a search for the truth while the defense attorney has a minimal role. The defense attorney can even be expected to assist the judge in a mutual search for the truth. The following description of the German legal system illustrates how the inquisitorial system operates:

> Although in theory the judges are neutral administrators, according to the rules of procedure they are not disinterested referees or umpires of court proceedings. They are expected to take an active role in fitting the law to the facts of the particular case and in ensuring that all relevant facts become known. Court observers accustomed to the Anglo-American system would be surprised by the active, inquisitorial posture assumed by German judges. At times they seem to be working with the prosecution against the defendant. But if one assumes, as the German legal system does, that it is the duty of all participants to discern the truth or facts of the case in order to ensure a just application of the law, this activist orientation of the judge is to be expected. Unlike the Anglo-American system, the process is not one of advocacy, with defense and prosecution each presenting their side of the case as forcefully and persuasively as possible, and with the judge or jury making the final decision. It is more inquisitorial, with all participants—defense, prosecution and judge—expected to join together in a mutual search for the truth, the real facts of the case.[2]

It is difficult for most Americans, especially members of the legal community, to envision the European model. We have been mired in the adversary system, having borrowed it from England, for over two hundred years. And even though we occasionally criticize its defects, we are unwilling to switch to an entirely new paradigm—even one that is used in the overwhelming majority of nations around the world, especially in the more advanced countries of Europe. The shocking fact to most Americans who make ethnocentric assumptions concerning the inevitable and inherent strength of the adversary system is that except for England and America, it is found almost nowhere else in the world.

Given human nature and one's reluctance to change a system that, despite its many flaws, continues to stagger along, it is more likely that our lawyers and politicians would prefer to work within a system they already know how to manipulate rather than come up with a new structure that might have great potential but they have not mastered. The scariest aspect of change, of course, is the uncertainty of how the new system will operate in the future and who will benefit.

It is important to note that in criminal cases the prosecutor is not under the same professional obligation as the defense attorney in terms of responsibility to protect his clients' best interests. Although it is obvious who the defense attorney is representing, the prosecution's client is the community. The prosecutor is under a broader professional responsibility not just to obtain a conviction but to seek justice. This broader obligation is clarified in the ABA *Standards for Criminal Justice: Prosecutor and Defense Function* under Standard 3–1.2. The commentary to this standard explains, "Although the prosecutor operates within the adversary system, it is fundamental that the prosecutor's obligation is to protect the innocent as well as to convict the guilty, to guard the rights of the accused as well as to enforce the rights of the public. Thus the prosecution has sometimes been described as a 'minister of justice' or occupying a quasi-judicial position."[3]

Many prosecutors do not follow the dictates of Standard 3–1.2. It is only a guideline, but if it were endorsed and enacted by state court systems, it might help to curb police misconduct and excessive prosecutorial zeal. It would certainly be a step in the right direction, reminding prosecutors that their ultimate responsibility is to truth and justice rather than blindly pursuing convictions at any costs.

LEGAL CONCLUSIONS

As noted at the beginning of this chapter, I believe that Carter and Artis were wrongfully convicted. I am, however, narrowly defining this term to mean that both juries failed to properly consider the evidence and that the prosecution failed to prove the defendants' guilt beyond a reasonable doubt. The defendants may or may not have committed the murders. Nevertheless, I am convinced that the prosecution failed to satisfy their heavy burden of proof.

The adversary system, which has just been discussed and characterized as creating a serious obstacle to uncovering the truth in this case, exerted its greatest influence upon the trial courts. It must be remembered, however, that the appellate courts (both state and federal) are also affected by this same adversarial struggle, but for several reasons are not as deeply affected by it: First, the purpose of the trial courts—to determine factual questions—is quite different from that of the appellate courts, which is to resolve issues of law. Rather than dealing with the elusive and arduous pursuit of the truth, the appellate courts review the trial court's performance to ensure that the defendant's legal rights have not been violated and that due process of law has been followed. Second, legal rulings in a trial court are made by a solitary judge and/or jury. In the appellate courts there is no jury. The legal adversaries must argue before a group of judges the legality of the trial court's performance. Their debate usually focuses upon differing interpretations of applicable legal precedents and/or statutory provisions.

The conclusion of a trial court is based upon a judge or jury deciding if there is sufficient evidence to convict the accused. Following their convictions in both trials (1967 and 1976), Carter and Artis appealed these New Jersey Superior Court decisions to the state appellate court, which is composed of intermediate courts of appeal and a state supreme court. The defendants and their lawyers labored for sixteen years within the New Jersey appellate system. They were completely unsuccessful, with the exception of their 1976 supreme court victory granting them a second trial following Bello's recantation. Finally, in 1983, after the defense successfully maneuvered the case into the federal system, the U.S. District Court for New Jersey overturned the conviction and ordered a new trial. Their decision was affirmed by both the Third Circuit Court of Appeals and the U.S. Supreme Court. By denying certiorari (choosing not to hear the case), the U.S. Supreme Court affirmed the circuit court's decision to grant the defendants a new trial because of the prosecution's *Brady* rule violation.

Technically speaking, these federal court decisions did not declare Carter's and Artis's innocence. They simply overturned the defendants' convictions at the second trial, thereby authorizing the Passaic County prosecutors, if they so chose, to conduct a third trial (although Judge Lee Sarokin did state in his 1983 decision that he thought it would serve the interests of justice if the Passaic County officials chose simply to dismiss the indictments).

One month after learning of the U.S. Supreme Court's rejection of their appeal (February 19, 1988), the Passaic County prosecutor, Joseph Falcone, announced that he would not seek a third trial and filed a motion to dismiss the original indictment. This decision did not indicate a change in the prosecution's belief in the guilt of Rubin Carter and John Artis. It was simply conceding victory in this extremely protracted adversarial struggle. These sentiments were reflected in a statement given by John Goceljak, the Passaic County prosecutor who had played a prominent role in the case since the second trial: "We had a good case. We think we had the right people (Carter and Artis). We took a lot of flak. In the end, after 20 or 30 rounds, the final result went against us."[4]

John Goceljak's statement accurately reflects the attitude of the Passaic County law enforcement establishment and many other New Jersey officials. Public sentiment appeared to wish for an end to the drawn-out legal battle. Local politicians may have desired just to let the matter rest rather than stoke the embers of old angers. Moreover, after twenty-two years many of the critical witnesses had either died or moved away, making it extremely difficult to rebuild a strong case.

There was no effort to initiate a new investigation of the Lafayette murders to see if there might be another pair of murderers besides Artis and Carter. This of course, is not surprising since to do so would be an admission that the prosecution and law enforcement officials had erred in focusing all of their attention on just Carter and Artis. The prosecutors still believe that Carter and Artis were the two men responsible for the Lafayette Bar and Grill slaughter.

A SERIES OF PARADOXES

The final section of this chapter presents a series of paradoxes that may help to explain the unique and complex aspects of Rubin Carter's struggle within the American justice system. The first one is Carter's celebrity status—a top-ranking professional boxer, a black man with a prior history of violence, a rebel who refused to be intimidated by Paterson's white establishment. Carter's status clearly benefited him in 1974 through 1976, when he was able to gain the support of national celebrities Bob Dylan, Muhammad Ali, and many others who rallied to his defense. Their efforts were critical in his winning a retrial in 1976. But within the Paterson community, the police, prosecutors, and judicial system were united in their commitment to keeping Carter in prison for the rest of his life. To them he was an abrasive, violent person who might one day catalyze the rage of the city's black community and who thus needed to be silenced—he was to them an embarrassment and a villain rather than a hero.

A second paradox relates to the question of how great an influence race bias and tension played in the case. On the one hand, it is obvious that

Paterson in 1966 was poised for a long hot summer in which the city's simmering racial tensions were likely to boil over. Carter himself had made an inflammatory comment a few years earlier, threatening to shoot some New York City police if they continued to brutalize blacks. Yet despite this reality and the shooting of a black bar owner by a white man a few hours earlier, the police and prosecutors were never able to specifically link Carter and Artis to a racially inspired motive. The Lafayette Bar and Grill was not a racist establishment, unwilling to serve blacks. Rather it was located in a racially mixed neighborhood, and bartender James Oliver was friendly with most of his black customers.

Rubin Carter himself is a paradoxical figure of great complexity. Despite his violent past and the many challenges he faced—spotty educational opportunities, a confidence-shattering stutter, and several years in a juvenile detention facility without any real instructional facilities, Carter went on to become an intelligent, self-educated, and loving father and husband. He spent most of his time in prison reading and writing, keeping in top physical condition, and working on his legal defense. One's view of Hurricane Carter depends on whether one speaks to friend or enemy, defense attorney or prosecutor. Even today, thirty-five years after the shootings, New Jersey criminal justice officials who were involved in the case speak of Carter in negative terms. They believe he was a violent predator who should have spent his entire life in prison for the Lafayette Bar murders. Carter's attorney, his Canadian friends, and acquaintances from his boxing career strongly object to this negative, narrow-minded characterization. To them, Rubin is a caring, intelligent individual committed to trying to ensure that other innocent defendants are not wrongfully convicted. Carter spends much of his time today lecturing and writing on behalf of the Association in Defense of the Wrongly Convicted, based in Canada, of which he is chairman. Even his supporters recognize Carter can be difficult and is a person of strong, intense convictions, but this does not diminish their respect and admiration for him. Even a neutral observer has to be greatly impressed by the strength of his character and all that he has had to endure.

It is one of the greatest ironies in this case that Lieutenant DeSimone, whose relentless efforts were critical in twice convicting Carter, was also indirectly responsible for the case being retried as well as its ultimately being reversed. DeSimone's overzealous commitment to convicting Hurricane Carter led him to engage in behavior that the federal courts and the

New Jersey Supreme Court found to be in unconstitutional violation of the defendant's Fourteenth-Amendment due-process rights.

What does the Carter case tell us about the American justice system? It concluded on a positive note, with Carter finally being released and having his name cleared, but only after he had served twenty-one years in prison. One wonders how other wrongfully convicted defendants have fared without Carter's unusual character strength as well as his celebrity status, a committed support group, and talented legal counsel. The case certainly places the federal courts in a positive light, since they came to Carter's rescue. But it took the defense team eighteen years to place their case before the federal system. Of course if one is not convinced of Carter's innocence, then the federal courts are not a savior but a meddling institution that allows violent criminals to be released on the basis of minor technicalities and procedural flaws. On this view they are an obstacle to the efforts of law-enforcement officials throughout this country who believe that federal-court decisions have limited their effectiveness by placing unwarranted restrictions on their crime-fighting responsibilities.

Although our system places a heavy burden of proof on the prosecution and the defendant is assumed innocent until proven otherwise, our justice system cannot guarantee that isolated instances of wrongful conviction will not continue to occur. Professor E. M. Morgan of Harvard Law School eloquently explains why our justice system can never be expected to completely eliminate the problem:

> Our system does not guarantee either the conviction of the guilty or the acquittal of the innocent. Certain safeguards are erected which make it more difficult to convict the innocent than to acquit the guilty, but all that our system guarantees is a fair trial. It is a price which every member of a civilized community must pay for the erection and maintenance of machinery for administering justice, that he may become the victim of its imperfect functioning.[5]

Our only hope for the future may then be that the members of the judiciary and prosecution will also recognize the imperfect nature of the criminal justice system and be committed to do everything possible to prevent a repetition of the legal nightmare experienced by John Artis and Rubin Carter.

Chronology

May 6, 1937	Carter born in Delawanna, New Jersey.
April 1943	Carter family moves to a home in Paterson on Twelfth Street.
March 1949	Carter arrested for the first time for stealing clothes from a haberdashery.
August 1951	Carter sentenced to three years at Jamesburg Reformatory for stabbing a man.
July 1954	Escaped from Jamesburg and enlisted in Army a few days later.
June 1956	Discharged from the army.
July 1957	Carter sentenced to a three-to-nine-year term at Trenton State Prison for a strong-arm robbery.
September 1961	Carter released from prison.
September 23, 1961	Carter has first professional fight, defeating Pike Reed in Annapolis, Maryland.
December 1964	Fought Joey Giardello for the middleweight championship in Philadelphia and lost in a fifteen-round decision.
June 17, 1966	Three people are shot to death at the Lafayette Bar and Grill. Carter and Artis are questioned and then released.
October 1966	Following Bello's identification, Carter and Artis are arrested and charged with the Lafayette murders.
June 29, 1967	Carter and Artis are sentenced to life imprisonment on their convictions for three counts of murder.
March 1976	New Jersey Supreme Court grants Carter and Artis a second trial.
December 1976	Carter and Artis convicted by jury at the second trial and again receive life sentences.

August 1982	New Jersey Supreme Court, in a 4–3, decision rejects appeal for a new trial.
January 1985	U.S. Federal Circuit Court of Appeals (3rd) affirms Judge Sarokin's decision to overturn the conviction.
November 1985	Federal District Court Judge Lee Sarokin overturns Carter's and Artis's second trial conviction.
January 1988	U.S. Supreme Court denies *certiorari* to the state appeal.
February 19, 1988	The Passaic County prosecutor, Joseph Falcone, announces that he will not seek a third trial and files a motion to dismiss the original indictments.
February 26, 1988	Passaic County Judge Ralph Martin officially dismisses the indictments.

Dramatis Personae

JUDGES

Ruggero Aldisert
Charles Alfano
Justice Robert Clifford
John Gibbons
Charles Joelson
Samuel Larner
Bruno Leopizzi
William Marchese
Leon Milmed
Lee Sarokin
Justice Sidney Schreiber
Justice Mark Sullivan
Chief Justice Joseph Weintraub
Joseph Weiss
Chief Justice Robert Wilentz

PROSECUTORS

John Goceljak
Joseph Gourley
Vincent Hull
Burrell Humphreys
Martin Kayne
Ron Marmo

PROSECUTION WITNESSES

Richard Arthur
Alfred Bello
Det. Edward Callahan
Sgt. Ted Capter

Lt. Vincent DeSimone
Det. Emil DiRobbio
Patl. Alexander Goodnough
Capt. Gourley
Annie Ruth Haggins
Leonard Harrelson
Carolyn Kelley
Philip LaPadura
Det. Al Lynch
Sgt. McGuire
Joseph Miller
Patricia Graham Valentine
Melvin Ziem

DEFENSE ATTORNEYS

Miles Alexander
Myron Beldock
Michael Blacker
Raymond Brown
Paul Feldman
Jeffrey Fogel
Lewis Steel
Arnold Stein
Stanley Van Ness

DEFENSE WITNESSES

George Andrews
Richard Caruso
Welton Deary
Bill Hardney

Cathy McGuire
Anna Mapes
Eddie Rawls
John Royster
Ronald Ruggiero
Erwin Schankerelli
Nathan Sermond
Elwood Tuck
Merrit Wimberly

OTHER CHARACTERS

Rev. Ralph D. Abernathy
Floyd Abrams
Paul Alberta
Muhammed Ali
David Anderson
Virgil Atkins
Georgie Benton
E. M. Borchard
Mae Thelma Bosket
Gov. Brendan Byrne
Thomas Cappucio
Bertha Carter
Lillian Carter
Annabelle Chandler
Avery Cockersham
Louise Cockersham
Frank Conforti
Joe Cooper
Rev. Roger Douglas
Margaret English
Florentino Fernandez
Joey Giardello

Jose Gonzalez
Mayor Frank Graves
Emile Griffith
Milt Gross
Barbara Haekja
Lenore Harkinson
Alfred Harris
Eldridge Hawkins
Emily Hoffman
Roy Holloway
William Hyland
Herschell Jacobs
Judi Kavanaugh
Buddy Leggett
George Lois
Lesra Martin
Captain Mendoza
William Metzler
Neil Morrison
Fred Nauyoks
Betty Panagia
Selwyn Raab
Arye Rattner
Evonne Seldon
George Shaw
Richard Solomon
Hazel Tanis
Carmen Tedeschi
Prentiss Thompson
Tom Trantino
Warden Vukevich
Ike Williams
Linda Yablonski

Research and Sources

The research for this book is based primarily upon newspaper accounts, trial transcripts, court decisions, and miscellaneous legal documents. They provide empirical evidence clarifying and describing the tortuous path followed by this highly controversial and emotional case, which took two decades to resolve. Although one may question the total reliability and impartiality of these primary sources—especially the newspaper accounts—they are nevertheless the best available. They provide a relatively clear picture of the chronology of "legal events" that are the central focus of this book.

I also conducted interviews. By speaking with lawyers, judges, and reporters, I was able to probe into the more puzzling aspects of this case. The interviews, however, were frustrating because many individuals who did speak were less than candid in their response to my questions. The long passage of time since the case began also proved to be a complicating factor. Many key individuals had either died, become very ill, moved away, or slipped into oblivion.

Another reason for the witnesses' reluctance to be interviewed was the unavailing emotionality of the case, even three decades after the shootings. Many people, especially former public officials in Passaic County, still regard the Carter case as controversial. The fact that a major Hollywood movie has been made about the case only ratchets up their paranoia another notch. These people did not wish to make a public statement about the case, even a personal opinion. Instead, they have referred me to earlier newspaper accounts that state their original position.

The inherent animosity between defense attorneys and prosecutors, an outgrowth of our adversarial system, also affected the quality and candor of the interviews. Interview difficulties arose whenever a sensitive issue was raised such as the possible planting of evidence by the police or the possible suborning of perjury by both defense and prosecution. Accusations of racism, anti-Semitism, political opportunism, and cowardice flew between the sides.

These intense feelings delimited the number and quality of my interviews. Half of the persons contacted declined to be interviewed. Their excuses ranged from being too busy to not having anything important to say ("It was all in the newspapers"). Several individuals from the first trial had little faith in the accuracy of their memories. Of those individuals who were willing to be interviewed, half were candid and half were cautiously guarded in their comments, even though much of what they refused to discuss could easily be found in court documents or newspaper accounts. I found that the most useful sources of information were newspaper accounts, trial transcripts, and court decisions. It should be noted, however, that even the newspapers had to be read carefully—I was constantly on the lookout for prejudices toward either the defendants or the prosecution. The two Paterson papers supported the prosecution while the *New York Times,* particularly articles by Selwyn Raab, favored the defense. The *Newark Star-Ledger,* which also covered both trials and all the appeals, assumed a relatively neutral position. By carefully reading all four papers, I gained a balanced overview of all proceedings.

This is the first book to examine this case comprehensively from the shooting on June 17, 1966, through the final successful appeal, which led to the dismissal of the indictments in February 1988. Carter wrote an autobiography entitled *The Sixteenth Round* (New York: Viking Press, 1974). Unfortunately, his story concluded shortly after his first trial, while he was serving his life sentence. A second book about the case focuses on the role of a group of Canadians aiding Carter during his successful federal appeal. This book was written by two of the Canadians, Terry Swinton and Sam Chaiton, and is entitled *Lazarus and the Hurricane* (Toronto: Penguin Books, 1991). The authors acknowledge early in their volume that they are not interested in offering the reader "a complete rehashing of the twenty-two year case because it would be neither practical nor fruitful nor is it the story of this book." Both books served as the basis for a movie based on Rubin Carter's life released in December 1999. The movie, *The Hurricane,* has received mixed reviews, in part because of its willingness to sacrifice factual accuracy for dramatic effect.

In order to gain a better understanding of the setting for this case, I read *About Paterson* by Christopher Norwood, published in 1974 (New

York: Saturday Review Press). Norwood offers a wonderful history of the city as well as an insightful description of the class and racial strife that have divided the city for over a hundred years. He also communicates the paranoia and parochialism that have plagued the city, a fear of outsiders that was deeply felt by the defense lawyers, Myron Beldock and Lewis Steel.

Two additional volumes were very helpful, particularly in the concluding chapter. Ann Strick's *Injustice for All* (New York: Penguin Books, 1977) is an incisive, thought-provoking critique of the adversary system. The second book is *Convicted but Innocent: Wrongful Conviction and Public Policy* by C. Ronald Huff, Arye Rattner, and Edward Sagarin (Thousand Oaks, Calif.: Sage, 1996). It is a thorough analysis of the wrongful conviction issue, presenting a comprehensive survey of the most responsible social science research on the topic. The authors' own study in Ohio was especially useful in understanding what factors contribute to a defendant being wrongfully convicted.

Although footnotes were not used in the traditional manner to document every possible reference source, there were, nevertheless, several points throughout the book where I deemed them necessary. The following list of citations is therefore offered to provide background or verification for those important and/or sensitive passages as chosen by the author.

Notes

1. THE FATEFUL NIGHT
1. "Former Tavern Owner Kills New Proprietor," *Paterson Evening News*, June 17, 1966.
2. Rubin Carter, *The Sixteenth Round* (New York: Viking Press, 1974), 244.

2. SETTING THE SCENE
1. Much of the information for this chapter was gathered from Rubin Carter's autobiography, *The Sixteenth Round* (New York: Viking Press, 1974). It was especially helpful for gathering details about Carter's childhood, early experiences with the law, and boxing career. The book ends with an account of the initial appeals and Carter's imprisonment after the first trial.
2. Carter, *The Sixteenth Round*, 226.
3. Elizabeth Kaming, "I Never Shot Anybody, Artis Tells Jury," *Paterson Morning Call*, May 24, 1967, 2.

3. THE FIRST TRIAL: MAY 1967
1. Leslie Maitland, "Witness at the Rubin Carter Trial Tells Hearing He Lied Often During the Case," *New York Times*, November 17, 1976, D-2 and "Rough Day for Witness," *Paterson News*, November 17, 1976, 14.
2. Dean Bender, "Jury Hears Tape on Offers by Detective DeSimone to Bello," *Paterson News*, November 20, 1976, 16.
3. *State v. Carter*. May 9, 1967, Trial transcript. 342. N.J. Superior Court, Passaic County.
4. Elizabeth Kaming, "Star Witness Puts Finger on Carter, Artis," *Paterson Morning Call*, May 12, 1967, 5.
5. *State v. Carter*. May 19, 1967. Trial transcript, 112. N.J. Superior Court, Passaic County.

4. BETWEEN TRIALS: 1967-1976
1. Rubin Carter, *The Sixteenth Round* (New York: Viking Press, 1974), 309.
2. Ibid., 310.

3. Ibid.

4. Ibid.

5. "Carter and Artis Given Life Terms," *Paterson Evening News*, June 30, 1967, 6.

6. State v. Carter. 255 A.2d. 746 (1969) at 752.

7. Carter, *The Sixteenth Round*, 317.

8. Tom Hester. "Rahway Riot Has a Mixed Legacy," *Newark Star-Ledger*, November 25, 1996, 19.

9. Carter, *The Sixteenth Round*, 336.

10. Dave Anderson, "Christmas at Rahway," *New York Times*, December 23, 1972.

11. This is from Selwyn Raab's testimony at the second trial.

12. Selwyn Raab, "Murder Case Witnesses Recant Seven Years after 2 Got Life Terms," *New York Times*, September 27, 1974, 1.

13. Ibid., 56.

14. "Byrne Will Discuss Request to Open Carter Case Today," *New York Times*, September 28, 1974, 20.

15. "Secret Recordings Played at Carter Trial," *New York Times*, November 5, 1974, 39.

16. Selwyn Raab, "Same Judge Gets Carter Appeal," *New York Times*, January 29, 1975, 37.

17. Selwyn Raab, "Appeal Filed for Retrial," *New York Times*, September 3, 1975, 41.

18. "State Won't Oppose Carter-Artis Appeal for a New Trial," *New York Times*, August 22, 1975, 36.

19. "Group Seeks New Trial for Carter," *New York Times*, September 1, 1975, 19.

20. "Ali Leads 1,600 at Rally for Freedom for Carter," *New York Times*, October 10, 1975, 33.

21. Phone interview with former Assemblyman Eldridge Hawkins, June 8, 1998.

22. Hawkins interview.

23. Selwyn Raab, "Report Says Rubin Carter Passed Lie Detector Test," *New York Times*, December 12, 1975, 43.

24. Ibid.

25. Phone interview with Hawkins.

26. Joseph Sullivan. "Supreme Court in New Jersey Told Carter Never Got a Fair Trial," *New York Times*, March 19, 1976, 36.

27. *State v. Carter*. 354 A.2d 627 (1976) at 632.

28. Selwyn Raab, "Rubin Carter and Artis Get New Trial in Murder Case," *New York Times*, March 19, 1976, 36.

29. Ibid.

5. THE SECOND TRIAL: PART I

1. Interview with Myron Beldock, June 18, 1998, New York City.

2. Selwyn Raab, "Bail Posted for Carter and Artis," *New York Times,* March 20, 1976, 56.

3. Selwyn Raab. "Carter and Artis Released on Bail after 9 Years," *New York Times,* March 21, 1976, 1.

4. Selwyn Raab, "Closed Court Weighs Change in Rubin Carter's Bail," *New York Times,* August 24, 1976, 36.

5. Selwyn Raab, "Rubin Carter Facing One Less Charge," *New York Times,* August 24, 1976, 36.

6. Robert Cohen, "Talk Is Legal: Court Again Removes a Carter Gag Order," *Newark Star-Ledger,* September 6, 1976, 5.

7. Selwyn Raab, "Judge Moves Rubin Carter Trial after Citing Prejudicial Publicity," *New York Times,* September 11, 1976, 23.

8. Selwyn Raab, "An Ex-associate of Rubin Carter Charges 'Pressure' by Prosecutor," *New York Times,* October 14, 1976, 43.

9. Dean Bender, "Carter Trial Begins," *Paterson Evening News,* November 12, 1976, D13.

10. Leslie Maitland, "2nd Trial of Rubin Carter Starts with Reporter Called as a Witness," *New York Times,* November 12, 1976, D13.

11. Bender, "Carter Trial Begins," 1.

12. "Defendants Displeased with Paterson Trial Site," *Paterson Evening News,* November 12, 1976, 4.

13. Interview with Louis Steel, May 27, 1998, New York City.

14. Leslie Maitland, "Witness at Rubin Carter Trial Tells Hearing He Lied Often during the Case," *New York Times,* November 16, 1976, D21.

15. Leslie Maitland, "Bello Again Testifies He Saw Carter and Artis at Slaying Scene," *New York Times,* November 18, 1976, 32.

16. Leslie Maitland, "Carter Jury Is Told about Bribe Offers," *New York Times,* November 21, 1976, 37.

17. Dean Bender, "Special Treatment for Bello Denied by County Judges," *Paterson Evening News,* November 11, 1976, 14.

6. THE SECOND TRIAL: PART II

1. Dean Bender, "Ammo Linked to Carter by Paterson Detective," *Paterson Evening News,* November 23, 1976, 3.

2. Dean Bender, "Policeman Denies Pressuring Bello," *Paterson Evening News,* November 24, 1976, 4.

3. Interview with Lewis Steel. May 27, 1998, New York City.

4. Leslie Maitland, "Two in Carter Trial Tell of Alibi Story," *New York Times,* November 29, 1976, 42.

5. "Witness Who Gave an Alibi Recants Testimony," *New York Times*, November 30, 1976, 25.

6. Ibid.

7. Leslie Maitland, "Testimony on Clothing Read in Rubin Carter Trial," *New York Times*, December 1, 1976, B24.

8. Ibid.

9. Dean Bender, "Carter-Artis Judge to Rule on Motivation Testimony," *Paterson Evening News*, December 2, 1976, 1.

10. Ibid.

11. Dean Bender, "Prosecution to Try to Prove Murders Racially Inspired," *Paterson Evening News*, December 3, 1976, 2.

12. Leslie Maitland, "Witness in Carter Trial Says He Heard No Talk of Revenge," *New York Times*, December 7, 1976, 35.

13. Dean Bender, "Carter Prosecutor Rests," *Paterson Evening News*, December 9, 1976, 8.

14. Leslie Maitland, "State Rests in Carter-Artis Trial, Judge Denies Dismissal Motions," *New York Times*, December 9, 1976, 36.

15. Leslie Maitland, "Times Reporter at Carter Trial Describes Bello Recantations," *New York Times*, December 15, 1976, B10.

16. Theodor Sherman, "Bello Bribe Story False, Raab Says," *Paterson Evening News*, December 15, 1976, 3.

17. Leslie Maitland, "Artis Goes on Stand, but Carter Decides He Will Not Testify," *New York Times*, December 16, 1976.

18. Ibid.

19. Leslie Maitland, "Artis Goes on Stand in Trial with Carter Denies Firing Any Gun at Anyone," *New York Times*, December 17, 1976, 28.

20. Dean Bender, "Defense Nears End," *Paterson Evening News*, December 17, 1976, 8.

21. Leslie Maitland, "Carter-Artis Trial Is Expected to Go to Jury Thursday," *New York Times*, December 18, 1976, 28.

22. Ibid.

23. Dean Bender, "Jury Gets Carter Case," *Paterson Evening News*, December 21, 1976, 1.

24. Dean Bender, "Carter and Artis Appeal Likely," *Paterson Evening News*, December 22, 1976, 6.

25. Ibid.

7. POSTSCRIPTS AND SIDESHOWS

1. Leslie Maitland, "Carter and Artis Shocked by Second Verdict," *New York Times*, December 23, 1976, 24.

2. Ibid.

3. Ibid.

4. Leslie Matiland, "Carter and Artis: Life Again," *New York Times*, February 10, 1977, 1.

5. Ibid., 32.

6. Ibid.

7. Stuart Marques, "Eye of Hurricane: Carter Wages a Lonely Fight for Freedom," *Newark Star-Ledger*, November 27, 1972, 48.

8. Ibid.

9. Interview with Myron Beldock, June 18, 1998, New York City.

10. Ibid.

11. Interview with Lewis Steel, May 27, 1998, New York City.

12. *N.J. v. Carter and Artis*. Superior Court, Passaic County. Indictment 167-66, opinion rendered May 31, 1979.

13. Interview with Beldock.

14. *State v. Carter*. 426 A.2d 501 (1981).

15. Sam Chaiton and Terry Swinton, *Lazarus and the Hurricane* (Toronto, Canada: Penguin Books, 1991), 184, 201.

8. The Appelate Labyrinth

1. "Plea for Third Trial by Carter and Artis," *Newark Star-Ledger*, March 10, 1982, 28.

2. *State v. Carter*. 449 A.2d 1286 (1982) at 1292.

3. Ibid.

4. *State v. Carter*. 1309.

5. Robert G. Seidenstein, "Justices Narrowly Reject Bid for a Third Carter-Artis Trial," *Newark Star-Ledger*, August 18, 1982, 17.

6. Sam Chaiton and Terry Swinton, *Lazarus and the Hurricane* (Toronto, Canada: Penguin Books, 1991), 165.

7. James S. Hirsch, *Hurricane* (New York: Houghton Mifflin, 2000), 228.

8. Scott Ladd, "Carter Seeks New Trial, Cites Withheld Evidence," *Newark Star-Ledger*, November 2, 1983, 29.

9. Chaiton and Swinton. *Lazarus and the Hurricane*, 202.

10. Ibid., 206.

11. Ibid., 208.

12. Ibid., 210.

13. Ibid., 271.

14. "Judge Uses a Sharp Pen to Help the Underdog," *National Law Journal*, May 20, 1985, 1.

15. Chaiton and Swinton, *Lazarus and the Hurricane*, 292; transcript of oral arguments of *Carter v. Rafferty*. U.S. Federal District Court, Newark, New Jersey. July 26, 1985.

16. *State v. Rafferty*. 621 F. Supp. 533 (1985) at 534.

17. *State v. Rafferty* at 560.

18. Robert Rudolph, "Carter Goes Free," *Newark Star-Ledger*, November 11, 1985, 1.

19. Earl Caldwell, "Justice under Pressure," *New York Daily News*, November 9, 1985.

20. Adam Sommers and Karl Johnson, "Many React Angrily to Judge's Ruling," *North Jersey News*, November 8, 1985, 2.

21. Scott Ladd, "Hurricane Carter Release Opposed as Passaic Prosecutor Files Appeal," *Newark Star-Ledger*, December 19, 1985, 4.

22. Robert Rudolph, "Court Rejects Evidence against Carter," *Newark Star-Ledger*, May 1, 1986, 1.

23. Robert Cohen, "Hurricane Carter Wins Final Round," *Newark Star-Ledger*, January 12, 1988, 1.

24. Karl Johnson, "Legacy of Carter Prosecution Lingers in Paterson," *Newark Star-Ledger*, March 6, 1988, 46.

9. FINAL JUDGMENT

1. Martin Erdmann, quoted in Anne Strick, *Injustice for All* (New York: Penguin Books, 1977), 128.

2. David P. Conradt, *The German Polity*, 6th ed. (White Plains, N.Y.: Longman, 1996), 238.

3. *ABA Standards for Criminal Justice: Prosecutor and Defense Function*, 3rd ed. (Chicago: ABA, 1993), 5.

4. Transcript of *The Hurricane Carter Story*, *American Justice* series (7448) (New York: Arts and Entertainment Television Network, 1996).

5. Arye Rattner, "Convicting the Innocent: When Justice Goes Wrong" (Ph.D. diss., Ohio State University, 1983), 5.

Index

About the Author

PAUL WICE is a professor of political science at Drew University in Madison, New Jersey. He received his undergraduate degree from Bucknell University and his doctorate from the University of Illinois–Urbana. Professor Wice has published eight previous books dealing with the American legal system as well as numerous monographs and articles. The recipient of several teaching awards, he has held visiting scholar positions at the U.S. Department of Justice, the New Jersey Administrative Office of the Courts, and the Center for the Study of Law and Society of the University of California, Berkeley.